Sex and Violence

Sex and Violence

The Hollywood Censorship Wars

TOM POLLARD

Paradigm Publishers

Boulder • London

Copyright © 2009 Paradigm Publishers

Published in the United States by Paradigm Publishers, 3360 Mitchell Lane Suite E, Boulder, CO 80301 USA.

Paradigm Publishers is the trade name of Birkenkamp & Company, LLC, Dean Birkenkamp, President and Publisher.

Library of Congress Cataloging-in-Publication Data

Pollard, Tom (Leslie Thomas)
   Sex and violence : the Hollywood censorship wars / by Tom Pollard.
      p. cm.
   Includes bibliographical references and index.
   ISBN 978-1-59451-635-1 (hardcover : alk. paper)
   ISBN 978-1-59451-636-8 (paperback : alk. paper)
   1. Motion pictures—Censorship—United States—History.
2. Sex in motion pictures.   3. Violence in motion pictures.   I. Title.
PN1995.62.P65 2009
363.3'10973—dc22

2008042260

Printed and bound in the United States of America on acid free paper that meets the standards of the American National Standard for Permanence of Paper for Printed Library Materials.

Design and composition by Cynthia Young.

14 13 12 11 10   2 3 4 5

Contents

Preface

This book has its antecedents during the fifties and sixties as my family piled into the family station wagon on Friday nights and headed out to the local drive-in to watch some of Hollywood's most memorable movies (along with some of its most forgettable). We watched Westerns, gangster films, Sci-Fi, thrillers, film noir, musical comedies, social problem films, and documentaries. For me that experience forever associated movies with adventure, fun, family, community, and entertainment. After a lifetime of watching movies, I discovered I could learn even more about them by organizing film festivals, interviewing filmmakers, and writing books and articles about film. For the past twelve years I have also worked on documentary films as a writer, researcher, and occasional host. Throughout all of these activities, however, I never lost my early fascination and enthusiasm with film.

Motion pictures attract many by providing fictional glimpses into imaginative, exotic, dangerous, or otherwise interesting worlds, while they repel others. The resulting controversies constitute an illuminating chapter in social history. This book examines Hollywood's most explosive censorship controversies. It surveys banned and censored movies and the struggles surrounding them. The study begins with the "precode" era, the powerful Hays Code period, and the Motion Picture Association of America's current regulatory system. In addition, this study examines unofficial censorship imposed by social movements, including McCarthyism during the late forties and fifties and the more recent evangelicalism. The study regards filmmaking and movie censorship as closely intertwined and constantly evolving. It assesses movies as social indices, cultural artifacts, socializing agents, and culture war battlefronts.

I wish to acknowledge the invaluable assistance of Dr. Carl Boggs, friend, colleague, and collaborator, who taught me to probe for deeper sociological and political meanings, as well as Sue Dickey, who greatly assisted in this study. In addition, I wish to thank the distinguished Canadian filmmaker Eva Wunderman, who taught me volumes about the film business from an insider's perspective. Also I wish to acknowledge author Dr. Michael Parenti for his insightful advice, and I wish to thank Dr. Jerry C. Lee, National University chancellor; Dr. Dana L. Gibson,

National University president; Dr. Thomas Green, National University provost; Dr. Michael McAnear, dean, National University College of Letters and Sciences; Dr. Jacquelynn Foltyn, chair, Department of Social Sciences, National University; and Dr. Charlene Ashton, associate regional dean, National University San Jose, for their unwavering support of this project. Finally, I wish to thank my family, including my father, C. Les Pollard, and my mother, Mercedes Pollard, for providing abundant opportunities to view films playing at the local theaters in Modesto, California, and my brother and sister-in-law Steven and Kathie Pollard and my brother Michael and sister-in-law Lenndey Pollard for supporting this project in a number of important ways. Finally, I wish to acknowledge the insightful comments of Sir Richard and Lady Feachem, Nan Sandusky, Julie Tsoi, and Edna Espanol.

CHAPTER ONE

Introduction to Movie Censorship

When audiences sit down in theaters, on airplanes, or in the privacy of their homes and hotel rooms to watch Hollywood films they rarely consider the rules and regulations governing the form, content, and advertising of the motion pictures they view. Most recognize that ratings provide information about the acceptable age of film audiences, although few know the complex assessment structure behind the ratings—currently ranging from G (general audiences, all ages admitted) through NC-17 (no one seventeen and under admitted). Few ponder the tense, behind-the-scenes negotiations between filmmakers and the Classification and Rating Administration (CARA) of the Motion Picture Association of America (MPAA), the outcome of which determines a film's financial success or failure, or realize the unofficial power of lobbyists, journalists, clergymen, and powerful organizations that pressure studio executives and film raters advocating their own agendas. Even fewer know of the historic struggles involving censorship, sexism, and racism that periodically embroil the film industry.

From the very birth of motion pictures filmmakers faced censorship. They swiftly adapted by inventing ingenious strategies to minimize artistic restrictions. With some modification, this early dynamic between censors, producers, and audiences remains operational today. The level of controversy over film ratings continues unabated, and interactions between producers and regulators can turn contentious at any stage of the rating process. By learning to evade censorship filmmakers crafted some of cinema's greatest classics and most enduring genres, and their evasion strategies remain vital to the filmmaking process even today.

Conflicts surrounding film ratings reflect broader sociopolitical "culture wars" that continue to flare even today. Current conflicts often pit "conservatives" against "liberals," terms that defy precise definitions, although conservatives traditionally demand strictly enforced regulations aimed at sanitizing movies from offensive scenes, episodes, images, and dialogue, claiming that a "liberal media" dominates movie content. Liberals grant filmmakers greater latitude to craft their movies. Film critic Michael Medved charges that currently liberal movie critics undermine traditional social values. Medved writes:

1

> Why is the critical fraternity so liberal now? It didn't used to be. There used to be very conservative critics and they put out reviews from a specifically moralistic point of view. What's amazing to me was how that entire voice representing that third of America who consider themselves conservative is basically not represented other than by myself in the film commentary business.[1]

Conservative commentators like Medved often assume a liberally biased media without attempting to prove or justify these views, and the term *liberal media* has acquired a life of its own. An online journal, *NewsBusters: Exposing and Combating Media Bias,* recently embarked on a mission to expose "liberal bias" in media without bothering to prove the existence of the alleged bias. Such charges frequently occur, usually without proof or justification.

Noam Chomsky refutes the "liberal bias" claims as a myth, given the enormous cloud of large media corporations headed by conservatives like Rupert Murdoch. Chomsky refuted charges of liberal bias in a 1997 documentary titled *The Myth of a Liberal Media.* And, despite the frequent cry of liberal bias, the conservative Fox News currently outpolls all other television news programs. Other cable news channels, including CNN, increasingly reflect Fox News's conservative bias. These corporations also control movie theaters and movie ratings services. In addition, religious movie ratings services currently provide mass audiences with their spin on the latest movies. Established periodicals including *The Christian Century, Movieguide, The Conservative Voice,* and *The American Conservative* currently host online movie ratings services. Recently, critic Roger Ebert appealed to both sides of the debate to moderate the level of acrimony in their writings and embrace critical diversity: "I think both the left and the right should celebrate people who have different opinions, and disagree with them, and argue with them, and differ with them, but don't just try to shut them up."[2] Unfortunately, if the past is any indication, Ebert's pleas may go unheeded, as political and religious beliefs continue to affect movies as they always have.

Production Codes Defined

Movie ratings derive from Production Codes, systems of rules and regulations governing film form and content. In order to placate detractors, Hollywood periodically reinvents Production Codes, which then play powerful roles in forming film genres, conventions, and social and political messages. Clashing social movements promote competing codes, each reflecting popularly held values and beliefs, which ultimately result in film censorship. For example, during the permissive pre-code period of the late twenties and early thirties weakly enforced rules allowed filmmakers to depict the newly emancipated female "flappers" as well as the bootleggers who supplied them with abundant alcohol. Heroes of this period included seductive vamps and flamboyant gangsters, but by 1934, fueled by a massive religious boycott, a more restrictive code appeared that forbade the popular "gold diggers," flapperlike female characters who seduce men, as well as bootleggers, rum runners, and other Prohibition-era protagonists. In response, filmmakers created more subtle characters who still managed to evoke the forbidden lifestyles. These struggles over film form and content constitute Hollywood's "censorship wars" in action.

Critics often employ the term *Production Code* synonymously with "Hays Code," which applies to one particular set of industry rules and regulations in effect during 1934–1968. However, Production Codes existed long before the Hays Code, and other codes arose after the Hays Code's demise. Today, Production Codes continue to exercise considerable influence on film form and content. In this study the term *Production Code* describes any system—formal or informal—that influences and attempts to regulate motion picture form, content, and advertising. Formal Production Codes date back as early as 1909, and informal ones arose even earlier. Before 1909, court cases, state and local governmental actions, and influential individuals and organizations created informal "codes" by which filmmakers learned the often painful limits of their art. Formal codes appeared in 1922, 1927, 1930, and 1968. The Hays Code (1934–1968) embodied portions of former codes, and today's MPAA Code retains many of the same basic issues, updated for contemporary tastes. A study of the history of Production Codes and the surrounding controversies exposes aspects of the film industry normally hidden from public view. In fact, wars between producers and censors provide graphic evidence of society's most taboo issues.

A few codes eventually grew stronger and more effective than others at censoring films. The Hays Code exercised the most influence, but the current MPAA "Valenti Code," which arose in 1968, remains in many respects equally potent. Whether weak or strong, codes function as effective buffers between the film industry and its more obstreperous critics. The existence of codes presents the appearance of vigorous self-censorship, often staving off more restrictive governmental intervention. There are other unstated rules and regulations, like the potent McCarthy code and the current evangelical code. All of these codes, whether formal or informal, wield a form of control over film form and content, as the following chapters reveal.

Initially, codes arose informally through mutual understandings between producers and outside pressure groups and eventually formalized into written documents and organizations designed to enforce rules. Formal codes censored film content, distribution, and advertising, functioning at times as virtual laws regulating film content, while at other times performing as weak negotiating bodies armed with little real authority. Today most code "enforcement" more closely resembles "negotiation" than adherence to formal laws, a dynamic process of give-and-take between producers and censors.

Hidden Censorship

As Gerald Gardner observes, "not all censorship originated in Hollywood and the state censor boards." From the beginning, he notes, "pressure groups that represent special interests" constituted "some of the most powerful forces for censorship."[3] Lobbyists, pressure groups, and political and military spokespersons pressure studio executives to suppress various plot elements and controversial subjects. For example, liquor industry lobbyists urge producers to include scenes of alcohol consumption and suppress scenes depicting the harms of alcoholism, while tobacco representatives and soft drink manufacturers persuade producers to focus on the pleasures of their products. The cumulative effect of the presence of lobbyists and pressure groups functions as a hidden "code." The McCarthy movement and the evangelical movements exemplify this hidden censorship. McCarthyism profoundly influenced film form and content for an entire generation. At the same time filmmakers learned to code their films with symbolic attacks on McCarthyism that often escaped attention. As a result, many McCarthy-era films share a defiant yet symbolic subtext. Today another powerful code demands family-oriented films and strict limits on movie sex. Producers ignore this large group, constituting more than one-third of film audiences, at their peril. Hollywood obligingly produces a growing number of evangelical-oriented family values films designed with this audience in mind, and in so doing practices a kind of self-censorship regarding film form and content.

Movies' powerful role in youth socialization remains the most often-cited rationale for regulating motion pictures. Even more than novels, motion pictures engender efforts to protect children from exposure to features with "adult" content. Although novels may ridicule or satirize sacrosanct values and beliefs, films pose a far greater threat to the status quo due to their ability to reach mass audiences, causing mounting pressures to reflect conservative social values. Critics often cite the hypnotic attraction of movies to justify censorship and control, assuming that movies function essentially as a form of brainwashing. In fact, motion pictures always fascinate children, who flocked to the earliest nickelodeon features, composing around one-third of early audiences. Today, children, especially teenagers, dominate movie audiences as never before.

Censorship Wars

A fascinating history of controversial social and political beliefs emerges from an examination of Production Codes. At times, conflicts focus intensely on political values and beliefs, while at other times they evoke religious or social issues. The conflicts surrounding film regulation reflect widespread social change, dissension, dissatisfaction, and turmoil. As a part of the larger cultural battles, conflicts over movie ratings punctuate the history of motion pictures, providing valuable insights into social taboos and sensitive issues and ideas. Ultimately, hero types reflect restrictions imposed by Production Codes, as different codes encourage different heroes. As codes change, so do the protagonists and villains. Tami D. Cowden, Caro LaFever, and Sue Vidors postulate the existence of eight "archetypes" for both male and female characters in popular media. Male archetypes include the chief, the bad boy, the best friend, the charmer, the lost soul, the professor, the swashbuckler, and the warrior. Female archetypes include the boss, the seductress, the spunky kid, the free spirit, the waif, the librarian, the crusader, and the nurturer.[4] Film ratings conflicts in the past focused on the appropriateness of one or more of these archetypes.

Filmmakers inevitably adapt to new codes, undermining their original purpose as they do so. As standards erode, critics call for new, stricter codes. In every era creative filmmakers learn to crack the codes, avoiding or at least blunting their restrictions. The process of circumventing codes often yields movie classics. In fact, many of the films that challenged prevailing codes are now recognized as classics, in part because filmmakers of necessity relied on inventiveness and adaptability in their efforts to thwart the codes. In order to attract audiences in the highly competitive film industry, producers managed through their own ingenuity to expand permissible limits, thereby further challenging and eroding the codes.

Not surprisingly, censorship wars erupt most often during periods of rapid social change in which pressure groups confront each other. At times, filmmakers choose to defy the Production Code, in effect refusing to submit to censorship. During the forties, fifties, and sixties a few producers defied the code and released unrated, uncensored films rather than submit to the changes demanded by the censors, generating controversies and affecting changes in the Production Code. In the long run, unrated films undermine regulators and may help affect changes and reforms in ratings systems.

Censorship Defined

Movie censorship exists in every age, and major censorship cases have occurred throughout film history. Censors may ban movies or, more often, may force filmmakers to edit, remove, or otherwise alter or obscure words, behavior, or images. Censorship bodies police ideas, images, scenarios, situations, and language. Suppression may commence early in the production process, as soon as producers negotiate for the screen rights to popular novels or Broadway plays. Legal scholars label the attempts to influence films or other works of art prior to their completion as *prior censorship* or *prior restraint. Postcensorship*, on the other hand, refers to efforts to edit, rewrite, excise, or ban films after production. In the postcensorship system filmmakers may reedit and resubmit their movies. Both kinds of censorship have enjoyed popularity with regulators and censorship advocates at various points in history. And movie censorship still exists, although in altered appearance. Despite the U.S.

Supreme Court ruling against prior censorship, Production Codes continue to define moviemakers' boundaries.

Censorship subdivides readily into several distinct categories:

- Moral censorship. Producers remove or alter subject matter deemed "immoral" or contrary to prevailing moral codes.
- Political censorship. Censors ban or edit films containing references to sensitive political issues including unionization, communism, socialism, or depicting government corruption.
- Religious censorship. Films attacking or belittling religious organizations or leaders may succumb to religious censorship.
- Special interest censorship. Trade organizations or other powerful groups and individuals apply pressure to filmmakers to depict their self-interests positively and avoid negative depictions.
- Self-censorship. Producers often organize industry-dominated agencies to limit and censor films in order to forestall official government intervention in the film industry.
- Prior censorship (prior restraint), ruled unconstitutional in 1965, involves censoring movies while still in the production stages.
- Hidden censorship. Producers respond to hostile forces by altering or otherwise obfuscating censorable content even before submitting their films for ratings.

Sex

The moment motion pictures arrived in theaters, opposition to sexual depictions in movies crystallized. During the eighteen nineties and nineteen hundreds pioneer filmmakers routinely deleted or obscured nudity and seductive dancing to placate censors. Later, the sexy "pre-code" films produced from 1930 through the summer of 1934 presented sexual relations fairly realistically, as normal, natural events. Seductresses played by Clara Bow, Marlene Dietrich, Jean Harlow, and Mae West made indelible impressions on audiences. Eventually the Hays Code banned the kinds of characters they depicted. Thereafter, promiscuity, adultery, miscegenation, prostitution, homosexuality, and nymphomania appeared in films only obliquely, through innuendo, symbolism, and double entendre. In the nineteen sixties, in response to the relaxing of earlier censorship, sexuality once again appeared in films, openly depicted by characters played by Marilyn Monroe, Elizabeth Taylor, and Jane Russell.

Today movie sexuality constitutes cinema's most controversial issue. The current Production Code proved vigilant in protecting teenagers from frank, realistic depictions of sexuality and sexual relationships. Currently, only small independent studios risk making realistic depictions of sexual relations, creating a two-tiered system with only a handful of filmmakers willing to undertake the risks of having their films banned from mall theaters, video rental outlets, and large retail outlets. Therefore, the Production Code itself is responsible for today's relatively paltry movie depictions of sexuality.

Violence

Although sex constitutes Hollywood's chief allure, violence functions as a close second. Filmmakers long ago discovered the allure of graphic violence and learned to include images of murder and mayhem in order to sell movie tickets as early as 1900. Today's violent features also rely on graphic images to allure audiences. Violence provided a safer financial strategy than sex. Recent films like *The Hills Have Eyes, The Passion of the Christ,* the *Saw* series, *Henry: Portrait of a Serial Killer, Hannibal, Seven, A History of Violence, Hostel, Irreversible,* and *Rambo* depict ultraviolent images. Like sex, violence sells tickets, and, because of antisex censorship, violence continues to be a safer bet financially. Historically, violent movies receive more favorable ratings than films featuring sex. Therefore, today's movies often contain more violent images than sexual ones.

Religion and Politics

Beyond sex and violence, religion and politics present filmmakers with some of their greatest challenges. Religious values lie at the heart of many strident calls for censorship and threats of government intervention. Religion generates most audience boycotts, but politics also unnerves censors, from official regulatory agencies like the MPAA to congressional subcommittees during the McCarthy era. When filmmakers rely on controversial political and social issues to attract audiences conservatives predictably react with anger, indignation, and calls for censorship. The resulting culture wars then erupt, revealing in sharp detail bitterly contested sociopolitical terrain containing society's most sensitive issues.

Films often reference political and social issues without containing overt political subject matter. For instance, melodramas in which the hero overcomes the villains and reestablishes the social order, the most broadly popular motion picture genre, implicitly endorse and reinforce the status quo (reverence for the family, government, religion, and business). In these films, heroes (traditionally males) fight to preserve the established order. The very nature of melodramas dictates a return to order and normalcy after a period of chaos. Accordingly, these films reference and reinforce conservative values and beliefs. Often the most interesting social issues appear invisible because everyone assumes their validity. However, rapid social changes undermine this stability and often launch new genres depicting these changes symbolically.

Pioneering filmmakers of the early twentieth century quickly found themselves embroiled in explosive conflicts over depictions of such issues as crime, slavery, racism, fascism, communism, and socialism. Behind calls for movie censorship lurked not only perceived offenses against public morality but also challenges to the dominant political values of the age. Voices of protest raised against depictions of sexuality (*Fatima, The Dolorita Passion Dance, The Plastic Age, She Done Him Wrong*) are similar to ones raised against depictions of other sensitive issues, like drug addiction (*The Man with a Golden Arm*), alcoholism (*The Lost Weekend*), anti-Semitism (*Gentlemen's Agreement*), racial inequality (*A Patch of Blue*), homosexuality (*Brokeback Mountain*), and many others. Each of the above-mentioned films expresses provocative sociopolitical themes, and each provoked ratings controversies and censorship wars.

Gender Roles

Many of the fiercest code conflicts focus on the limits of acceptable roles for women and men. Behind many debates over film sexuality lurks the deeper issue of "proper" and "acceptable" gender roles. Censors' prohibitions against prostitution, nudity, adultery, homosexuality, and childhood sexuality involve gender issues as well as definitions of family. Prostitutes present particularly disturbing female models that poses a threat to the Victorian concept of a proper family. Censors often act to prohibit female adultery, though they display greater tolerance for male transgressors. These disturbing female characters, despite their obvious box office attractiveness, threaten the nuclear, male-dominated family. They represent the perennial "seductress" archetype, which dates back to the birth of cinema. Long revered in literature and opera, seductresses proved irresistible to early filmmakers, just as they do today. Code restrictions against prostitution typically banned seductresses of all types. Film raters preferred images of women as loyal, dutiful wives and dedicated, loving mothers and often censored any deviations from these norms. The seductresses that employ sexuality to compete with or profit from males pose a particularly potent threat to patriarchal family values.

Male roles may also spawn heated controversy and censorship. Gangsters and the criminal lifestyle often raise concerns with movie censors who fear that audiences might be tempted to follow these "bad boy" role models. Code enforcers worry about the temptations for impressionable youth viewing characters with exciting, antisocial criminal lifestyles. For that reason, most codes prohibit glorification of criminals, although depictions of romantic, outlaw heroes thrive despite code restrictions. However, because of their attractiveness filmmakers often depict con artists, gangsters, psychopaths, rogue police, and other out-of-control males. Because of censorship practices, filmmakers find it easier to create sexualized male characters than their female counterparts. Males sewing masculine wild oats, if followed by a change of heart and reformed behavior, may be permitted, while female transgressors usually pay steep penalties. The earliest codes explicitly prohibited "sexual perversions," which usually meant homosexuality, and openly gay characters remain a rarity even today despite relaxing standards.

Creating the Couple

In most films the internal tensions focus on two characters of the opposite sex. Virginia Wright Wexman estimates that 95 percent of all films reference this social dynamic. In the past, the newly formed "couples" formalized their union with marriage bonds, but today a growing number of couples appear whose bonds consist solely of their love for each other. Whether couples are formally bonded in holy matrimony or conjoined into nontraditional postmodern relationships, a final union usually occurs. The resulting couples reveal insights about contemporary social values and beliefs. Wexman observes that "movies define and demonstrate socially sanctioned ways of falling in love." Films not only define but also demonstrate types of relationships that are already socially sanctioned. They do not create those sanctions; they merely contribute to them.[5]

Of course, couple formation lies at the heart of family values. Loving couples constitute the reproductive backbone of society, upon which families and societies arise. Therefore, it should come as no surprise that couple formation turns out to be one of the most contentious and sensitive issues in cinema. Production Codes, it turns out, exert a very powerful effect on movie couples, determining the social acceptability of a variety of relationships. Who marries whom or who lives with whom matters very much in society, and movies help identify and define acceptable relationships. In more conservative times, relationships tend to be limited to marriages between two people of the opposite sex but the same race, religion, and economic and social class. In other periods, nonstandard relationships abound between members of diverse races, classes, and age categories. Even homosexual relationships may be tolerated during some periods and censored during other periods. For example, Todd Haynes's *Far From Heaven* (2002) dissects 1950s-era restrictions on couple formation in ways that would have been permitted in some eras and forbidden in others. In Haynes's film a married couple, Cathy and Frank Whitaker (Julianne Moore and Dennis Quaid), find their assumptions about each other failing after Cathy discovers Frank kissing another man, which launches her into a journey of sexual discovery as she in turn becomes attracted to an African American gardener (Dennis Haysbert). Homosexuality and miscegenation appear in films of the late twenties and early thirties but disappear from 1934 until 1968, depending upon the Production Code in force at the time.

The issues discussed in this book raise urgent questions about the role of motion picture regulation. The relationship between film producers, film consumers, and the larger community remains dynamic and conflicted, despite over a century of experience with industry self-regulation. This study explores the constantly fluid dynamics between producers and consumers. For more than one hundred years that dynamic has exposed sensitive, often taboo subjects and issues.

CHAPTER TWO

Pre-Code Hollywood

Vamps, Gangsters, and Scandals

The term *pre-code* officially denotes the brief period from 1930 to 1934 between the drafting of the film industry Production Code adopted by the Motion Picture Producers and Distributors of America (MPPDA) and its eventual enforcement. Although the period lasted only four years, during that short span talented directors created some of the screen's most revered classics, as well as some of its more controversial films. Giants like Cecil B. DeMille, Louis Milestone, Josef von Sternberg, and Charles Chaplin, among others, crafted unique films featuring stars like Jean Harlow, Mae West, Clara Bow, Marlene Dietrich, Douglas Fairbanks, Sr. and Rudolph Valentino. Relatively unbounded by censorship, the pre-code period continues to enjoy popularity among critics and film buffs for its daring, sexy, and often scandalous classics.

However, the relationship between filmmaker and censor evolved for more than three decades before the official "pre-code" period. This early film history, lasting from the eighteen nineties through 1930, also qualifies as pre-code because it preceded the Hays Code. The heated battles over film ratings that marked the end of the official pre-code period in 1934 served merely as an epilogue to conflicts involving earlier Production Codes.

Soon after movies arrived in primitive theaters, alarmed citizens formed local and state censorship boards. City councils established early censorship boards in Chicago (1907) and New York City (1908). During the teens and twenties state legislatures in Pennsylvania, Ohio, Kansas, New York, Virginia, Massachusetts, Maryland, and Florida created censorship boards. These boards decided which films could be screened and arranged and received payment from producers for excising offensive scenes and segments. By cutting and banning, censorship boards effectively created their own Production Codes as producers adapted to their standards or risked expensive alterations and limited access to theaters. The boards rewarded filmmakers with incentives for cooperation if they cut or modified offensive scenes and situations.

Working-class Americans, including recent immigrants, became target audiences for early movies. At that point the motion picture industry consisted of tiny theaters showing one-reel films available for individual viewing in "peep hole" lenses. Working-class audiences speaking a variety of languages experienced no difficulty in decoding these early "flicks" (so called because of their jerky appearance), many of which appealed directly to their baser instincts. These short features depicted aspects of eastern urban life as well as westward migration, train robberies and murders, and exotic singing and dancing. Audiences flocked to these little films, which played in tiny theaters, on vaudeville, or as warm-ups for circuses, offering low-cost entertainment for the masses. As industrialization and urbanization expanded, Victorian mores weakened. Early features often included exotic subject matter, sexuality, sensational current events, and graphic violence.

Luring Audiences

The film industry embraced sexuality as a major audience lure. *Fatima: Muscle Dancer,* an early Thomas Edison Kinetoscope production exhibited at the Chicago World's Fair in 1893, features a Middle Eastern female dancer gyrating on stage in a revealing costume. Some viewers and World's Fair officials objected to Fatima's suggestive gyrations, so Edison created a less offensive version using cross-hatchings that obscured much of the dancer's body, providing enough modesty to silence critics while retaining some of the allure of her youthful, scantily clad figure.[1] In 1896 Edison updated Fatima's dance with *Fatima's Coochee-Coochee Dance*, which played in arcades and neighborhood theaters. This film spawned even later versions, which ultimately triggered censorship. In 1907, by order of a Chicago censorship committee, a stain (allegedly looking like New England) covered Fatima's scantily clad, gyrating body.[2] In 1897, a controversial arcade film with a strikingly similar theme, *The Dolorita Passion Dance*, raised the ire of a prominent Atlantic City minister after he noticed a crowd of men lining up to view it. The film features a young woman dancing the "Danse-du-Ventre, the famous Oriental muscle dance" in front of some seated musicians. Without bothering to investigate the film's contents, the minister petitioned the city government to close the peep show. The Atlantic City Council complied and banned the film sight unseen.[3]

Thus early censorship failed to deter filmmakers from venturing into forbidden territory. Edison, for one, continued to experiment with sexual lures in his early features. One of the most shocking scenes of the period occurred in Edison's *The Kiss* (1896), in which middle-aged actors May Irwin and John Rice engage in a lip-locked, sloppy kiss lasting 20 seconds. The film, which contains only one scene, proved to be one of the most popular of the early Vitascope offerings (early projected films) and one of the most controversial. Edison followed it with a longer version in 1900. Both versions raised the ire of social conservatives aghast at public displays of kissing.[4]

As pioneering filmmakers used sexuality as audience lures, they aroused unwanted attention from conservative individuals and groups, including ministers, women's clubs, religious organizations, newspaper editors, and law enforcement officers. These groups became a powerful obstacle to filmmakers wishing to use sex to lure audiences to their films. Early on, conservatives kept watchful eyes on the new "flicks." Early censors found sympathetic police chiefs, judges, mayors, and city councils willing to ban any film deemed objectionable. These censorship efforts, though spontaneous and unorganized, constituted de facto codes discouraging filmmakers from scenes that could lead to censorship and outright banning. Unwilling to take economic risks, filmmakers learned to avoid nudity and overly graphic sexuality, replacing them with more nuanced, indirect sexuality and sensuality.

In order to continue attracting audiences, pioneering filmmakers invented strategies to elude the censors but still attract audiences. Edwin S. Porter's *The Gay Shoe Clerk* (1903) employs one of the popular strategies used by filmmakers to fend off censorship: sexualizing an otherwise innocuous activity. Porter's short film, lasting only two minutes, features a young shoe customer slowly raising her long dress above her ankles, revealing her calf to a young shoe clerk (Edward Boulden). As he laces a pair of high-heeled shoes on her feet, his hands tremble, revealing his attraction to the woman. She appears drawn to him as well, and the two soon embrace and kiss, whereupon the young lady's chaperone, probably her mother, strikes the clerk and flees the shop indignantly with the young woman. The film stopped far short of what today would be deemed indecent exposure, but when Porter's film appeared audiences flocked to see a kiss, stocking-clad ankles, and a woman's calf.[5] The film's seemingly innocuous format prevented local censors from doing much damage, yet it evoked sexuality. The makers of the *Sex and the City* television show employed a remarkably similar plot in one episode in which a male shoe clerk steals glances underneath women's dresses. *The Gay Shoe Clerk, Fatima, Dolorita's Passion Dance,* and *The Kiss* each exemplify early efforts to entice audiences. Edison blurred Fatima's nudity with cross-hatchings, while Dolorita suffered banning. *The Gay Shoe Clerk* titillated audiences as he leered at nude ankles. These films evoke Victorian-era taboos while revealing the limits of permissible filmmaking at the time. They reveal a society deep in the throes of social conflict over the limits of sexuality. Immigrants enjoyed these sexy films, while many ministers and government officials chafed at the alleged indecencies they depict.

Pioneer filmmaker Thomas Edison, one of the first filmmakers to endure censorship of his films. (Copyright 1917 Thomas Edison.com)

Penny Arcades

These popular establishments contained pinball machines along with kinetoscopes with peepholes for individual viewing. Films and slides rented for one cent, placing them well within the reach of working-class audiences. The little films that played in arcades usually lasted for only a few minutes and featured only one continuously looped scene. The subjects depicted ranged from mundane scenes of planes flying, ships launching, and trains running through mountains, to a man squirted by a garden hose. Also, some of these little films contained sexy shots of scantily clad girls, including a nude emerging from a giant clam.[6] Although hardly full-fledged motion pictures, they popularized the new medium and exposed millions to the thrills of movie viewing. These short films proved popular for a time, but by 1896 audiences began to tire of the arcade format, and inventors realized that a projection system would prove more profitable. Edison's Kinetoscope Company purchased a new projector invented by C. Francis Jenkins and Thomas Armat in 1896. The Edison Company dubbed the new projector system Vitascope, and it revolutionized the film industry.[7]

Nickelodeons

Nickelodeons originated in 1900 in Pittsburgh when an enterprising businessman decided to charge people five cents to view one of the little films that were beginning to appear at that time inside a small theater instead of in a machine-filled arcade. He reportedly paid $40,000 to construct a theater, in which he installed a large phonograph, hiring a "drummer" or barker to advertise.[8] His venture proved so popular with audiences that theaters suddenly blossomed all across the United States. By 1905 the new fad of going to the "flicks" stimulated the creation of makeshift theaters in converted storefronts and other unused commercial spaces. Owners promptly posted billboards and flyers advertising the new "featurettes" and brought in as many chairs as they could stuff into their new theaters. Although 1905 witnessed only a few of these theaters, by 1906 nickelodeons had spread across thirty-five states. By 1910, 26 million people attended nickelodeon theaters each week, and motion pictures became the first truly mass entertainment medium.

A growing movement of ministers and other concerned citizens began to claim that movies and theater owners constituted public menaces because they endangered public morals. These critics objected not only to sex but also to the "blood and thunder" type of film, including those depicting murders, train robberies, and sensational crimes.[9] Within a year cities witnessed massive theater closures and the arrest of theater owners as the first full-fledged censorship war erupted.

This war began in earnest in 1907 when the Chicago Arts Council voted to allow the chief of police to censor penny arcades and nickelodeons throughout the city. No film could be shown without the signature of the general superintendent of police. In that same year, censorship also appeared in New York when the New York Children's Society caused the arrest of a theater owner for showing *The Great Thaw Trial,* a feature depicting the Henry K. Thaw–Stanford White–Evelyn Nesbit love triangle that led to the murder of White, a prominent New York architect. It included a scene in Ms. Nesbit's mirrored boudoir. This film, and others that the era's conservatives found shocking, prompted fiery antimovie sermons, and a few advocated banning films altogether.[10]

In 1908 the New York City Council voted to close all arcades and nickelodeons beginning at midnight on Christmas Eve. Theater owners united against this order and won a court injunction against it. The mayor then invoked the city's Blue Laws and banned the screening of any films on Sundays except for those of educational value. The resilient owners then staffed theaters with announcers to highlight the educational aspect of each film shown on Sunday by, for example, pointing out, "these are railroad tracks" and "we are passing a mountain."[11] This early example reveals surprising strategies used by exhibitors and filmmakers to circumvent censors. Meanwhile, in New York just a month after the 1908 Christmas Eve banning, a meeting of concerned citizens, led by Christian ministers, convened at New York's Marble Collegiate Church to thwart the growing power of theater owners. Shortly thereafter, the newly formed People's Institute in New York announced the formation of a censorship board consisting of Christian ministers, educators, and labor leaders. This group became the first formalized censorship board in the country.[12] The board served as a model for later Christian censors, including the Catholic Legion of Decency and the Catholic Bishops' motion picture ratings. It also preempted efforts in the state legislature to create a statewide censorship board. The precedent of church involvement signaled the advent of Christians taking an active role in the motion picture rating process.

In Chicago two hundred theater owners sued the city for banning two Westerns, *The James Boys in Illinois* (1908), written and directed by Gilbert M. "Bronco Billy" Anderson, and *Night Riders* (1908). Both depict gangs of train robbers, common during that period. City censors banned *Night Riders* because of "the evil influence of obscene and immoral representations."[13] The case traveled to the Supreme Court, which issued its ruling in *Black v. Chicago* (1909), which ruled that Chicago possessed the legal right to ban films deemed "immoral" and "obscene." Furthermore, the Court ruled that the films in question, because they depicted criminal details, "represent nothing but malicious mischief."[14] Thus the Court established a legal precedent for film censorship, and as a result an anti–motion picture bias prevailed for nearly fifty years.

Edwin S. Porter's *The Great Train Robbery* (1903), an earlier depiction of the James gang robberies, assiduously avoided the controversies engendered by *The James*

Boys in Illinois and *Night Riders*. Although Porter's film depicts a train robbery and includes such details as having gunmen knock out a telegraph operator and commandeer a speeding locomotive, his film clearly sides with the posse instead of the train robbers. Audiences watched rapturously as the posse pursues and eventually overtakes the gang as they meet to split up the loot. After a gunfight, the posse takes the gang into custody. By taking pains not to glorify the outlaws, Porter avoided the fate of these later films while retaining the excitement and audience allures of a dramatic robbery.

National Board of Censorship

Seeking to resolve these censorship battles, which appeared with increasing frequency, in 1909 producer Charles Sprague launched the National Board of Censorship of Motion Pictures (NBC) to review all films and create lists of those found acceptable to parents and teachers for children. Producers paid a small fee for every foot of film reviewed. The NBC first met in 1909 and screened five hours of film. Of the eighteen thousand feet reviewed, only four hundred failed to pass muster. The board banned only one film outright, *Every Lass a Queen*, which depicted a roving sailor who keeps a different girl in every port.[15] The first of many industry-controlled self-censoring bodies, the NBC served primarily to forestall efforts to establish real government censorship. The NBC served the industry well until the advent of feature films during the teens. Thus an enduring pattern emerged between self-regulation and government censorship, with the NBC censors allowing the film industry to keep critics at bay with the appearance, not the reality, of censorship.

In 1910 the NBC added a "Censorship Board" consisting of volunteers from the YMCA, the YWCA, the Children's Aid Society, the Women's Municipal League, the SPCA, the Purity League, the Women's Christian Temperance Union, and a variety of church-related organizations. The board voted either to pass films, cut offending sections, or ban films altogether. During the organization's first year it reviewed an average of thirty-five films per week, mandating cuts in many films and banning roughly one-fifth of all films submitted. One board member described the simple criteria for banning films: "All obscene subjects are strictly taboo." In addition, the board banned all crime films "showing gruesome details or tending to teach the techniques of crime." Also, it banned "all suggestive crime . . . like arson or suicide," and it banned all films it felt contained "unmitigated sensationalism and malicious mischief." The NBC banned most kidnapping films as well as most films dealing with marital infidelity.[16] Each of these issues became enshrined in the Production Codes that arose during the twenties and thirties.

Gradually, filmmakers adapted as the NBC banned or cut their films to placate the censors. Initially, the NBC banned as many as 20 percent of the films it reviewed. The era's producers quickly adapted to the Censorship Board's preferences and avoided those issues it found offensive. In addition, local communities continued to censor and often banned even films the NBC approved. For example, even though the NBC passed it unanimously, the city of Chicago banned an early adaptation of Jules Verne's novel *Michael Strogoff* depicting life in Siberia because the film contained one disturbing scene in which assailants burn Strogoff's eyes out. The ban forced the filmmakers to cut out the offending scene and reedit the movie.[17] Novels, of course, also suffer banning. Schools and library boards attempted to ban novels like *The Grapes of Wrath, As I Lay Dying, The Great Gatsby, The Catcher in the Rye, Native Son, Ulysses, To Kill a Mockingbird*, and *Huckleberry Finn*, but these actions often stimulated instead of stifled book sales. Movies, however, unlike novels, require theatrical release, a process tightly controlled by Production Codes.

The first two-reel films appeared in the teens, signaling a new era in motion pictures. Instead of quick, cheap views, the new features required greater audience commitments. Prices jumped from a nickel to as much as a dollar, depending upon the movie and the seating. Filmmakers often tapped Broadway for movie adaptations, since Broadway plays were much longer than the earlier nickelodeon movies. During the 1913–1914 season Famous Players Lasky, the largest production company, made movie adaptations of *Queen Elizabeth, The Prisoner of Zenda, Tess of the D'Urbervilles, In the Bishop's Carriage, Chelsea 7750, The Count of Monte Cristo, Caprice*, and over a dozen other Broadway plays. The "two-reelers" allowed audiences intermissions between reels, much like Broadway intermissions, marking a new era in filmmaking.[18] The practice of "picturizing" Broadway plays proved both popular and controversial as censors sought to protect moviegoers from bawdy Broadway fare.

In the United States the emerging film industry successfully convinced the public that it was doing an adequate job of self-regulation. British filmmakers, lacking an industry-led alternative to governmental regulation, submitted to real government control after Parliament enacted the Cinematograph Act of 1909. The act regulated theaters exhibiting motion pictures primarily for fire safety due to the flammability of motion picture stock. Despite widespread discussion of the safety issue, however, there was never a single fire at a British theater, despite cramped viewing conditions and the volatility of film stock. The law required theaters to be licensed and inspected by local governmental agencies. Immediately, however, authorities used the law to force theater closings on Sundays and religious holidays and to impose age restrictions on admissions. During the teens authorities expanded the law to cover film content, particularly sexuality. The law affected not only British productions but U.S. films as well, since over one-third of the films showing in British theaters were U.S. productions.[19]

The threat of federal U.S. censorship receded during the teens due to the existence of the NBC. The organization provided much of the substance as well as the appearance of strict censorship, and filmmakers happily cooperated with the volunteer agency rather than submit to dreaded federal censorship. Eventually, some of the industry's harshest critics began to suspect that the NBC served merely as an instrument for producers, so a movement spearheaded by reform-minded editors and politicians demanded the establishment of statewide and even federal censorship boards. In 1911 Pennsylvania became the first state to regulate movies, and in 1913 Ohio and Kansas created censorship boards. At that time, many legal scholars assumed that the First Amendment guaranteeing free speech applied only to federal legislation, not to states. An early motion picture distribution company challenged the Ohio and Kansas laws as unconstitutional, but the action failed after the U.S. Supreme Court ruled in 1915 against the distribution company and firmly established the government's right to prior censorship of motion picture content. Justice Joseph McKenna, writing for the conservative majority, created a legal defense of censorship by concluding that "there are some things which should not have pictorial representation in public places and to all audiences."[20] Unfortunately for the film industry, however, the ruling failed to define those "things which should not have pictorial representation." The ruling provided not guidance and restraint for regulators but legal justification for their censorship activities.[21]

In 1919 the threat of federal regulation reappeared after conservative Christian ministers once more railed against film sex. Responding to the threat of governmental censorship, film producers quickly expanded the NBC to screen all films and ascertain their acceptability. Although the NBC mandated minor cuts in films and managed to ban a few outright, it exercised no real authority. Its primary purpose was to blunt calls for more serious censorship, and, in fact, it delayed the imposition of stringent governmental intervention. By the twenties, five states—Kansas, Maryland, Ohio, Pennsylvania, and Virginia—had established censorship boards. The boards banned films, in whole or in part, sending a message to producers that the boards were a force to be reckoned with. Three other states—New York, Massachusetts, and Florida—soon created their own censorship boards. Over ninety municipal censorship bodies followed the states' examples. Individuals who worked for the boards could earn $200 per month from producers, a princely salary at the time. Censorship boards routinely cut out scenes that offended them, reedited films, or even wrote new intertitles. Producers paid three dollars per thousand feet of cut film and five dollars for rewritten intertitles. Subsequently, state and local censorship earned substantial revenue from Hollywood. By 1928 the Virginia Censorship Board reported receipts of $27,625. The board exulted in the substantial sum earned. "Never before in the history of censorship," it reported, "has the volume of business been so great."[22]

Although the NBC banned a large number of films, it lacked the power to fine filmmakers for evasion of the code. Therefore, the organization ultimately proved ineffective in controlling filmic depictions and subject matter. Seizing upon the opportunities to produce films with relative freedom, during the late teens and twenties talented directors like D. W. Griffith, Buster Keaton, Charles Chaplin, and Cecil B. DeMille created several screen classics, some of which relied on sexuality and violence to attract audiences (*Way Down East, The General, The Gold Rush, The Ten Commandments*).

Since the beginning of film, influential clergy had pressured filmmakers through sermons, sometimes delivered by powerful church officials. Filmmakers began offering churchgoers Christian-oriented films. Thomas Ince's popular *Civilization* (1916), for example, depicts a savage war between countries in which Jesus himself returns to earth to put an end to the strife. In 1916 the American Catholic Church, incensed with A. M. Kennelly's *The Power of the Cross,* forbade Catholics from viewing it and threatened to excommunicate Kennelly over doctrinal issues.[23] This action set the precedent for Catholic involvement in censorship in subsequent decades.

By 1917, when D. W. Griffith included a Passion section in his epic film *Intolerance,* the growing power of the Temperance Movement demanded he insert a disclaimer title in the scene in which Jesus transforms water into wine, explaining wine's sacramental use (not recreational) in biblical times. Despite the disclaimer about wine, Griffin's film contains erotic elements, permissible because they were set in the past.[24] In 1922 the Catholic Church began publishing lists of recommended films, further increasing the church's influence on filmmakers.[25]

Race

In 1915 D. W. Griffith released *The Birth of a Nation,* one of the first feature-length productions. In this film Griffith depicts the South as being saved from the evils of Reconstruction by the Ku Klux Klan (KKK). Griffith adapted Reverand Thomas Dixon's *The Clansman,* a popular novel glorifying the Klan's formation and post–Civil War exploits in wresting control of the region from African Americans and their allies. Although many whites during the teens may have found Griffith's message acceptable or even heroic, depicting the KKK as saviors of southern civilization proved too much for many African Americans to bear, especially in light of the Klan's role in enforcing Jim Crow. Bowing to pressure from vociferous African Americans and their allies, Ohio's board of censorship immediately banned Griffith's film. The National Association for the Advancement of Colored People (NAACP), founded five years earlier, promptly labeled Griffith's film racist. The NAACP threw picket lines around theaters showing Griffith's film, but the effort did little to dampen audience enthusiasm. Riots broke out in Boston, Philadelphia, and other major cities between supporters and detractors of the film, and Chicago censors banned it outright, as did Denver, Pittsburgh, and Minneapolis. The governor of

Ohio also banned it upon recommendation of the state Board of Censors. The new Kansas State Board of Review banned the film even though all three board members praised its artistic merit.[26] In Lafayette, Indiana, gangs of whites roamed the streets looking for blacks, and in the ensuing melee a white man killed a black teenager.

Despite these controversies, or perhaps partly because of all of the publicity, the film proved popular, and audiences waited in long lines to see it. They paid not five cents but two dollars, an unheard-of ticket price for that period. Despite the high ticket price, and despite its two-and-a-half-hour running time, *The Birth of a Nation* became the first box office "blockbuster." President Woodrow Wilson demanded a private screening in the White House, the first time such an honor was awarded. As for the film's racism, white audiences, including Wilson, either ignored or endorsed the film's racist messages, reflecting the widespread bigotry of the Progressive era. Griffith's film continues to stimulate controversies today and has become the most banned motion picture in history, stimulating controversy as late as 1978, when a riot broke out at a screening in Oxnard, California.[27]

Griffith, stunned by protests, charges of racism, and censorship, published at his own expense a pamphlet, in which he explained that he was not a racist and defended himself from charges of racism engendered by the film. His next film, *Intolerance,* was intended to prove that Griffith was, in fact, tolerant. This film presents four stories of intolerance and inhumanity, the most famous of which is set in ancient Babylon. This new film may have promoted tolerance, but it did little to diminish the controversy surrounding *The Birth of a Nation.* Even today, many would approve of the action of the early censors in banning Griffith's film. As Robert Sklar observes, audiences are still torn between admiration for *The Birth of a Nation*'s dramatic structure and abhorrence of its racism, regarding it either as "a work of racist propaganda or a work of consummate artistic skill." Griffith's film appears "as remarkable, and as flawed, in its art as in its theme of white supremacy."[28] Griffith's film graphically illuminates the chasm that existed between whites and African Americans during this period.

Sex

Sex easily proved the most sensitive issue for critics of movies, including clergy, women's groups, and journalists, who increased or decreased the pressure on Hollywood depending upon how Hollywood responded to their demands. Despite constant criticism from these groups, however, early filmmakers found it difficult to resist using sex as audience enticements. In the absence of a strong Production Code, producers enjoyed relative freedom to employ sexuality in their films without censorship. For example, Cecil B. DeMille's *The Cheat* (1915), considered an early classic, exemplifies the relative freedom enjoyed by producers to express sexual content. DeMille's unconventional married heroine, Edith Hardy (Fanny Ward), dallies with a young Asian businessman, Haku Arakau (Sessue Hayakawa), dubbed the "Burmese ivory king." Tolerated by high society due to his wealth, impeccable manners, and palatial estate, Arakau poses a potent threat to the marriage. He drives a sporty convertible and takes great pleasure in taking the lovely Edith to parties and fairs. Richard (Jack Dean), Edith's husband, provides lavish material and emotional support, despite her liaison with Arakau. Richard's support proves crucial after Edith shoots Arakau with his own pistol to prevent his raping her. To save her from a death sentence Richard gallantly shoulders the blame, but after a jury convicts him of attempted murder she makes a public admission, exonerating her husband. In the final dramatic courtroom scene Edith tears off part of her dress to reveal Arakau's mark on her shoulder, baring a partially nude breast in addition to her scar. DeMille's camera lingers on Edith in close-up for several minutes, allowing audiences to enjoy what must have been a shocking scene for the period. In *The Cheat* DeMille relied on one of his favorite scenarios, the undermining and weakening of a marriage. He injected the exotic lure of the Far East and the idea that sex has a hypnotic effect on its participants. DeMille's film features a juxtaposition of cross-cuts between Richard and Edith in which he berates her for carrying on with Arakau, who embodies her self-indulgent profligacy. DeMille's other sexually embellished films from this period include *The Squaw Man* (1914, 1918), *Don't Change Your Husband* (1919), and *Why Change Your Wife?* (1920). Each depicts unconventional relationships that would have been unacceptable under the later Hays Code.

Maurice Tourneur's *A Girl's Folly* (1917) bears the message "Passed by the National Board of Review," the new name for the old National Board of Censorship. Tourneur's film stars Robert Warwick as Kenneth Driscoll, a popular motion picture actor. While on location shooting a Western (in New Jersey), Driscoll meets Mary (Doris Kenyon), a vivacious local girl who, predictably, falls in love with the handsome movie actor. He promises her a screen test if she will remain with him in New York. Heartbroken after failing her screen test, and temporarily seized by guilt for agreeing to live with Driscoll, Mary vows to return to New Jersey, although she admits that she despises it. Driscoll confides soothingly, "Little girl, you know I love you, suppose you stay here—with me—I can give you everything and perhaps you'll be happier?" Although she is tempted at first to move in with Driscoll, her shame at violating sexual taboos temporarily overcomes her infatuation with glamour, and she waves good-bye and heads toward home. Filled with fresh resolve, she rejoins Driscoll in the dining hall. "You see," she tells him, "I've changed my mind. I'm never going home!" An alternate version exists in which Mary dutifully returns to her mother, in case local censors refused to allow the original.

World War I proved a powerful stimulant to filmmakers, who gradually began producing antiwar features. King Vidor's *The Big Parade* (1925) pillories the war as a

Edith Hardy (Fanny Ward), a married woman, dallies with a young Asian businessman, Haku Arakau (Sessue Hayakawa), dubbed the "Burmese Ivory King," in Cecil B. DeMille's *The Cheat* (1915), an example of sexy pre–Hays Code films. (Copyright 1915 Jesse L. Lasky Feature Play Company)

needless waste of human potential. While in France Vidor's hero Jim Apperson (John Gilbert) encounters Melisande (Renee Adoree), a French peasant girl, who watches him and his friends bathing themselves in the great outdoors. Louis Milestone's *All Quiet on the Western Front* (1930) includes a controversial scene in which Paul Baumer (Lew Ayres) and two other soldiers receive food from three French-women living alone and then spend the night with them. In their bedroom, Paul tells one of the women that he will always remember her. "Toujours. Oh, if only you could know how different this is from the women we soldiers meet." The Ohio board of censors demanded that Milestone cut the offending scene. Eight years later, during the much stricter Hays Code, Joseph Breen, head of the Production Code Administration, demanded deletion of the same scenes before the film could be rereleased.[29]

During the twenties and early thirties many commentators, from ministers to journalists, debated the issue of film censorship, with one side arguing that censorship was necessary in order to safeguard children from exposure to "immorality" in films. Then as now, no consensus existed about what constituted immorality. This proved particularly true regarding depiction of forbidden female body parts, passionate kissing, drug use, and prostitution. Was depicting a crime in all its professional details, thereby possibly supplying real criminals with vital information, immoral? In the absence of a strong Production Code filmmakers found themselves at the mercy of state and local censorship boards. The National Board of Review (NBR) and its predecessors provided Hollywood with the semblance of censorship while freeing filmmakers to depict popular Jazz Age themes, from handsome, roguish bootleggers and buccaneers played by Douglas Fairbanks and Rudolph Valentino to sexy "flappers" and "vamps" played by Theda Bara, Carol Lombard, Marlene Dietrich, and Clara Bow.

Rudolph Valentino popularized a male "vamp" image during the twenties in a powerful variation of the "bad boy" archetype. His seductive roles in *Four Horsemen of the Apocalypse* (1921), *The Sheik* (1922), *Blood and Sand* (1922), and *Son of the Sheik* (1925) established an erotic screen persona that parallels the blatant sexuality of the female vamps. Valentino was young for a leading man, only twenty-five when he made *Horsemen*, which no doubt added to his allure. He also dressed audaciously, wearing either a wild-looking gaucho costume or tuxedo in *Horsemen,* and his sheik costumes, according to Ashton D. Trice and Samuel A. Holland, seem "straight out of the Ballet Russe staging of *Scheherazade.*" Handsome and authentic, he acts threateningly toward women at first, even abducting them, but then seduces them voluntarily through a combination of bold actions, audacity, and natural good looks.[30] Douglas Fairbanks Sr. also seduced women more directly and conventionally in the swashbuckler genre. Fairbanks's films include *Robin Hood* (1922), *The Mark of Zorro* (1922), *The Black Pirate* (1929), and *The Gaucho* (1929). Only Valentino rivaled Fairbanks for free-spirited seduction and quiet machismo. These stars added a distinctive flavor to films of the period, providing a considerable amount of sexual energy to their films. The male heroes of pre-code Hollywood served as masculine reflections of their female counterparts. Both genders indulged in lighthearted seduction and bold adventures. In this respect, the films of Clara Bow, Theda Barrett, and Rudolph Valentino appear remarkably similar. Each features either seductresses or male vamps, popular icons of the day.

Nineteen-Twenties and Early Nineteen-Thirties

Cecil B. DeMille's *The Ten Commandments* (1923) appealed to Christian audiences not only by depicting the story of Christian laws but also by including a modern parable of two brothers, one a saint and the other a sinner. DeMille relied on dazzling special effects to depict the parting of the Red Sea and other Mosaic miracles.

Sheik Ahmed Ben Hassan (Rudolph Valentino) seduces Yasmine (Vilma Bank) in George Melford's *The Sheik* (1921). Valentino has been labeled a pre-code "male vamp" who excelled at seducing women. (Copyright 1926 United Artists)

El Zorro (Douglas Fairbanks, Sr.) in Fred Niblo's *Mark of Zorro* (1920). Fairbanks, like Valentino, served as a popular sex icon during the twenties. (Copyright 1920 United Artists)

The huge financial success of this film prompted DeMille to return to biblical themes in 1927 with *The King of Kings.* DeMille starred H. B. Warner as Jesus and employed a two-color process for the final Resurrection scene. In order to enhance the film's realism, he shot on location in Egypt. To set a properly pious tone, DeMille led the cast and crew in daily prayers throughout production. Wishing to avoid all taint of Hollywood scandals, which had already plagued the industry, DeMille forbade everyone to frequent nightclubs or be seen drinking and carousing. He well understood the power of scandal to undo all of his artistic efforts.[31]

Realizing that biblical settings afforded an excuse for nudity and other forms of sexuality, DeMille created yet another biblical epic, this time taking full advantage of the new talking format. He set *The Sign of the Cross* (1932) in ancient Rome in the time of the Emperor Nero's ruthless persecution of the early Christians. By setting this epic in the ancient past DeMille slipped in some rather shocking scenes for the period, even including nudity. A lesbian-themed dance scene in which a nearly nude pagan woman attempts to seduce a young Christian female raised the ire of the Hays Office, which lobbied hard to keep it out of the film. However, since the Studio Relations Board possessed little enforcement power, DeMille overruled objections, and the sex lures no doubt helped the film achieve substantial box office success. When he decided to rerelease the film a few years later, however, a stronger Production Code forced DeMille to remove the offending scenes.[32] DeMille, like Milestone, discovered that a few years made all the difference regarding the Production Code.

In 1921 a movement arose of conservative Christian clergy deeply offended by what they viewed as Hollywood's sexual laxity and general moral turpitude, which they believed promoted "sex, crime, and immoral activity."[33] Their concerns stemmed partially from some sensational trials exposing a Hollywood of orgy and adultery. The first occurred when director/comedian Roscoe "Fatty" Arbuckle found himself accused of raping and murdering starlet Virginia Rappe, who died under mysterious circumstances during one of Arbuckle's notoriously wild parties. Already saddled with a reputation for wild drinking binges with beautiful young women, Arbuckle became a victim of a media campaign that strongly implied that the 320-pound filmmaker raped Rappe, fiancée of friend and director Henry "Pathe" Lehrman, during one particularly over-the-top drinking orgy. Even after it was later revealed that Rappe's death actually occurred as a result of a ruptured bladder, charges of manslaughter against Arbuckle persisted. The jury failed to reach a verdict in two separate trials, even after learning of Ms. Rappe's botched abortion prior to attending the party. Arbuckle was eventually exonerated legally, but his dissipated public image, weak even before the Rappe incident, received a fatal blow as newspapers wallowed in sensational coverage of the trials. Arbuckle's persona, which challenged conventional morality, coupled with the lavish media attention paid to the criminal proceedings, provided potent ammunition for

Comedian Roscoe (Fatty) Arbuckle prior to the scandal that erupted in 1921 after a young starlet, Virginia Rappe, died after attending one of the actor's notorious parties. (Copyright 1920 Paramount Pictures)

censorship advocates. From that point onward Arbuckle found studio work only as a cameraman. Forgotten by his former admirers, most of whom probably assumed his guilt, Arbuckle died in 1933.

In 1922, only one year after the Arbuckle case, another sensational Hollywood scandal erupted that exposed even more sordid details about Hollywood's debauched elite. It involved popular director William Desmond Taylor and two young stars, Mabel Normand and Mary Miles Minter. The thirty-eight-year-old Norman had starred in dozens of films, the first in 1911, while the twenty-year-old Minter had also played in several movies. In February 1922, Taylor was found shot to death in his Hollywood mansion. The inquest revealed intimate relationships with several popular stars, including Normand and Minter, both of whom had mysteriously visited him on the night of the shooting. Although neither star was ever charged with Taylor's murder, the revelation of illicit sexual relations between directors and stars, coupled with rumors of binge drinking and illegal drugs, added to a growing concern among many that Hollywood was spiraling out of control.

As if all this bad news wasn't enough, later in 1922 yet another sensational industry scandal garnered national headlines after actor/director/writer Wallace Reid, addicted to morphine after receiving head injuries in a train crash, began treatment for drug and alcohol addiction. Reid, a tall, handsome actor who performed in dozens of films starting in 1910, including a small part in *The Birth of a Nation,* died soon afterward. The resulting scandal boosted growing anti-Hollywood sentiments and galvanized attempts to regulate the film industry. The state legislatures in thirty-two states began debating bills setting up state censorship boards. In Massachusetts the legislation passed. Furthermore, incensed at Hollywood licentiousness, censorship advocates compiled the first blacklist of stars they planned to boycott.[34] By 1922 the studios' hopes of remaining free of governmental censorship had greatly diminished.

Nineteen-Twenties Production Codes

In order to ward off federal censorship, producers formed the Motion Picture Producers and Distributors of America (MPPDA), a reprisal of the National Board of Review, in 1922. To create a sense of conservatism and probity to the outside world the MPPDA hired William "Will" Hays, who possessed a sober reputation for moral and religious conservatism, to present a suitable public face. Hays, a Presbyterian elder and former National Republican Party chairman who then served as Warren G. Harding's U.S. postmaster general, headed the watchdog agency designed to purify movies. He received a $100,000 salary, a huge amount in those days. Within months Hays released the Motion Picture Production Code, which instituted preproduction scrutiny. The code presented "Ten Commandments" of situations that filmmakers must follow. The commandments prohibited:

1. depictions of crimes against the law,
2. sexuality and vulgarity (nudity, revealing costumes, provocative dancing),
3. obscenity (in titles or subtitles—this was the silent age),
4. attacks against religion,
5. public hangings and electrocutions,
6. cruelty to children or animals,
7. the sale of women (prostitution or "white slavery"),
8. depictions of addictive drugs,
9. sexual "perversions," including homosexuality, and
10. miscegenation.

The MPPDA code apparently mandated the complete absence of the kind of controversial subject matter needed to attract audiences. Studio executives feared being forced by censors to produce staid, conservative pictures that few would pay to see, threatening their ability to attract the large audiences necessary for financial survival. At that point Hollywood also faced fierce competition from radio, a far cheaper form of mass entertainment, as well as leisure activities like driving around in the era's new mass-produced automobiles. All of these forces threatened Hollywood's lifeblood: box office receipts. Like earlier censorship agencies, the MPPDA relied upon a "gentleman's agreement" between representatives of the churches and of the motion picture industry, but the fact that it was a voluntary agreement meant that it could be broken. The MPPDA code, like previous codes, proved toothless and easily evaded by the studios, thus joining a long line of failed attempts to force the film industry to conform to conservative, church-dictated morality. Hollywood emerged untouched from the early confrontations between conservatives and filmmakers, and the remainder of the twenties witnessed relative peace between filmmakers and social critics.

In 1927, in response to continued complaints by social conservatives about movies' permissiveness, the MPPDA issued eleven "Don'ts" and twenty-five "Be Carefuls" for studios. The "Don'ts" included the original "Ten Commandments," and banned profanity, nudity, drugs, and sexual "perversions." In addition, the list forbade offending any race or creed, occasioned by some foreign governments' banning films with negative depictions of their natives. The "Be Carefuls" warned filmmakers to avoid bad taste when depicting sexuality or violence. Since the lists did not include any consequences for noncompliance, studios once again found it easy to ignore and evade a moral code that would surely decrease box office profitability. The "Don'ts" and "Be Carefuls" soon transformed into "Why nots?" and "Let's pull out all the stops!" for many filmmakers.

The code coincided with Prohibition (the Volstead Act), which transformed twenties and early thirties America by substituting illegal alcohol sales and consumption for the previous legal channels. Prohibition spawned bootleg beer, rum runners, speakeasies, and organized crime. Soon rival gangs warred with each other over the lucrative new markets. Hollywood responded to the general mood of lawlessness by flagrantly ignoring the code, just as it had earlier ones. In order to appeal to mass audiences, producers turned out films filled with attractive, scantily clad women and daring, romantic bootleggers. The code once again proved effective at discouraging conservative groups from achieving government censorship, as it served as a politically expedient buffer between filmmakers and those incensed with Hollywood's orgies. The Production Code at that time presented the appearance of conservatism and allowed Hollywood and Hays to fend off censorship for several more years.

Filmmakers continued embellishing movies with sex and shocking subject matter to attract mass audiences, but in 1930 their efforts proved increasingly futile as the Great Depression devastated movie attendance. During this time of crisis, as Hollywood moguls anguished over the future of their studios, an influential Jesuit priest and professor of religious studies, Father Daniel Lord, along with Martin Quigley, prominent lay Catholic and editor of the *Motion Picture Herald*, crafted a new Production Code for the MPPDA designed to cleanse the system once and for all. Reputedly encouraged privately by Hays himself, Lord and Quigley threatened a massive boycott against all films should the studio heads fail to agree to real censorship. Their document, known as the Lord Code, prohibited glorifying gangsters and other undesirables, including adulterers and prostitutes, and demanded that films present government and religious institutions favorably. It also mandated conservative "family values" in movies. Father Lord argued that motion pictures were lawfully subject to prior censorship and did not enjoy the same First Amendment protection as books, periodicals, or theatrical performances because of their reach to mass audiences of every age and class. His arguments were consistent with the Supreme Court ruling in *Black v. Chicago*, and the MPPDA adopted the new code, which mandated clean, conservative motion pictures. However, the self-censorship board also included an appeals process, which made it all too easy to circumvent the code. Once more, like its predecessors, the Lord Code succeeded only as a means of pacifying critics and forestalling governmental censorship

Because the Lord Code included an industry-dominated appeals board, enforcement of its lofty principles consisted more of appearance than reality. In fact, the Production Code enforcement became so lax that today the period is known as the official pre-code era. During this period Hollywood moguls felt freer than ever before to embellish their movies with provocative themes and scantily clad actresses to maximize box office appeal. The era today is famous for thrillers and comedies that often ooze sex and violence, and Hays appeared unable or unwilling to stifle or control it. During this period Hays functioned essentially as a public relations agent for Hollywood. In fact, Hays proved to be the consummate public relations front. Today, the pre-code era remains popular with scholars and film buffs and is widely studied and appreciated by large audiences. With contemporary mass video distribution networks, it is probable that many pre-code films receive wider distribution now than they did when they exhibited in theaters. For the most part, films from this period reflect a high level of ingenuity and creativity, especially those by such talented directors as Lewis Milestone, D. W. Griffith, Buster Keaton, Charles Chaplin, and Cecil B. DeMille.

Despite its reputation for permissiveness, however, the pre-code period actually witnessed many behind-the-scenes negotiations between producers and the MPPDA. Jason Joy, a retired colonel, served as chief censor. He wrote pleading letters to producers urging them to tone down some of their characterizations, particularly the sexy vamps and romantic gangsters. Lea Jacobs argues that the MPPDA often proved successful in persuading producers to tone down graphic scenes and soften some of the more glaring violations of conventional morality in order to forestall and placate state and local censorship boards.[35] For example, Colonel Joy explained to one producer that "the important thing is to leave the audience with the definite conclusion that immorality is not justifiable, that society is not wrong in demanding certain standards of its women, and that the guilty woman, through realization of her error, does not tempt other women in the audience to follow suit.[36] Despite Joy's pronouncement, the MPPDA found it difficult to withstand industry pressure for permissiveness, particularly in the midst of the Great Depression. Struggling for their very survival, Hollywood studios turned to sensational, edgy subject matter and the sex appeal of attractive stars. They produced films that explored premarital sex, adultery, serial monogamy, and miscegenation including *The Bitter Tea of General Yen* (1933), *The Emperor Jones* (1933), and *Massacre* (1934). Sexual desire, promiscuity, and adultery proliferated in films like *Red-Headed Woman* (1932), *Call Her Savage* (1932), and *Baby Face* (1933). Thomas Doherty observes that "for four years, the code commandments were violated with impunity in a series of wildly eccentric films." Films of this period explored taboo subject matter with frankness, realism, and candor that have yet to be equaled. To Doherty, "pre-Code Hollywood is from another universe. It lays bare what Hollywood under the later Hays Code did its best to cover up and push off screen."[37]

Cecil B. DeMille's *Madam Satan* (1930) exemplifies the latitude filmmakers enjoyed during the pre-code era. DeMille enjoyed a well-deserved reputation for creating edgy, provocative films (*The Cheat, Squaw Man, The Ten Commandments, The Plainsman*). *Madam Satan* depicts a wealthy married man, Bob Brooks (Reginald Denny), who enjoys reveling in alcohol-steeped orgies, complete with mistress. His prim wife, Angela (Kay Johnson), who initially adheres to the "librarian" archetype, accidentally uncovers one of her husband's adulterous affairs. After she confronts him he replies that he had little choice because she had lost her allure by turning into a "schoolteacher," not a sexually attractive mate. When Angela confronts her husband's mistress she, too, accuses Angela of having abandoned her sexuality. Faced with her failure as a lover, Angela transforms into a masked Madam Satan for a masquerade. She dresses in a sheer, revealing costume that leaves little to the imagination. At the party Bob finds himself enthralled by the sexual, aggressive Madam Satan. After pursuing the masked beauty, he finally discovers that it is Angela, who has succeeded in transforming herself from an angel into a devil in order to become sexually attractive. In the end, Bob and Angela reunite during a long, orgiastic party scene peopled with other scantily clad women. This film, like many other sexuality-laced productions of the period, succeeded well at the box office. DeMille achieves surprising results by reversing traditional sexual roles and features Madam Satan as the sexual predator, not her husband, who serves as the hapless victim.

Robert Z. Leonard's *The Divorcee* (1930) presents yet another broken marriage story, adapted from Ursula Parrot's controversial novel *Ex-Wife*. This time the dramatic tension surrounds Jerry (Norma Shearer) and Ted (Chester Morris), young lovers who marry and settle down after a whirlwind courtship. That is, Jerry settles down, but Ted soon strays with another young woman. After Jerry discovers their affair, which amounted to a single encounter never repeated, she decides to even the score and strays one night with Ted's best friend Don (Robert Montgomery). Ted returns from a business trip anxious to patch up their marriage but changes his mind after Jerry confesses without naming the man involved. Furious and betrayed, Ted leaves Jerry and sues for divorce. Deeply stung, Jerry continues to "even the score." "From now on," she warns, "you're the only man in the world that my door is closed to." After both characters embark on debauched lives Jerry realizes that she still loves Ted and takes a job in London so she can be closer to Paris, where he now resides. Finally, Jerry encounters Ted in a Parisian nightclub on New Year's Eve. After hearing Jerry's tearful protestations of love, Ted declares, "I'd give my right arm for you!" Jerry replies, "I like that right arm, Ted. How about putting it around me?" The film ends with their heartfelt embrace. A message emerges about true love trumping everything else, even an extramarital transgression or two. This film, like DeMille's, advocates marriage and tolerance of occasional flings and sexual transgressions.

Jack Conway's *Red-Headed Woman* (1932) ventures even further in tolerating and even seemingly advocating extramarital sexuality. It also features a beautiful, seductive woman, but this time she is not pretending. Jean Harlow stars as Lil, a gold digger from the wrong side of the tracks who explains to her friend Sally (Una Merkel), "I made up my mind a long time ago. I'm not going to spend my life on the wrong side of the railroad tracks." Sally warns, "Well, I hope you don't get hit by a train while you're crossin' over." Lil escapes being hit by a train, but she manages to completely disrupt the lives of several wealthy men, particularly Bill Legendre, Jr. (Chester Morris), a wealthy small-town businessman. She forces herself on Legendre, repeatedly and shamelessly, finally causing his wife, Irene (Leila Hyams), to sue for divorce. After he is divorced, Lil persuades Bill to marry her, but she soon loses interest and focuses her sights on a wealthier, older man from New York, Mr. Gaersle (Henry Stephenson).

These men serve merely to enrich Lil, but she reserves her true affections for Albert (Charles Boyer), Gaersle's French chauffer. Next, his suspicions up, Bill hires a private detective to spy on Lil, and the detective provides photographic evidence of her faithlessness. Bill divorces Lil, and Gaersle throws her out and fires Albert. If this film had been made just two years later, it might have ended with Lil's disgrace as a "fallen woman." However, Conway and scriptwriter Anita Loos included an epilogue in Paris in which Bill spots Lil at a horse race, where she receives first prize for her horse. This time speaking fluent French, Lil leaves with an older, wealthy Frenchman in a limo driven by none other than her paramour Albert. She achieves her dream of crossing the tracks and still keeps her lover, achieving wealth, status, and love, becoming the ultimate gold digger. This kind of character disappeared entirely after the Hays Code went into effect two years later. Even in 1932 the censorship boards of Massachusetts and Pennsylvania cut out the scenes with Albert, and Ohio removed the ending. England banned the film altogether.[38]

Alfred Green's *Baby Face* (1933) depicts still another femme fatale sleeping her way to the top. Green's film features a sweet-faced young woman named Lily (Barbara Stanwyck) who decides to become wealthy after reading Fredrick Nietzsche's *The Will to Power*. Lily rapidly rises through the corporate ranks, at one point accepting a transfer to Paris, where she continues her seductive ways. Even with Hays Code censorship still in the future, producer Raymond Griffith agreed to cut some controversial scenes and change the original conclusion, featuring Lily's triumph, into her defeat. Despite these changes, the newly formed Catholic League of Decency placed the film on its banned list in Chicago. When the Hays Code went into effect one year later *Baby Face*, even in its altered form, remained banned until its release on videotape in 1980. Recently the uncut version reappeared at the Library of Congress Archives, and it now appears on the DVD version.

Josef von Sternberg starred German bombshell Marlene Dietrich in *Blonde Venus* (1932), a heart-wrenching narrative of a devoted wife, Helen "Jones," who decides to return to her original career as a nightclub performer to raise money for her sick husband Ned Faraday (Herbert Marshall). Billed as "Blonde Venus," Dietrich sizzles as an entertainer, most notably in "Hot Voodoo." In that song she appears in an abbreviated African costume embellished with hundreds of tiny mirrors while singing, "Hot voodoo makes me wild!" The lyrics exude seduction, equating sex with exotic subjects like cannibalism and magic. Soon, her song and sultry delivery succeed in attracting Nick Townsend (Cary Grant), a wealthy playboy who, smitten by her beauty and talent, decides to subsidize her from then on. He forces her to quit the stage and provides an apartment for her and her young son Johnny. Thus, she becomes a "kept woman," causing the neighbors to gossip. When her husband recovers in Europe and announces his return, Helen decides to renounce her relationship with Townsend and return to Faraday. Nick suggests a farewell cruise, and she misses meeting Faraday's ship. When he returns home unexpectedly he finds her gone and

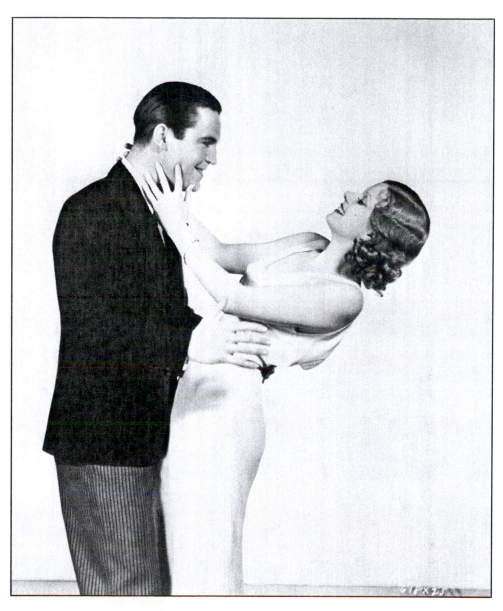

Lilian Andrews Legendre (Jean Harlow) toys with William Legendre (Chester Morris), whom she marries and quickly forms relationships with more powerful men in her rise in society in Jack Conway's *Red-Headed Woman* (1932). Lilian became one of the most notorious "gold digger" characters in film history. (Copyright 1932 Metro-Goldyn-Mayer)

Barbara Stanwyck's career as a femme fatale spans the pre-code era (*Baby Face*) through the classic film noir period (*Double Indemnity, The Strange Loves of Martha Ivers*). (Copyright 1939 Columbia Studios)

deduces the rest. When she finally returns from the cruise Ned uncovers her infidelity and can't rest until he divorces her, despite the fact that she accepted money from Nick only to save Ned. Ned proves unforgiving and pursues her with detectives to seize custody of Johnny. Alone and destitute, Helen briefly contemplates suicide, but instead turns once again to the cabaret, and this time she becomes an international sensation. While performing in Paris she runs into Nick, who eventually convinces her to become his fiancée.

At this point, von Sternberg changes the conventional ending of reunited married couple, as in *Madam Satan* and *The Divorcee*, and allows Helen and her lover to unite. The film contains much that would not have passed muster during the Hays Code, which would be enforced in two more years. Dietrich's *Blonde Venus* still excites and titillates today. Helen's affair with Nick clearly violates the prohibition

Helen Faraday (Marlene Dietrich), stage name "Blonde Venus," performs a sensual song titled "Hot Voodoo" in Joseph von Sternberg's pre-code classic *Blonde Venus* (1932). Dietrich's role as a desperate wife driven to prostitution to pay her husband's medical bills proved controversial and added to the rising agitation for stricter censorship of movies. (Copyright 1932 Paramount Studios)

Helen Faraday (Marlene Dietrich) seduces wealthy Nick Townsend (Cary Grant) in Joseph von Sternberg's *Blonde Venus* (1932). (Copyright 1932 Paramount Studios)

against adultery, yet studios ignored the MPPDA with impunity at that time. Even today, ratings difficulties might arise from the opening scene, censored from television broadcast versions, of Dietrich and five other beautiful maidens swimming in the nude. Although von Sternberg photographed no breasts from the front, he panned sensuously over the young girls' naked behinds and legs in the first scene, quite titillating at the time. Helen's methods of raising money, including petty theft and prostitution, appear brazen. *Blonde Venus*, like other sexy pre-code films, received a pass from the MPPDA. However, two years later, with the advent of the Hays Code, the MPPDA banned the film.[39]

Pre-code female characters reflected social advances for women, including suffrage and enhanced freedoms like driving, smoking, drinking, and dancing. Films appeared that reflected these changes. Many pre-code female characters enjoyed greater freedom than screen heroines of later decades and were often depicted in speakeasies with mirrored chandeliers reflecting short-skirted flappers with bobbed hair dancing the Charleston. Characters like Lily, Blonde Venus, Helen, and Madam Satan combine sexual liberation with material acquisitiveness and a rise in social class. The motif of achieving material wealth and status through sex proved especially potent to Depression-era audiences, and they flocked to these films, much to the growing dismay of social and religious conservatives.

Classic Gangsters

The pre-code period, coinciding with unpopular Prohibition, witnessed the birth of a new genre featuring bootleggers as heroes. Pre-code laxness in code enforcement coincides with a rise of organized crime, due largely to the unpopularity of Prohibition. Otherwise law-abiding Americans tolerated and patronized illegal speakeasies, swilled bootleg gin, and smuggled alcohol home from their vacations. This situation ended up glorifying the mobsters who stepped in to fill the sudden need for illegal alcohol and created the ideal conditions for a new genre: the classic gangster film. As Thomas Schatz observes, the classic "gangster genre" seemed to spring from nowhere in the early thirties because, responding to real gangland wars, the genre was "lifted from the headlines."[40] These films featured tales of urban crime and the rise of criminal empires using gangsters as heroes. Films by Howard Hawks, Mervyn LeRoy, and William Wellman (*Scarface, The Public Enemy, Little Caesar, I Am a Fugitive from a Chain Gang*) feature robust, attractive characters played by such actors as Paul Muni, James Cagney, and George Raft who engage in exciting, antiestablishment, forbidden activities. The unpopularity of Prohibition, spurred on by sensational newspaper accounts of gang warfare and bootlegged alcohol, ensured ready audiences. Illegal saloons and dance halls proliferated in residential neighborhoods, adding to the era's permissiveness. In fact, the classic gangster films perfectly embody public antipathy toward Prohibition.

The new genre arrived during the early days of talking pictures and continued to grow and develop in tandem with Prohibition-era mobs and crime lords. As increasing numbers of Americans enjoyed illegal bootlegged alcohol and patronized speakeasies, a culture war erupted between social and religious conservatives opposed to alcohol and average people who enjoyed social drinking. Bootleggers became more social heroes than villains. As an early version of the Production Code went into effect in 1930, the first of these new films, including *The Big House, The Criminal Code,* and *Doorway to Hell,* were already in production or being released. With box office losses due to the Depression, the code accomplished little to sanitize or censure these films. The genre turned classic with Mervyn LeRoy's *Little Caesar* (1930), William Wellman's *The Public Enemy* (1931), and Howard Hawks's *Scarface* (1932), each inspired by Chicago gang leader Al Capone. LeRoy's Rico (Edward G. Robinson), Wellman's Tom Powers (James Cagney), and Hawks's Tony Comate (Paul Muni) embody Capone's public persona at that time. These attractive stars provided gangsters with panache and almost iconic status.

Gang leader Rico (Edward G. Robinson) in Mervyn LeRoy's *Little Caesar* (1930).
After playing this Capone-like gangster, Robinson became an icon of the classic
gangster genre. (Copyright 1930 Warner Brothers)

Gangster Tom Powers (James Cagney) in William Wellman's *The Public Enemy*. Cagney also became an icon in the classic gangster genre. (Copyright 1931 Warner Brothers)

In *The Public Enemy*, Wellman cast James Cagney as Tom Powers, an obvious stand-in for Al Capone, the most charismatic of the Chicago gangsters. The film treats gangsters as if they were overgrown teenagers adept at exploiting lucrative illegal sources of income. Powers hijacks booze and runs bootlegged alcohol, making it seem fun and exciting. His criminal "honor" allows him to harm any gangster who attempts to stand in his way, but restricts him from harming outsiders. In his personal life, he seems attracted to flashy girlfriends, whom he treats heavy-handedly. After seeing the script, the Hays Office objected to a breakfast scene between Tom and Kitty (Mae Clarke) because both stars appear in pajamas, implying that they have spent the night together. That would mean that the two unmarried characters were engaging in a sexual affair. Wellman chose to include the scene anyway, as well as an even more sensational scene in which Powers, having become disillusioned with Kitty, explodes, "I wish you was a wishing well so I could tie a bucket to you and sink you," after which he grinds a half grapefruit into her face. That scene and others like it helped popularize Wellman's film among men, who in real life may have longed to express similar dominance over women. Later, Powers picks up Gwen Allen (Jean Harlow), a flashy, sexy blonde more to his liking. A sizzling Allen informs Powers, "You are different, very different from the men I know, and I've known dozens of 'em. Oh, they're so nice, so polished, so considerate. Most women like that type. I guess they're afraid of the other kind." Powers leaves no doubt that he is of that "other kind." Already in love, she tells Powers, "You're so strong. You don't give, you take. Oh, Tommy, I could love you to death!" Gangster protagonists like Powers and Tony Comate (Paul Muni) in *Scarface* proved effective at drawing audiences to theaters just when the Depression had resulted in decreased box office sales.

The rise of the gangster genre proved the last straw for religious conservatives like Father Lord and Martin Quigley. They quickly enlisted allies in other conservative groups and began agitating for censorship and outright banning of offensive films. The most vocal groups included the World War Veterans of Shenandoah Valley; the Exchange Club of Elizabeth, New Jersey; the Federal Council of Churches of Christ in America; and the Patrolman's Benevolent Association. These organizations expressed concern that gangster films would prove inspirational to young men and women, recruiting future gangsters into criminal careers. To allay these fears, Wellman, along with Darryl Zanuck, president of Warner Brothers, reassured the public by creating a special preface in which a police captain ostentatiously condemns organized criminal behavior.[41]

One of the most controversial crime films proved to be Mervyn LeRoy's *I Am a Fugitive from a Chain Gang* (1932). LeRoy's docudrama depicts a real person, Robert Burns (Paul Muni), who, after being convicted of petty theft and sentenced to a Georgia chain gang, endures inhuman prison conditions before escaping and fleeing to Chicago. Although he is successful under a new identity, Burns's wife informs the authorities, who promptly arrest him. In a bid to win exoneration, Burns reluctantly agrees to return to Georgia and serve a few months of his original sentence in exchange for a parole. However, prison authorities renege on their promises and rule that he must serve out the remainder of his sentence. At this point Burns engineers a second prison break. This time he writes several magazine articles and later a book about his experiences.

After LeRoy decided to film Burns's narrative, the MPPDA expressed deep concerns. The story's realistic depiction of prison conditions worried Colonel Joy. On February 26, 1932, Joy warned producers that the story's exposure of harsh prison conditions and depiction of Burns's two successful prison escapes ran the risk of offending Georgia authorities, who would likely retaliate by urging Georgia and other southern states with chain gang systems to ban the film. In a letter to Hays written on that same day he mused, "While it may be true that the [southern penal] systems are wrong, I very much doubt if it is our business as an entertainment force

Gangsters Tony Comante (Paul Muni) (left) and Guino Rinaldo (George Raft) in Howard Hawks's *Scarface* (1932). Comante served as another thinly disguised Al Capone in this classic gangster movie. (Copyright 1932 The Caddo Company)

to clear it up." Joy also objected to the prison scenes showing a majority of black prisoners, and after Warner Brothers decided to produce the film anyway Joy urged Zanuck to reverse the proportion of blacks versus whites because the preponderance of black prisoners made the film "unmistakably southern."[42] Zanuck, however, refused to make the required changes and because the Production Code was not yet enforced, LeRoy released the film without changes.

Early censors attempted to limit bawdy Broadway plays and sexually explicit novels from becoming "picturized," or adapted for the screen. During the twenties, filmmakers relied on Broadway for sensational, titillating scenarios. Mae West, Broadway's most popular sex icon, presented a one-person challenge to Production Codes, especially to the major Be Careful, which was never to present sexuality as vulgar or, in effect, as natural or animalistic. West was a veteran of burlesque, where she had played "Baby Vamp" as a child. At fourteen she graduated to vaudeville, and for the next few years, from 1907 to 1914, she achieved notoriety by performing raunchy reviews, introducing the shimmy to the stage, and writing her own sexually explicit dialogues.

West embodied the antithesis of conservative female role models. A part of the flapper generation, and yet older than most vamps, West crafted a persona that proved anathema to conservative gender expectations. In 1928 she further defied family values with *Diamond Lil*, also scripted by her, in which she starred as a madam with a passion for collecting diamond jewelry from wealthy lovers. Like West's previous works, *Diamond Lil* triumphed at the box office, and many expected it to be picturized. When the Hays Office produced a banned list of projects that Hays feared would be adapted to the screen, *Diamond Lil* topped it.[43] West's bawdy, suggestive delivery and the basic plot featuring a gold-digging female burlesque singer willing and able to use sex for personal gain pushed *Diamond Lil* to first place among the banned Broadway plays. Hays expressed his desire to exert a "special effort to prevent the prevalent type of book and play from becoming the prevalent type of picture." After Paramount purchased the screen rights in 1932 public furor over the decision helped launch the Hays Office into the next phase of Production Code development. West, working with director Lowell Sherman, proved adept at dodging the MPPDA's objections by deliberately introducing into the script outrageous scenes offered as sacrifices to Joy. West's strategy was to follow the advice from the MPPDA while subtly doing exactly what she wanted. In the end, West's sexy dialogue, vamp songs, and other titillating bits remain, even to the point of associating "Lady Lou" with an advertisement for diamonds, drawing an obvious parallel to the Broadway heroine.[44]

She Done Him Wrong became an instant box office hit, turning Mae West into a screen personality. In the film version "Lady Lou," a thinly disguised Diamond Lil from the Broadway play, persuades men smitten with her charms to give her expensive diamonds for her adornment. The film strongly implies that she barters

Mae West, a pre-code vamp who created a persona of a cynical, sensual gold digger who plied males for expensive presents, especially in Lowell Sherman's *She Done Him Wrong* (1933), a controversial pre-code film. (Copyright 1933 Paramount Pictures)

them in exchange for her body. Ample allusions to prostitution exist in this film. For example, after being greeted as a fine woman while walking downtown, Lou corrects her with, "best woman ever walked the streets!" As for gold digging, Lou explains, "I wasn't always rich. No, there was a time when I didn't know where my next husband was coming from." She attempts to seduce Captain Cummings (Cary Grant) with her oft-misquoted line, "Why don't you come up sometime and see me?" Even today, Lady Lou remains one of the most audacious characters in film history.[45] Gold diggers like Lady Lou anticipated the film noir seductresses of the forties and fifties.

The success of the pre-code sex films and classic gangster films, and the fact that the notorious West was starring in a Hollywood film based on the scandalous *Diamond Lil*, created a turning point in public opinion. In 1933 conservative Catholics demanded the imposition of the Lord Code, and Lord, with the support of the newly organized Catholic Legion of Decency (founded, some say, on Hays's unofficial advice), together with like-minded Christian and Jewish clergy from many denominations, demanded a national boycott of all Hollywood films. Studios faced a threat far more dire than government censorship. An audience boycott occurring during a period of already poor box office proceeds would end up costing millions. In fact, an audience boycott could well have proved fatal to many studios, so they finally submitted to strict production rules, and starting in July 1934, the Hays Code began.

Despite its name, the pre-code period teemed with production codes, but these proved largely ineffective. However, early production codes achieved some successes in modifying and softening film content. Even the official pre-code period of 1930–1934 provided far less freedom to filmmakers than many critics acknowledge, according to Lea Jacobs, who argues that Hollywood studios practiced a form of self-censorship during the pre-code period by anticipating objections from the MPPDA and adopting strategies to meet them. She reasons that the production codes wielded a powerful though indirect influence on films of the period. She concludes that self-regulation often corresponds with the aims of film producers. A cozy relationship developed between regulators and filmmakers in which the MPPDA often acted as an intermediary representing producers confronting hostile state censorship boards.[46]

Gender Roles

The late teens and twenties, like all postwar eras, teemed with nonconformist movie characters. Earlier films featured sweet "good girls" like Elsie Stoneman (Lillian Gish) in *The Birth of a Nation* or Mary Pickford's various roles. As Julie Burchill observes, during this time "girls changed their names to Blanche Sweet, Arlene Pretty, and even Louise Lovely in a bid to become the kind of kindergarten cutie." The first star, Mary Pickford, exuded wholesomeness and vulnerability. All that changed with the end of the war and the rise of the vamp.[47]

However, pre-code vamps, perfect embodiments of the seductress archetype, sported bobbed hair, smoked cigarettes, drank and danced in speakeasies, and seduced men. Hollywood depicted them as predatory femme fatales conquering men with seductive, saucy diction and alluring, unmistakably sexual gestures and posturing. Female characters throwing off traditional gender patterns provided women attractive, modern role models. Sexy, independent, and assertive, these nonconformist characters attracted audiences as never before, and the popularity of seductresses increased. Women admired and identified with Theda Bara, the first vamp, and her imitators, like the "It Girl" (Clara Bow), the clever sex diva Mae West, the audacious Jean Harlow, and the German "Blonde Venus," Marlene Dietrich. Characters like Harlow's red-headed woman, Diamond Lil, Dietrich's Blonde Venus, and West's Lady Lou ooze with sexuality while coldly manipulating all the males they encounter. Others, like Madam Satan, flaunt their sexuality to obtain goals and overcome obstacles. The period's gold diggers, who often slept their way to the top, appealed to women as well as men while infuriating social and religious conservatives. These popular vamp characters of the twenties and thirties in many ways resemble earlier "fallen woman" characters of nineteenth-century novels like *Tom Jones, Madame Bovary*, and *Lady Chatterley's Lover.* They serve as forerunners of the seductresses of pre-code Hollywood films.[48]

As for men, during the early thirties Hollywood resurrected the "bad boy" archetype of rebellious, attractive men flaunting society's gender restrictions. The male characters that stand out in pre-code cinema include the "male vamps" and swashbucklers portrayed by Douglas Fairbanks Sr. and Rudolph Valentino. These actors, inhabiting exotic settings and sexy, swashbuckling roles including sheikhs, matadors, and pirates, inspired audiences. By 1924 a survey of high school students found *The Four Horsemen of the Apocalypse* the most popular movie ever. Girls ranked *The Sheik* as their favorite movie besides *The Four Horsemen of the Apocalypse.* Even today, critics maintain that Valentino was the era's biggest box office name and, in fact, became America's first true "star" with the power to attract mass audiences.[49]

The classic gangster film provided viewers with sexy male mystique. James Cagney provided pre-code male audiences one of Hollywood's most self-centered, openly aggressive characters. The image of Cagney's bad boy Tom Powers's grinding a half-grapefruit into Kitty's (Mae Clarke) face in that breakfast scene in *The Public Enemy* remains a powerful statement of male dominance even today. That act of defiance against women resonated with those tired of the assertive, independent vamps and flappers. Powers's defiant act, along with similar macho actions by the protagonists of the classic gangster films, provided audiences tough male role models who were not afraid to express their views.

Pre-code male characters, especially in the gangster genre, enjoyed freedom to dominate women or flout social decorum. Hollywood's movie males acted a bit like some stars behaved in real life, that is, badly. Pre-code heroes avoided routine and conventional jobs, opting instead for more exciting lives as sheikhs, criminals, gold miners, and matadors. They often fell into the swashbuckler archetype as bold action heroes with auras of mystery and exoticism. However, bad boys, like seductresses, eventually proved unpopular with conservative religious groups, and were ultimately banished completely.

Creating the Couple

The two most popular character types of the pre-code era—assertive, aggressive males willing to flaunt authority and engage in violence, and aggressive females willing to use sex for self-advancement—outraged social and religious conservatives, who forced Hollywood to ban these characters. However, outrageously behaving pre-code characters inspired dozens of films and provided attractive, seductive faces to the pre-code period.[50] Many of these films remain popular today.

Pre-code couples evolved from the stodgy, middle-aged May Irwin and John Rise of *The Kiss* into sexy bombshells in films like *Blonde Venus, Red-Headed Woman,* and *She Done Him Wrong.* Popular movie scenarios changed from "boy meets girl" to "bad boy" meets "the seductress." Audiences found the combination irresistible. Pre-code couples include boyfriends and girlfriends, husbands and wives, husbands and lovers, and even wives and lovers. Early Production Codes struggled to keep films from offending powerful conservatives, but they ultimately proved unsuccessful. The two most popular character types of the pre-code era, aggressive males and sexually assertive females, often united to form couples, as in the James Cagney/Jean Harlow duo of *The Public Enemy.* By the early thirties opponents of these kinds of characters banded together and forced Hollywood to banish them for decades. However, outrageously behaving pre-code characters inspired dozens of films and provided attractive, seductive faces to the pre-code period.[51] They remain popular with film fans even today.

Marriage in pre-code films often seems weak, flawed, or nonexistent as filmmakers dispensed with Victorian stereotypes of silent, obedient ladies and sober, honest gentlemen. Instead, popular movies relied increasingly on seductresses encountering bad boys and swashbucklers. In many pre-code films men and women explore new roles and enjoy unprecedented freedoms. Several films depict marital infidelity, like *The Divorcee* and *Blonde Venus,* but extramarital cheating serves higher ends. In these films husbands and wives display the full range of human weaknesses, and, though they often pay heavily for their sins by experiencing poverty, jealousy, and hatred, ultimately the marital bonds, no matter how flawed, turn out to be stronger than expected, and couples survive infidelities just as they weather other trials of life.

CHAPTER THREE

The Hays Code

Historians usually employ the term *Production Code* to signify the period between 1934 and 1968 in which the Production Code Administration (PCA) held sway over film content and advertising. Will H. Hays, the first president of the Motion Picture Producers and Distributors of America (MPPDA), initiated and administered that code. Under Hays's leadership the older production codes discussed in the previous chapter underwent refinement and codification, with some new elements interjected in 1930 by Father Daniel Lord, a Catholic professor of religious studies. Finally, the Hays Code began functioning in July 1934.

From the beginning, the Hays Code imposed powerful rules and regulations governing motion picture content that constituted real censorship for the first time. For many, the rapidly evolving code became synonymous with Hays himself and eventually came to be referred to as the Hays Code, while Hays became known as "Mr. Hollywood." The Production Code Administration, which oversaw the day-to-day applications, soon came to be called the Hays Office. During no other period of film history has one man dominated the Production Codes like Hays did. To fully appreciate the ramifications and nuances of the 1934 Hays Code, we need to turn to Hays's earlier film regulator roles.

In 1922 he became the first president of MPPDA, an organization ostensibly formed by the major studios to regulate filmmaking policies and to represent the producers in their interactions with the public. In fact, the organization served to blunt criticism of Hollywood, allowing filmmakers freedom to use any means to entice audiences. Hays proved adept at assuaging public displeasure over Hollywood's scandals and permissiveness, negotiating with state and local censorship boards on behalf of producers and touting the agency's largely nonexistent power to force changes in films. However, under the threat of a Catholic and allied faiths' audience boycott and the behind-the-scenes machinations of powerful Catholic businessmen, studio executives reluctantly agreed to abide by a code that included serious provisions for enforcement. Hays then refined and adapted the latest iteration of previous codes that placed strict limitations on movie subject matter and advertising. The Hays Code eventually became the most long-lived set of filmmaking rules and regulations in motion picture history.

Don'ts and Be Carefuls

During the thirties filmmakers faced increasing criticism from unhappy ecclesiastics and women's groups. Hays attempted to deflect calls for government censorship by inaugurating an industry-controlled system, and in 1927 the MPPDA issued the first of its Production Codes. This code contained a list of "Don'ts and Be Carefuls" for filmmakers to follow. The Don'ts and Be Carefuls contained a list of prohibited activities, including:

1. Pointed profanity—by either title or lip—"God," "Lord," "Jesus," "Christ" (unless used in a religious context), "hell," "damn," "Gawd," and every other profane and vulgar expression, however it may be spelled.
2. Any licentious or suggestive nudity—in fact or in silhouette, and any lecherous or licentious notice thereof by other characters in the picture.
3. The illegal traffic in drugs.
4. Any reference of sex perversion.
5. White slavery.
6. Miscegenation.
7. Sex hygiene and venereal diseases.
8. Scenes of actual childbirth—in fact or in silhouette.
9. Children's sex organs.
10. Ridicule of the clergy.
11. Willful offense to any nation, race, or creed.

In addition to the Don'ts, the code also contained a long list of items that required special care:

1. The use of the flag.
2. International relations (avoiding picturization in an unfavorable light of another country's religion, history, institutions, prominent people, and citizenry).
3. Arson.
4. The use of firearms.
5. Theft, robbery, safecracking, and dynamiting of trains, mines, buildings, etc. (keeping in mind the effect that a too-detailed description of these may have upon the moron).
6. Brutality and possible gruesomeness.
7. Technique of committing murder by whatever method.

8. Methods of smuggling.
9. Third-degree methods.
10. Actual hangings or electrocutions as legal punishments for crime.
11. Sympathy for criminals.
12. Attitude toward public characters or institutions.
13. Sedition.
14. Apparent cruelty to children and animals.
15. Branding of people or criminals.
16. The sale of women or of a woman selling her virtue.
17. Rape or attempted rape.
18. First-night scenes.
19. Man and woman in bed together.
20. Deliberate seduction of girls.
21. The institution of marriage.
22. Surgical operations.
23. The use of drugs.
24. Titles or scenes having to do with law enforcement or law-enforcing officers.
25. Excessive or lustful kissing, particularly when one character or the other is a "heavy."[1]

Clearly, this early code contains most of the elements of the later production codes, including a rationale for regulating film content. Sexuality should be either avoided completely or handled "tastefully" according to the prevailing mores. Women, children, and animals were to be protected, and any realism regarding childbirth or the physical body was prohibited. The issue of homosexuality remained unstated and only implied under "sex perversions," which could also encompass other activities. At the time, homosexuality was simply too taboo even to include on the list.

Evasion occurred immediately. Although the code required producers to submit their scripts to the Hays Office for censorship, they merely appealed to the Producers' Appeals Board. At that point a jury consisting of Hollywood filmmakers who might well face similar censorship themselves ruled on script suitability, invariably in producers' favor. Therefore, this early censorship, though infused with tough-sounding regulations, functioned as a paper tiger lacking enforcement teeth. It provided badly needed cover for producers under increasing pressure to rid films of sex and violence. When confronted by procensorship organizations, studio spokesmen at the time pointed to the Don'ts and Be Carefuls, never mind that no one, certainly not Will Hays, planned on enforcing them.

In the long run the Don'ts and Be Carefuls proved just as vague as previous codes. Raymond Moley notes that even if the censors, headed by retired army colonel Jason Joy, desired vigorous enforcement, "the absence of a definite industry-law would have prevented its success."[2] The code was simply too vague, too subject to interpretation, and too lacking in enforcement provisions to be successful. Like earlier codes, it ultimately proved irrelevant, functioning primarily as window dressing and providing cover for filmmakers under pressure from social and religious conservatives.

During the Depression Hollywood audiences substituted listening to the radio, which was relatively inexpensive, for watching movies, and the resulting slump at the box office threatened the studios with bankruptcy. Faced with widespread economic uncertainty and industry layoffs, the moguls appealed to Hays to allow them to produce films unfettered by the restrictive code. Hays acquiesced by continuing to give them wide latitude in terms of subject matter and content. The resulting period, lasting from 1929 to July 1934, witnessed some of the freest, sexiest, most politicized, most violent films in motion picture history (see the previous chapter). As Gary Morris observes, during the early thirties "Hollywood films were rife with left-wing sentiments, anticapitalist rhetoric, images of the politicized poor, crime, sex, drugs, nudity, deviances of every description, and, yes, even the words 'damn' and 'hell.'"[3] The medium they competed with, radio, possessed many advantages, especially low cost. Once customers purchased radios, enjoying the programs cost nothing. Filmmakers responded to radio's threat by offering daring, sexy, violent programming designed to lure audiences back to theaters. With significantly less disposable income in audiences' hands, the task of attracting theater audiences became much more challenging.

Boycott

Predictably, pre-code permissiveness stimulated reaction from religious conservatives. In 1933 Amleto Giovanni Cicognani, apostolic delegate to the American Catholic Church, called upon American Catholics to unite against the immorality of the cinema. In response, the American Catholic Church announced the formation of the Legion of Decency that same year. The legion urged Catholics to avoid objectionable films as "occasions for sins." It charged that Hollywood had become "the pest hole that infects the entire country with its obscene and lascivious moving pictures." In 1934, in order to force studios to clean up movies, Cardinal Dougherty of Philadelphia called for a complete boycott of all Hollywood films. In an open latter to Catholics, Dougherty warned that "perhaps the greatest menace to faith and morals in America today is the motion picture theater." He complained that previous lobbying efforts to cleanse films of their prurient content had failed. Now, he concluded, "Nothing is left for us except the boycott."[4] In June, Cardinal Mundelein brought the Chicago Diocese into the boycott.[5] Protestant leaders immediately announced their support for Cardinal Mundelein's position, and Catholics were soon joined by like-minded Protestant and Jewish organizations, adding to the chorus raised against Hollywood. Finally, the legion enlisted the support of the Giannini brothers, heading up the Bank of America, which funded countless films. The brothers, conservative Catholics, agreed that Hollywood needed censorship and threatened to cut off production funds if Hollywood continued to delay code enforcement. Faced with a serious threat to motion picture financing and attendance at a time of dwindling Depression audiences, studio heads reluctantly acquiesced to a code armed with powerful enforcement teeth.[6] This new code forced Hollywood into rethinking its entire approach to crime, sexuality, religion, and a host of other sensitive issues. Long after the code went into effect, the Legion of Decency continued to play a prominent censorship role by condemning many films and forcing changes in many others.

The Hays Code

In July 1934 the heads of the major studios finally agreed to abide by the new Hays Code and to pay a huge (for the period) fine of $25,000 for failure to cooperate. On June 15, 1934, *Variety* announced the abolishment of the Producers' Appeals Board and stated, "Joe Breen is supreme pontiff of picture morals from now on. Only appeal from the Breen ruling is to the Hays directorate in New York."[7] Thus the laissez-faire pre-code period, witness to some of the best films ever made, ended, and an era of regulated film content and advertising began. Echoing the Don'ts and Be Carefuls of pre-code days, the code for the first time placed strict limitations on subject matter. Studios had no choice but to abide by its precepts and work with its enforcers. The Hays Code would remain in force, though greatly altered, for thirty-four years.

The Production Code adopted by Hays largely originated with Father Daniel Lord, a professor and Catholic priest working with Martin Quigley, a wealthy lay Catholic and publisher of the influential *Motion Picture Herald*. Quigley believed strongly that "the function of art is to ennoble." He disliked films that depicted earthy, realistic human behavior, believing that they dragged humanity down. Instead, he demanded that movies provide spiritual and moral uplift to audiences.[8] This perspective not only resulted in the establishment of the Hays Code, it also stimulated newer, more conservative genres.

To assist him with his new enforcement powers, Hays enlisted Joseph Breen, a prominent lay Catholic, to head the new Production Code Administration (PCA), the MPPDA's enforcement arm. The Breen Office, located in Hollywood instead of New York, tracked scripts from the beginning of the production process until their completion. Like Colonel Joy of the pre-code days, Breen and other PCA officials wrote detailed letters to producers outlining their reactions, often their objections, to each script. In order to obtain the all-important MPAA "Seal of Approval," producers reluctantly complied with PCA directives. If any studio ignored the PCA and released a film without a seal, it would have to pay the steep $25,000 fine and face expulsion from the MPPDA. That carried an additional threat of retaliation by bankers, drying up funding for producers. Studios that abandoned the code also faced the powerful Catholic Legion of Decency, poised to impose a boycott against any that failed to conform to the code.

The Hays Code contained some significant shocks for producers, who soon discovered that the code banned many of the most successful strategies for attracting audiences, or at least severely limited their use. The code's three overarching principles express the essence of Hays morality:

1. No picture shall be produced which will lower the moral standards of those who see it.
2. Correct standards of life, subject only to the requirements of drama and entertainment, shall be presented.
3. Law—divine, natural, or human—shall not be ridiculed nor shall sympathy be created for its violation.

The code retained most elements of the Don'ts and Be Carefuls, and, in fact, enforcement proved the greatest difference between it and the earlier Lord Code. In addition to the general principles, the Hays Code prohibited graphic depictions of crime and famously mandated that crime must never pay. In Hays Code movies, criminals must always suffer for their misdeeds. The code banned depictions of drug addiction and, remembering the Charles Lindbergh case, also banned depictions of kidnappings of children. In terms of violence, the Hays Code prohibited "extreme brutality," but, like obscenity and profanity, it left those concepts undefined. Primarily, the code censored sexuality and profanity. It demanded that films uphold marriage and avoid depicting adultery, particularly making adultery appear justified or pleasurable. It demanded that filmmakers avoid depictions of lustful, open-mouthed kissing (in practice, no kissing over thirty seconds) as well as the seduction of women, rape, and abortion. It prohibited depictions of sexual "perversions" of any kind, especially homosexuality, and it prohibited depictions of venereal disease and children's sexuality. Finally, in response to intense lobbying from the church, it banned obscenity, blasphemy, and profanity, although it also left those concepts murky and undefined. In addition to subject matter, the new code also regulated dialogue and advertising, making it by far the most comprehensive Production Code in film history.

In depictions of sensitive material, the Hays Code demanded "that evil is not presented alluringly." The code acknowledged that "sin and evil enter into the society of human beings," so they cannot be forbidden. However, filmmakers must make sin and evil repellent. That goal long eluded creative writers, including John Milton, who made Satan a strangely fascinating character in *Paradise Lost*. The code banned "the presentation of scenes, episodes, plots" that are "deliberately meant to excite" sex and passion among audiences, thereby banning some of filmmakers' chief allures while admitting that "sex and passion exist and consequently must sometimes enter into the stories which deal with human beings." Ultimately the code sternly warned that passion, even if excited by "pure love" between a man and a woman "is not the subject for plots." Of course, this also proved difficult to enforce and even to define. Sexuality between characters courting but not yet married, or between those who were no longer married, was forbidden. In fact, sexuality of any kind, even between married couples, was never permitted. Thereafter, it would be impossible to receive a Seal of Approval for the "gold digger" films so popular during the pre-code era, and Hollywood was prohibited from using its most successful strategies for enticing audiences.

On the subject of crime, the code censored far less stringently than on sex. It required that "criminals should not be made heroes, even if they are historical criminals." Also, it warned that "law and justice must not by the treatment they receive from criminals be made to seem wrong or ridiculous." That codicil reminds us of the humorous Keystone Cops of the twenties. Of course, this segment of the code effectively outlawed the gangster genre, as well as the swashbuckler genre, which formerly featured films about buccaneers, pirates, and the like. The code also prohibited positive depictions of communism and strongly opposed negative portrayals of capitalism. Joseph Breen reportedly regarded communism and socialism as closely akin to criminal behavior and never tolerated positive depictions of these systems. Breen also opposed sympathetic depictions of labor unions. He demanded "balanced" depictions of Adolf Hitler and Benito Mussolini, meaning no direct attacks on them or on their actions. Privately, he admired Francisco Franco. His own anti-Semitism actually parallels that of Nazi Germany, and he wrote privately that "these Jews seem to think of nothing but money making and sexual indulgence. They are," he concluded, "probably the scum of the earth."9

The films of the Hays period provide a detailed record of changing mores and attitudes during Hollywood's Golden Age. The PCA shielded audiences from sensitive, potentially explosive issues like organized crime, extramarital and premarital sex, drug use, prostitution, violence, and government corruption. It protected the institution of the family, organized religion, large corporations, and even foreign governments from unfavorable treatment in films. Its framers intended the code to arbitrate and mandate proper depictions of evolving family relations, criminal activity, and anything else challenging to the status quo. The code offered hope to the general public that motion pictures and movie advertisements would provide a bulwark against disturbing social changes then taking place. The social portrait that the code's framers promulgated was of stable, docile, law-abiding, monogamous citizens more at home in agricultural America than in its industrialized cities.

Screwball Comedy

For the moment filmmakers were forced to adhere to the Hays Code, but a few innovative directors quickly invented some clever evasion strategies, adhering to the letter but not the spirit of the regulations. Between 1934 and 1938 a handful of innovative directors created an entirely new genre that appealed to audiences grown accustomed to sexy, provocative films. Frank Capra invented the new genre, since labeled screwball comedy, in 1934. Capra's *It Happened One Night* served as a prototype for a genre exploiting erotically tinged differences in social class. Screwball comedies relied on the forbidden. When the protagonists, Peter Warne (Clark Gable) and Ellie Andrews (Claudette Colbert), find themselves sharing the same room in an auto camp, Andrews demands they erect a wall of sheets to divide them, as if any such flimsy obstacle could prevent them from falling in love in a Hollywood movie. Colbert plays a willful millionaire's daughter who ran away from her father's yacht in Miami because he did not approve of her new husband, King Wesley (Jameson Thomas). Andrews buys a bus ticket to New York, but before she can go there she meets newspaper correspondent Warne, who has just been fired. A palpable undercurrent of sexual attraction quickly develops between them. These tensions at first glance seem improper because Andrews is technically married and therefore forbidden fruit. However, her marriage was never consummated, so her liaison with Warne does not quite qualify as adulterous. As the sexual tension between them increases audiences realize that the flimsy room divider will never suffice. In one scene, as Andrews quickly retreats to her side of the sheet, Warne undresses, observing, "Perhaps you're interested in how a man undresses. You know, it's a funny thing about that. Quite a study in psychology. No two men do it alike." Later, in another scandalous scene (for the time), Andrews hikes up her skirt and exposes her thigh alongside the highway in order to secure a ride. After several drivers slam on their brakes she observes proudly, "Well, I proved once and for all that the limb is mightier than the thumb." Warne replies, "Why didn't you take off all your clothes? You could have stopped forty cars!" Like *The Gay Shoe Clerk* thirty years earlier, Capra's film exposes just enough flesh to titillate but not enough to trigger censorship.

Screwball comedy dialogue barely skirted the edges of acceptability, but it provided a sense of permissiveness and deviancy. Later the pair feigns a domestic quarrel to convince the motel manager and his wife that they are truly married. After witnessing their spat the motel manager remarks, "I told you they were a perfectly nice married couple." Marriage in this film becomes synonymous with misery, while the feigned marriage between these two socially mismatched protagonists ultimately blossoms into love, as the following dialogue illustrates. Warne complains to Andrews's father, "A normal human being couldn't live under the same roof with her

Peter Warne (Clark Gable) and Ellie Andrews (Claudette Colbert) finally get together after several false starts in Frank Capra's *It Happened One Night* (1934). Capra's film pioneered a new genre labeled screwball comedy that arose due to stricter censorship of movie sexuality. (Copyright 1934 Columbia Pictures)

without going nutty." When asked whether or not Warne loves his daughter, Warne responds, "Yes, but don't hold that against me. I'm a little screwy myself!" In Capra's film, suggestive dialogue and tantalizing situations substitute for the more direct expressions of sexuality of the pre-code period.

It Happened One Night illustrates the central tension of screwball comedy: between officially sanctioned marriages and more casual, less officially acceptable versions. In screwball comedy formal weddings get put off and eventually abandoned, while chance encounters lead to contentious though exciting romances rendered through innuendo, symbolism, and double entendre. Classic screwball couples indulge in verbal teasing, divorce with impunity, remarry, and generally violate Victorian notions of proper relationships while nominally remaining within acceptable social limits. Capra's film tweaks conservative, middle-class values by evoking sympathy for a young couple on the social fringes, with no money (for the moment), and who travel in the company of a variety of nonconformist characters. Andrews, a runaway from both husband and father, represents the quintessential rebellious young woman who rejects the social conventions that demand her subservience to father and husband.

Had Capra chosen a more directly sexual approach to the love affair of his two stars, the film would have failed to receive a production seal. If Capra had made this film one year earlier the relaxed code would have allowed the couple to dispense with the "Wall of Jericho" and other accommodations to conservative sensibilities. Despite this, the film proved enormously popular with audiences and critics alike, becoming the first motion picture to sweep the major Academy Awards (Best Picture: Columbia; Best Actor: Gable; Best Actress: Colbert; Best Director: Capra; Best Adaptation: Samuel Hopkins Adams). The success of *It Happened One Night* soon inspired a host of imitators, including Gregory La Cava's *My Man Godfrey* (1936) and Howard Hawks's *Bringing Up Baby* (1938) and *His Girl Friday* (1941), each of which features protagonists from diverse social classes in the time-honored manner of screwball comedies.

Despite the best efforts of Hays censors, filmmakers continued to produce sexy films that survived PCA scrutiny by inventing a genre of mismatched lovers that come across as naughty, teasing, and subtly deviant yet officially safe. Filmmakers charged these comedies with a powerful symbolic and sexy undercurrent that violated social class taboos. As Christopher Beach points out, in screwball comedy "class relationships are often sexualized or eroticized."[10] Similar effects occur from the genre's rapid-fire dialogue, particularly in the form of saucy, suggestive remarks by the sexy, female lead characters. These modernized vamps became one of the genre's most recognizable icons. As Maria DiBattista observes, fast-talking women often translate socially as having loose morals. She notes that "so quickly do words come flying out of mouths that it is difficult to follow what is being said." The

"Hildy" Johnson (Rosalind Russell) in Howard Hawks's *His Girl Friday* (1940). Russell plays the ultimate "fast-talking dame" in this screwball comedy classic. (Copyright 1940 Columbia Pictures)

resulting cacophony of verbal barrages launched by both heroes and heroines served as a symbolic representation of more intimate relationships that were not permitted by the code. Fast-talking characters presented an acceptable substitute for more overt sexual depictions.[11]

Although marriage provided the only acceptable sexual relationship during the Hays period, matrimony fares very poorly in screwball comedy. As Katherina Glitire observes, "Marriage is commonly understood in the screwball world to involve oppression and confinement." In fact, marriages in screwball comedies are rare. As Glitire notes, "marriage is never a 'beautiful thing' in screwball comedy. It is always a problem." In some classic screwball comedies, the central couple only *pretend* to be married (*If You Could Only Cook*, 1935; *Midnight*, 1939), pretend that they are not married (*The Palm Beach Story*, 1942), believe incorrectly that they are married (*Mr. and Mrs. Smith*, 1941), or get divorced and reunite later (*His Girl Friday*, 1940). Some engagements break off in screwball comedies (*My Man Godfrey*, 1936;

Bringing Up Baby, 1938; *Holiday*, 1938). Other comedies feature characters that commit implied adultery (*She Married Her Boss*, 1935; *The Awful Truth*, 1937). Even bigamy figures in some plots (*Libeled Lady*, 1936; *My Favorite Wife*, 1940; *Too Many Husbands*, 1940).[12]

Broadway Musicals

Broadway musical comedies remained the bane of Hays censors but, nevertheless, provided many allures for Hays Code audiences. Usually, musicals featured attractive, seductive young women, providing motivation for male audiences. To attract women, these films also featured debonair leading men, like Fred Astaire and Dick Powell, who could not only act but also sing and dance. Ray Enright's *Dames* (1934) exemplifies the musicals forced to conform to the Production Code. This Busby Berkeley–arranged film goes by the unofficial name of *Gold Diggers of 1934*, referring to Mervyn Leroy's successful, exciting *Gold Diggers of 1933*, also choreographed by Berkeley. Both films feature dozens of scantily clad females performing extravagant songs and dances, but in the 1933 pre-code version the girls wear even less clothing than they were allowed to wear in 1934. Busby Berkeley's *Gold Diggers of 1935* also flirted with the boundaries imposed by Hays Code censors. It still shows dozens of beautiful women singing and playing identical pianos, but the amount of skin tolerated in 1935 pales in comparison to the skin allowed in Lloyd Bacon's *42nd Street* (1933). In that pre-code film, released prior to harsher Hays Code restrictions, the weak censors had allowed Bacon, with Berkeley's assistance, to show female dancers stripping down to lace panties and brassieres. The same level of nudity was unacceptable just two years later, but by then Berkeley had simply substituted elaborate staging for the naughty costuming of the pre-code era.

After 1934, audiences continued to attend musicals, and filmmakers learned to substitute double-entendre dialogue, virtuoso performance scenes, and elaborate staging in order to compensate for the reduced sensuality of the characters. Hays Code audiences may have missed the sexy costuming and dialogue of earlier musicals, but they were enthralled by Astaire's and Rogers's dancing and Dick Powell's singing. Thirties musicals also served as escapism, keeping people's minds off the Depression and disturbing world events. These glitzy musicals allowed audiences to escape from the harsh realities of daily life.

Astaire's reputation, along with Powell's, soared during the Hays Code. One of Astaire's most virtuoso performances occurs in Mark Sandrich's *Top Hat* (1935), in which Astaire stars as Jerry Travers, who falls for Dale Tremont (Ginger Rogers) while staying in London. Their renditions of Irving Berlin's "Cheek to Cheek," "Isn't This a Lovely Day to Be Caught in the Rain?" and "Top Hat, White Tie, and Tails" rank among the screen's all-time best performances. Sandrich skirted the Hays

Code's prohibition of obscenity, which included "damn," in one memorable scene in which Travers impersonates the driver of a horse-drawn cab. Travers responds to Tremont's request that he make the horse go faster. "Well, it's like this, Miss. You see, the horse is kind of tired today on account of he won the Grand National on Friday." When Tremont questions whether the Hansen horse is really a racehorse, Travers answers, "Yes, Miss, and I've got his pedigree, too. As a matter of fact, his sire was Man O' War." Tremont then asks, "Well, who was his dam?" After pretending not to hear the question, he finally replies, "Oh, I don't know, Miss, he didn't give a . . ." At that point the word "dam," an obvious double entendre for the banned obscenity "damn," is nearly drowned out by the sudden speeding up of the horse. The code remained inviolate, and Sandrich escaped detection with this "obscene" reference. Audiences, grown accustomed to Hays Code censorship by then, must have thought it hilarious.

Gangsters

Hollywood's filmmakers proved especially nimble in sanitizing the gangster genre, one of the chief reasons for the rise of the Hays Code. Pre-code gangster films like Mervyn LeRoy's *Little Caesar* (1930), William Wellman's *The Public Enemy* (1931), and Howard Hawks's *Scarface* (1932) raised the ire of conservatives, and for that reason the Hays Code outlawed all films glorifying crime. The Hays Code mandated that criminals pay for their crimes, often with their own blood, but sometimes even that failed to satisfy code requirements if the PCA felt the criminals were being glorified during most of the movie. However, after only three years resourceful Hollywood filmmakers devised a gangster film that even Joseph Breen liked.

William Keighley's *G-Men* (1935) inaugurated a new genre formula emphasizing the exploits of law enforcement officers, not organized criminals. After an explosion of bank robberies in 1934, the public seemed ready for a different kind of crime drama, and censors obliged them. In an abrupt genre change Keighley's film showcases FBI agent Brick Davis (James Cagney), not a bootlegger like in pre-code films. Instead of bootlegging, Davis starts out as an unsuccessful lawyer who applies for the FBI after gunmen kill his college friend. He proves amazingly adept at fist and gun fighting, skills acquired during his rise from the ghetto. To further strengthen the connection between Davis and the pre-code bootleggers, Keighley provides Brick with a convenient gangster background. At first, Cagney wanted to play this role with gentlemanly polish, but producer Hal Wallis demanded that he play it rough and unrefined, more like his portrayal of gangster Tom Powers in *The Public Enemy.* Wallis also demanded that Keighley shoot the film as darkly as possible, using shadows and low lighting. The finished film manages to retain many elements of the older gangster genre, substituting a tough law enforcement officer for a hardened criminal. Warner Brothers, fearful of competition from other studios, avoided using the *G-Men* title throughout the production process, substituting instead the eponymous title *Mr. Farrell*, named for Agent Hugh Farrell (Lloyd Nolan), a senior FBI detective who ends up shot by the criminals. Warner feared that other studios would follow their new formula for skirting the Hays Code. In fact, from that point onward filmmakers from other studios began making violent gangster films, only now their heroes fought on the right side of the law.[13]

In 1937 William Wyler released *Dead End*, a gangster film costarring Humphrey Bogart as Baby Face Martin, a small-time hoodlum who decides to kidnap a rich child and hold him for ransom. Bogart's character behaves as more villain than hero, a far cry from the glorification of bootleggers during the pre-code period. In 1938 Warner Brothers created a more traditional gangster film that was still permissible to the Hays Code. Michael Curtiz directed *Angels with Dirty Faces*, starring James Cagney as gangster Rocky Sullivan and Pat O'Brien as his childhood-friend-turned priest Jerry Connolly. Joseph Breen responded quickly to the script submitted in January 1938. In a letter to Warner Brothers, he warned the studio that "it is important to avoid any flavor of making a hero and sympathetic character of a man who is, at the same time, shown to be a criminal, a murderer, and a kidnapper." In order to pass the censors, Breen advised that "great care will be needed both in the writing and actual shooting of the picture."[14] Curtiz took Breen's advice and included a scene in which Sullivan pretends to be afraid at his electrocution in order to provide a suitable unglamorous model to the Dead End Kids, a neighborhood youth gang. In fact, Sullivan dies unafraid, as he explains to Connolly shortly before his execution, "In order to be afraid, I think you've got to have a heart. I don't think I got one. I got it cut out of me a long time ago."

Film Noir

Even before 1941 the country plunged into a pessimistic mood and Hays censors began relaxing some of their most stringent restrictions. As long as movies seemed to reflect patriotism the Breen office began allowing more overt expressions of sexuality. Preston Sturges's *The Miracle of Morgan's Creek* (1944) stars Betty Hutton as sexy Trudy Kockenlocker, who goes dancing with some soldiers leaving for the war, loses her memory, gets married, becomes pregnant, and asks her gullible admirer, Norval Jones (Eddie Bracken), for assistance. Sturges thwarted the censors' demand that Trudy remain sober by having her hit her head and stagger dizzily through several scenes. He satisfied censors by having Trudy marry while spoofing the code by filming it as a comic, mock wedding.

With the Breen office seemingly distracted by the war, a new genre arose that expressed the era's pessimism and willingness for frank sexuality. These films feature neither gangsters nor law enforcement officers, banned by censors, but instead show-case private detectives, returning soldiers, boxers, and rogue cops—prohibited characters just a few years earlier. Directors working in this genre invented clever stratagems for depicting forbidden behavior. For example, in this genre, dubbed *film noir*, or "black film," by French critics, men and women do not engage in sexual behavior on screen. Instead, they perform sex symbolically in a code widely understood by audiences. They may walk off screen together, signifying a much deeper intimacy, or enter a bedroom with each other, and audiences easily filled in the details.

Film noir benefited from recent technological developments in the industry. Wartime newsreels demanded the development of smaller, lighter, hand-held cameras that relied on outdoor lighting for filming battlefield documentaries. Filmmakers soon embraced the new cameras, which needed neither expensive studio sets nor artificial lighting. The new cameras were capable of using available lighting, and even allowed for night shots without artificial lighting, called night-for-night photography. Therefore, at a time when the public began to demand realistic, hard-boiled thrillers, the new outdoor cameras allowed filmmakers to dispense with elaborate sets and expensive lighting.

Today many attribute John Huston's *The Maltese Falcon* (1941) as the pioneer and model for the film noir genre, although Boris Ingster's *Stranger on the Third Floor* (1940), a low-budget offering, preceded it by a year. Huston based his film on Dashiell Hammett's best-selling dark novel about Sam Spade, a cynical private detective who finds himself immersed in a caldron of sex and violence. Huston cast Humphrey Bogart in the lead role, relying on his expertise with gritty, hard-boiled characters. Huston's film, with its seedy San Francisco underworld settings and dark, night-for-night photography, is remembered today not only for being the first of a creative new genre but for its sheer darkness—both morally and physically. Bogart seems perfect in the role of Spade, a hard-bitten detective, a role made darker and bleaker by Hammett's dialogue. In the first scene, when Spade is interviewing Brigid O'Shaughnessy (Mary Astor), he reveals his cynicism by accepting her bribe in the form of a retainer to investigate a murder. "We didn't exactly believe your story, Miss O'Shaughnessy, we believed your two hundred dollars. . . . I mean, you paid us more than if you'd been telling us the truth, and enough more to make it all right."

Huston's film depicts Brigid O'Shaughnessy as a criminal of loose morals who serves as one of the film's villains and, as a consequence, pays a heavy criminal penalty for her wickedness. Joseph Breen wrote to Warner Brothers that "the fade-out of Spade (Humphrey Bogart) and Brigid is unacceptable because of the definite indication of an illicit sex affair." Furthermore, the film's downbeat detective conducts a clandestine extramarital affair with Ida Archer, his partner Miles's wife, until Miles turns up murdered, at which point Spade dumps her. In his letter Breen

Detective Sam Spade (Humphrey Bogart) confronts femme fatale Brigid O'Shaughnessy (Mary Astor) in John Huston's 1941 film noir classic *The Maltese Falcon* (1941). Spade outsmarts and defeats the femme fatale in this film, a rare occurrence in the film noir genre. (Copyright 1941 Warner Brothers)

warned, "It is essential that Spade should not be characterized as having had a sex affair with Ida."[15] Ultimately, Spade relinquishes both of his paramours, first by dumping Ida and later by turning Brigid over to the police for the murder of Miles. "Yes, Angel," he explains ironically, "I'm going to send you over." When she protests that they love each other, he replies, "Maybe I do. I'll have some rotten nights after I've sent you." Lest she think that he hasn't sacrificed much, Spade explains that he won't let her go free "because all of me wants to regardless of consequences, and because you counted on that with me, just like you did with all the others." Only by sacrificing Ida and Brigid, his illicit lovers, does Spade find redemption. The climax occurs when Spade informs the police about O'Shaughnessy's guilt for murdering his former partner. As she is taken away by the police Spade descends a staircase, headed down to a lower level that seems symbolic of hell. Audiences loved the blatant cynicism and macho actions of Spade and many of the other characters in the film, and Hollywood immediately began turning out other dark films modeled after this one.

As novelist Raymond Chandler, author of many noir novels (*Time to Kill, Murder My Sweet, Farewell My Lovely, The Big Sleep, Lady in the Lake, Marlow, The Long Goodbye*), observed, film noir depicts "a world gone wrong, a world in which long before the atom bomb, civilization had created the machinery for its own destruction and was learning to use it with all the moronic delight of a gangster trying out his first machine gun. The law was something to be manipulated for profit and power. The streets were dark with something more than night."[16]

Although the first film noirs appeared during the war, the genre accelerated rapidly during the postwar period. The movement's dark, brooding, pessimistic films reflect perfectly the angst-ridden postwar period as Americans began to cope with immense wartime losses, especially the human casualties, not to mention a new, menacing cold war developing with the USSR. The war's effects, however, did not end with the cessation of hostilities. Returning soldiers, exhausted from long years of combat, encountered marital infidelity, wartime profiteering, social dislocations, newly assertive women, and restive minorities. As with all wars, a large number of veterans experienced battle fatigue and the lingering effects of shell shock.

Other sexually titillating notable noirs of this period include Billy Wilder's *Double Indemnity* (1943), featuring Barbara Stanwyck as an adulterous, murderous wife; Michael Curtiz's *Mildred Pierce* (1945), with Joan Crawford in the title role and Ann Blyth as the daughter who competes with her mother for the love of a wealthy playboy; Charles Vidor's *Gilda* (1946), starring Rita Hayworth as a promiscuous, adulterous wife; and Billy Wilder's *Sunset Boulevard* (1950), featuring Gloria Swanson as an aging former Hollywood star who attempts to buy the love of a young writer, played by William Holden.

Hollywood scriptwriters honed their skills at creating sexually suggestive dialogue that barely avoided Hays Office censorship. Examples include the speech in which "Slim" (Lauren Bacall) tells "Steve" (Humphrey Bogart) in Howard Hawks's *To Have and Have Not* (1944), "You know, you don't have to act with me, Steve. You don't have to say anything and you don't have to do anything. Oh, maybe just whistle. You know how to whistle, don't you Steve? You just put your lips together and blow." In this case the dialogue was coscripted by William Faulkner from an Ernest Hemingway novel. In Hawks's *The Big Sleep* (1946), also coscripted by Faulkner, Bogart, again as Marlowe, compares Bacall to a horse: "You've got a lot of class, but I don't know how far you can go." Bacall (as Vivian Sternwood), replies, "A lot depends on who's in the saddle." There was no need to spell it out. Sex forms the subject of much of the dialogue in film noir, yet it was permitted because it was never addressed bluntly or directly. Despite the Hays Code, film noir, like screwball comedy, stands out as one of Hollywood's sexiest genres. Both of these genres owe much of their power and dynamism to their indirect employment of sexually laced dramatic situations and dialogue.

Tay Garnett's *The Postman Always Rings Twice* (1946) tested the Hays Code as few others had. Garnett based his film on James M. Cain's steamy Depression-era novel featuring an adulterous relationship that develops between a drifter and the wife of a roadside restaurant owner, who eventually murder the husband. As early as 1934 Joseph Breen wrote to the Radio-Keith-Orpheum Studio (RKO), which was then considering optioning the book, "It is our considered judgment that the story . . . is definitely unsuited to motion picture production and we strongly recommend that you pass it up." He was incensed when MGM, ignoring the stiff opposition, obtained the option a few weeks later. Hays himself, fearful that the other studios he had dissuaded from purchasing the story would blame him for having lost out to a rival, wrote to MGM in a last-ditch effort to persuade them to drop the project. His efforts appeared successful, but in the postwar era other studios, including Paramount, made inquiries about producing it. After Louis B. Mayer decided to go ahead with production, Breen wrote once more, pointing out the "unacceptability of the script in its present form." This time, he outlined the conditions under which the film could be made. First, the filmmakers had to reduce "the overall flavor of lust." He suggested cutting out all scenes involving physical contact between the stars.[17] Garnett hired Lana Turner to play Cora Smith and John Garfield to play her lover, Frank Chambers. In order to comply with Breen's admonition not to include scenes of physical contact, Garnett has Cora refuse to kiss Frank until far into the picture, after they successfully murder Cora's husband (Cecil Kellaway). "When we get home, Frank, then there'll be kisses. Kisses with life and not death." Flush with lust and victory, however, Frank refuses to wait, turning to Cora for his kiss. With his eyes off the road Frank fails to notice a curve, sending the car careening over a bridge. Frank survives to face murder charges for killing Cora, though not for murdering her husband. Frank's conviction and execution placated Breen; yet the censored film exudes sexuality in every scene. By forcing Garnett to substitute symbolism and innuendo for graphic realism, the PCA probably improved the film's quality.

During the film noir movement character after character engage in "illicit sex affairs," but they do so discreetly, consummating their often-adulterous relationships offscreen, and audiences learned to decode the clues and foreshadowing that filmmakers were forced to rely on. In the end, noir protagonists always lost their lovers, if not their lives, thereby redeeming themselves as far as the censors were concerned, while at the same time endowing them with tragic overtones. As long as they abided by the rules, filmmakers were allowed to create characters that engage in both premarital and extramarital affairs. However, the code demanded that they ultimately renounce their sins and transgressions and pay a heavy penalty for their illicit pleasures. As William Marling observes, even Joseph Breen's censorship powers failed to eliminate sexuality from film noir. In fact, sex merely went underground. Marling

Film noir seductress Cora Kellaway (Lana Turner) seduces a gullible Frank Chambers (John Garfield) into murdering her husband in Tay Garnett's *The Postman Always Rings Twice* (1946). The couple succeeds in beating the murder charges levied against them, but Cora dies in a fatal car accident caused by Frank's negligence in kissing her while driving. (Copyright 1946 Metro-Goldwyn-Mayer)

Femme fatale Annie Laurie Starr (Peggy Cummins) lures men into violent crimes in Joseph H. Lewis's classic film noir *Gun Crazy* (1950), originally released as *Deadly Is the Female*. Starr, an ace marksman, convinces Bart Tare (John Dahl) to join her in a series of bank robberies. (Copyright 1950 United Artists)

notes, "Salacious events had to be figured in icons, symbols, gestures, stage business, costuming, lighting, expression, and intonation." Film noir accomplished this by inventing its own style that exuded sexuality by resorting to such devices as "the manipulation of cigarettes and lighters, telephones and guns, doors and windows."[18]

Femmes fatales, or "femmes noir," instead of marrying and living conventional lives, flit scandalously from one sexual dalliance to another, often instigating murders and other acts of violence in the process. Incredibly, the PCA allowed this since the films only hinted at sexuality, and only if the characters paid dearly for their indiscretions. Forced into invention and innuendo, noir filmmakers imparted a powerful new sexuality to their films. Femmes noir come in different patterns: some may be sexual predators, others nymphomaniacs, and still others opportunists. Noir females could even be thinly disguised prostitutes, labeled "B-girls." Like their pre-code predecessors, femmes noir functioned as seductresses and embodied a newly realistic attitude far different from Victorian values. The effect on female role models was stunning. "Film noir," summarized Eddie Muller, "is where Pollyanna went after payback, in spades."[19]

Social Problems

Many returning soldiers discovered that the country they had defended was itself riddled with problems that had been forgotten or swept under the rug during the war. With the cessation of hostilities journalists and filmmakers alike began exploring some of these hidden issues using the social problem format. These films were shot in the new noir style and so are usually classified as noirs. Audiences began demanding more of these new, profoundly disturbing film noirs exposing long-festering social problems, including alcoholism in Billy Wilder's *The Lost Weekend* (1945); returning soldiers trying to adopt to peacetime, including William Wyler's *The Best Years of Our Lives* (1946) and Edward Dmytryk's *Till the End of Time* (1946); anti-Semitism, particularly Elia Kazan's *Gentleman's Agreement* (1947) and Edward Dmytryk's *Crossfire* (1947); and prejudice against minorities. These problem films proved popular with postwar audiences and shared many stylistic and thematic commonalities with the contemporary film noir movement.

Social problem films faced stiff opposition, not only from the Hays Office but also from powerful pressure groups outside the MPAA. Billy Wilder's *The Lost Weekend* (1945), which depicts the debilitating effects of alcoholism, caught the attention of the powerful liquor industry. Wilder cast Ray Milland as Don Birnam, an archetypical lost soul who suffers from severe alcoholism. At one point Birnam confesses his alcoholism to his girlfriend, Helen St. James (Jane Wyman), explaining, "What I'm trying to say is, I'm not a drinker, I'm a drunk." During a weekend-long binge Birnam comes down with delirium tremors and attempts suicide. At the end, Birnam describes his alcoholic state, delivering as he does a powerful indictment against the harmful effects of alcohol:

> My mind was hanging outside the window. It was suspended just about eighteen inches below. And out there is that great big concrete jungle. I wonder how many others there are like me. Those poor bedeviled guys on fire with thirst. Such comical figures to the rest of the world as they stagger blindly towards another binge, another bender, another spree.

Paramount Studios paid Charles Jackson $100,000 for the screen rights to his controversial novel and hired Wilder to direct the film. As production began Stanley Baer, executive vice president of Allied Liquor Industries, an industry lobby group, wrote a threatening letter to Paramount in which he claimed that the film would have "adverse effects on the liquor industry." Baer warned Paramount to reconsider producing the film and indirectly threatened to involve the Hays Office. Perhaps influenced by Baer, the Pennsylvania Board of Censors demanded that Paramount cut out many of the binge scenes and present those episodes with less graphic realism. Paramount resisted diluting the film. However, the Hays Office added to the pressure by disallowing the film's sexual depictions of prostitution and for showing a toilet.[20] Films like Wilder's, including those mentioned above, added ammunition for conservative forces confronting what they perceived as disturbing political elements in the film noir and social problem genres.

Defiance

At first, gangster films ran into a brick wall with the Hays Code. As time went on, even Westerns encountered problems with the PCA. In 1940 Howard Hughes sent Joseph Breen a copy of *The Outlaw* (1941), a Western loosely based on the legend of Billy the Kid. Hughes wished to star Jack Buetel as Billy and then unknown Jane Russell as Rio, Billy's girlfriend. Hughes hired Howard Hawks to direct the film. At Hughes's suggestion, Hawks features shot after shot of Russell's ample bosom as she alternates between her other boyfriend, Doc Holliday (Walter Huston), and Billy. Breen had not yet seen Russell's performances, so he had no way of knowing how much Hughes would expose her breasts in the movie. However, he found plenty to criticize in the screenplay alone. He wrote: "The present version seems to contain various elements which seem to be in violation of the Production Code and whose inclusion in the finished picture we believe would render it unacceptable."[21]

Unfazed, Hughes continued with his project, even designing a special bra for Russell to enhance her cleavage. Hughes's insistence on flaunting Russell's breasts finally proved too much for Breen, who refused to give the film a seal of approval. Hughes appealed the decision, and his appeal proved successful. Finally, in 1943, he decided to release the film. San Francisco's independent Gaiety Theater premiered the controversial feature, but audiences were unimpressed with Hughes's product. Today, *The Outlaw* is remembered as a quirky, minor classic that glorifies the bad boy and seductress archetypes, yet it pioneered a growing rebellion against Hays Code restrictions. When Maryland's state censorship board banned it completely, Hughes challenged the ruling in court, but the unsympathetic judge ruled against him, charging that Russell's breasts "hung over the picture like a thunderstorm spread out over the landscape."[22] By today's standards, *The Outlaw* seems tame, although no one can miss Russell's ample breasts. Unlike some of today's female characters, those breasts remain fully yet thinly covered (at least the nipples) throughout the entire film. Rio's

Jane Russell wearing a daring bra designed by Howard Hughes in his 1943 film *The Outlaw*. Hughes eventually released this film independently because of its failure to appease Hays Code censors. (Copyright 1943 Howard Hughes Productions)

ménage à trois with Billy the Kid and Doc Holliday also seems far from shocking today given contemporary dating standards.

During the forties shocking sexuality spread from film noir and Westerns to ordinary thrillers. In April 1941 a Warner Brothers' script based on Henry Bellaman's best-selling novel *King's Row,* depicting small-town aberrant sexuality, ignited a censorship firestorm. Joseph Breen sternly informed the studio that "the material, in our judgment, is quite definitely unacceptable under the provisions of the Production Code and cannot be approved." He added, "Before this picture can be approved . . . all the illicit sex will have to be entirely removed." His concerns included scenes depicting incest, rape, and premarital sex. Breen also objected to a mercy killing and the characterization of sadistic Dr. Gordon (Charles Coburn), who operates without anesthetics, amputates limbs needlessly, and brutalizes his own family. Finally, he warned, "to attempt to translate such a story to the screen, even though it be rewritten to conform to the provisions of the Production Code, is in our judgment a very questionable undertaking from the standpoint of the good and welfare of this industry." He argued that no matter how many changes the studio initiated, "the fact that it stems from so thoroughly questionable a novel is likely to bring down upon the industry, as a whole, the condemnation of all decent people."[23]

The project that created such controversy amounted to an early version of *Peyton Place,* in which citizens of a small midwestern town misbehave sexually. The story surrounds two young men, Parris Mitchell (Bob Cummings) and Drake McHugh (Ronald Reagan), who grow up together in the town of King's Row. They both eventually fall in love with women their age, but not always with the right women. Parris's lifelong love for Cassandra Tower (Betty Field) proves disastrous for her after her father, Dr. Tower (Claude Rains), poisons her out of personal jealousy. The film implies that Dr. Tower's incestuous affair with Cassie resulted in her becoming a nymphomaniac, and she subsequently fixates on Parris. For his part, Drake carries on sex affairs with two loose sisters before falling for Randy Monaghan (Ann Sheridan), who admits, "I have given him everything, with gladness." Finally, Parris, now a doctor, decides to end his grandmother's (Maria Ouspenskaya) life through a mercy killing.

Producer Hal Wallis agreed to the strict changes demanded by Breen in order to sanitize the film sufficiently, which included omission of Cassie's nymphomania, omission of Cassie's and Parris's nude bathing while children, insertion of Parris's remorse for his affair with Cassie, omission of Drake's and Randy's sex affair, omission of the mercy killing of Parris's aunt, and depicting Dr. Tower as a jealous father rather than a jealous lover. Warner Brothers agreed to these changes, which all occurred, except for a scene that remains of Parris and Cassie's childhood nude bathing early in the film. Cassie's nymphomania remains, though only implied.[24]

Director Sam Wood managed to convey Cassie's sexuality through Betty Field's spirited acting and other plot details. Tantalizing elements of the forbidden sex remain in this movie, which received Academy Award nominations for Best Cinematography (James Wong Howe), Best Director, and Best Picture.

Supreme Court

In 1948 the U.S. Supreme Court rendered a decision in *United States v. Paramount* that reverberated throughout the fifties as the major studios were forced to divest themselves of movie theaters. The Court ruled that studios and their theater subsidiaries violated the Sherman Anti-Trust Act. With this ruling Hollywood studios lost control of motion picture distribution, and when that occurred, MPAA control over the film industry was badly weakened. Even more disconcerting for the MPAA was Justice William O. Douglas's opinion that forced divestment did not imply restrictions against film content. "We have no doubt," he wrote, "that movie producers, like newspapers and radio, are included in the press whose freedom is guaranteed by the First Amendment."[25] Thus, the Supreme Court reversed itself from its earlier opinion in 1915 that films were "entertainment" and therefore not protected by the First Amendment.

In *Burstyn v. Wilson* (1952), or the *Miracle* case, the Court reversed a New York State Supreme Court ruling that had banned Roberto Rossellini's *The Miracle* from screening in New York. Rossellini's film depicts a simple-minded Italian woman's belief that the child she bore was the "son of God." Although the film received warm reviews from secular critics, the Catholic Church denounced it as sacrilegious. Cardinal Spellman blasted the film as "a subversion of the very word of God," and the Legion of Decency condemned it, as did Martin Quigley's *Motion Picture Herald,* which held that it was communist propaganda.[26] The Court ruled on fairly narrow grounds, arguing that the New York statute banning sacrilege in films was too narrow. The Court ruled that "liberty of expression by means of motion pictures is guaranteed by the First and Fourteenth Amendments." This decision emboldened a few filmmakers to begin defying the Production Code, just as Howard Hughes had pushed it to the limits with *The Outlaw.*

Social changes in public opinion unleashed by the war's end, coupled with the strains that often accompany social and economic fluctuations, would soon find expression in Hollywood films. The rise of television also challenged Hollywood, just as radio had done in the twenties. In 1937, 61 percent of the population attended a movie theater daily. By 1963, daily movie attendance had fallen to just 23 percent.[27] Lost audiences still enjoyed media, but from the comfort of their own homes. Their exodus from the theaters, the worst since the Depression, made filmmakers desperate to invent new strategies to lure them back. Much of fifties' censorship wars represented reactions against increasingly daring strategies to woo and entice lost audiences.

Nuanced Westerns

Fred Zinneman's *High Noon* (1952) is warmly remembered as one of the best of the classic fifties' Westerns. The film stars Gary Cooper as Marshall Will Kane, the chief law enforcement officer in a small western town. As the film opens, Kane marries Amy (Grace Kelly), a Quaker pacifist. Immediately, word arrives that Frank Miller, a hardened criminal, has just been released from prison. Miller had vowed to avenge himself upon Kane, and the entire town awaits Miller and his gang. Kane decides to stay and face the outlaws, alienating his new pacifist wife in the process. The Hays Office objected strenuously to Kane's former relationship, or sex affair, with Helen Ramirez (Katy Jurado) as well as to Kane's deputy Harvey Pell's (Lloyd Bridges) current relationship with Ramirez. Breen wrote to the producer and stated that the premarital relationships were "unacceptable." In addition, Breen warned Zinneman to take special care in handling Amy's religion, especially since she is obliged to kill Miller herself in the climax in order to save Kane. Despite Breen's prohibitions, Zinneman left the scene in which Amy kills Miller, as well as the premarital relationships, intact.[28] PCA approval of this film, which would not have been tolerated a decade earlier, is another sign of Hays Code decline.

In 1953 Otto Preminger, abandoning all hope of receiving a seal, decided to release *The Moon Is Blue* without it. Preminger secured the screen rights to F. Hugh Herbert's slightly risqué play about two middle-aged men who vie for the attentions of a young woman. Preminger, fearful that the MPAA would not grant the seal of approval (Breen had already indicated as much in an early letter), decided to increase his chances to make the film by casting two A-list male actors, William Holden as Don Gresham and David Niven as David Slater, in the lead roles. He also cast Maggie McNamara, a pretty young starlet, as Patty O'Neil. Preminger knew that with a sizzling screenplay and A-list actors he stood a much better chance of securing funding. In fact, after some negotiations Preminger eventually secured the support of United Artists for the picturized version of his hit Broadway play.

Although the film failed to win approval from the PCA, it appears tame and almost cerebral by today's standards. Although it contains some sexy dialogue, much of it appears as double-entendre and innuendo. For instance, Gresham suggests to O'Neil that their first date end with "ham and eggs," a not-so-veiled reference to a tryst. When Slater appears he, too, attempts to seduce O'Neil. The incensed Breen flatly refused a seal of approval, and the Legion of Decency promptly condemned it.

Amy Fowler Kane (Grace Kelly), Marshal Will Kane (Gary Cooper), Helen Ramirez (Katy Jurado), and Deputy Marshal Harvey Pell (Lloyd Bridges) in Fred Zinnemann's *High Noon* (1952). The audience knows about a previous relationship between Ramirez and Will Kane before the marshal married Amy Fowler. As the story begins Ramirez is in another romantic relationship, this time with Deputy Pell. Censors hated these extramarital relationships, yet Zinnemann managed to keep them in the final cut. (Copyright 1952 United Artists)

It was also widely cut or banned by state censorship boards. In the end, United Artists withdrew from the MPAA over the matter. Brisk box-office receipts helped assuage UA, and Preminger's film ranked in the top twenty in total revenue for 1953.[29] *The Moon Is Blue* proved to filmmakers and audiences that movies did not necessarily need a seal to succeed financially. As Hollywood faced stiff competition for audiences from television, UA's example of withdrawing from the MPAA rather than passing up a potential moneymaker occasioned many in Hollywood to take notice.

To PCA film rater Jack Vizzard, Preminger's film attacked the very premise of the code by implying that sexuality, or "free love," "was something outside the scope of morality altogether, was a matter of moral indifference." Had Gresham chosen to bed Cynthia Slater, the other single female character, the movie implied that "that was his business." That brought Preminger's film directly into conflict with the code

Free-spirited Cindy Slater (Dawn Addams) comforts her dog in Otto Preminger's *The Moon Is Blue* (1953). Slater attempts to seduce Donald Gresham (William Holden), who spurns her and falls for Patty O'Neil (Maggie McNamara). However, bachelor David Slater (David Niven) also attempts to seduce O'Neil. This was too much for censors, and they refused to give Preminger's film a seal of approval. He decided to release it without the seal. (Copyright 1953 United Artists)

warning that "pictures shall not infer that low forms of sex relationship are the accepted or common things." Ultimately, the gap between the Hays Code philosophy and the lifestyle depicted in the movie proved unbridgeable.[30]

Youth Rebellion

In the postwar period filmmakers increasingly defied the censors. Laslo Benedek's *The Wild One* (1954), produced by Stanley Kramer, depicts a youth motorcycle gang at war with society. Benedek starred Marlon Brando as Johnny, a macho biker gang leader. The gang takes over Hollister, California, and terrorizes the citizenry while thrilling the town's young women. A woman in a bar asks, "Hey, Johnny, what are you rebelling against?" Johnny replies, "What have you got?" Since the code forbade glorification of criminals, Joseph Breen cast doubt on the script's suitability: "The callousness of the young hoodlums in upsetting the moral tenor of life in a small town, the manner in which they panic the citizens, the ineffectiveness of law and order for the majority of the script, the brawling, drunkenness, vandalism and irresponsibility of the young men are, in our opinion, all very dangerous elements."

The problem was that the film blatantly violated the code's provisions by making juvenile delinquency seem attractive and exciting. It prohibited films that served to "inspire potential criminals with a desire for imitation" and "make criminals seem heroic and justified." However, rather than refuse *The Wild One* a seal and create another crisis like *The Moon Is Blue* had occasioned, Breen agreed to grant a seal if Kramer agreed to insert a cautionary prologue. This resulted in the county sheriff's admonition of Johnny as the film's coda: "I don't get you, I don't get your act at all. And I don't think you do, either. I don't think you know what you're trying to do or how to go about it. I think you're stupid, real stupid!"[31]

The sheriff's coda and a new prologue do little to change the nature of this film. However, the speech provided Breen with justification to grant an exception and allow it to be released with a seal of approval. At this point, compromise was essential in keeping the code from losing what remaining legitimacy it still possessed.

Preminger's next film, *The Man with the Golden Arm* (1955), chronicles the misfortunes of a heroin addict, Frankie Machine (Frank Sinatra). Machine struggles with his addiction, eventually managing to kick the habit by going cold turkey and winning the love of Kim Novak. However, the code explicitly prohibited any depictions of drug addiction. As early as 1950 Breen wrote to the producer, explaining that "we can see no possibility of handling the subject of drug addiction." Five years later, Preminger again requested a seal of approval for his finished film, but to no avail. The MPAA remained adamant. Finally, Preminger persuaded United Artists to allow him to shoot the film anyway. The MPAA once again refused to give its seal to the film, so the studio released it unrated. Interestingly, the Catholic Legion of Decency, normally even more conservative than the MPAA, declined to condemn Preminger's film.[32] Perhaps the legion believed that the time had arrived for the problem of drug addiction to come out in the open.

Tennessee Williams

Tennessee Williams, more than any other screenwriter, appears responsible for movies' increasing defiance of the old code restrictions. Movie versions of Williams's plays challenged the Hays Office even more than film versions of Eugene O'Neil's plays, including *The Emperor Jones* (1933), *The Hairy Ape* (1944), and *Desire Under the Elms* (1958). In fact, Elia Kazan's adaptation of Williams's *A Streetcar Named*

Desire (1951) caused the Hays Office the most consternation, even more than the other picturizations of Williams's screenplays (*The Glass Menagerie* [1950], *Baby Doll* [1956], and *Cat on a Hot Tin Roof* [1958]). Of these, *Streetcar* incurred the most opposition from the PCA. Joseph Breen strenuously objected to the film. Breen's concerns included the sexuality between Stanley Kowalski (Marlon Brando) and his sister-in-law Blanche DuBois (Vivien Leigh), as well as to steamy sex between Kowalski and his wife, Stella (Kim Hunter). Breen outlined his objections to Warner Brothers in a letter. They included an unacceptable aura of "sex perversion" (homosexuality) regarding Blanche's husband, Blanche's "nymphomania" and "attention to young boys," and the presentation of Stanley's rape of Blanche as justified. Finally, Warner Brothers agreed to cut four minutes from the film to avoid a "Condemned" label from the Catholic Legion of Decency.[33]

Williams's scripts no doubt reflected social changes then taking place, and the most sensitive issues evoked the most vehement responses from the Hays Office. During the postwar period audiences grew accustomed to even greater liberties with the Hays Code. Hays retired in 1945, devoting himself to anticommunist activities. Joseph Breen, head of the Production Code Administration, took over as head of the MPAA. Social changes occasioned by World War II loosened public morality, and fifties' films began expressing taboo subjects with unheard-of freedom. Joseph L. Mankewicz's *Guys and Dolls* (1955), for example, stars Marlon Brando as Sky Masterson, a high-rolling gambler, and Jean Simmons as Sister Sarah, a Salvation Army officer. Their romance captures screwball comedy's venerable tension between social classes, in this case a middle-class church woman and an outlaw gambler. Joseph Breen complained to producer Samuel Goldwyn that the original Broadway script contained unacceptable shots of streetwalkers. Furthermore, Breen warned Goldwyn that Sister Sarah should not be depicted as getting drunk in Cuba with Masterson. Also, he warned that Adelade's (Vivian Blaine) song "Take Back Your Mink" in which she strips off her expensive clothes and jewelry on stage was "unacceptably suggestive." In January 1955 Geoffrey Shurlock succeeded Breen as chief censor. Shurlock's chief concern was the use of "sin" and "sinner" in reference to gamblers attending Sister Sarah's revival meeting.[34]

Catholic Boycott

Geoff Shurlock proved a far more lenient code administrator than Breen had been. In his first year he allowed Elia Kazan's *Baby Doll* (1956), written by Tennessee Williams, to receive a code approval, despite the fact that the film's basic plot presents a clear violation of the Hays Code. It revolves around a nineteen-year-old child bride named Baby Doll Meighan (Caroll Baker), who is legally married to Archie Lee Meighan (Karl Malden), yet her marriage contract stipulates she remain a virgin

Archie Lee Meighan (Karl Malden) struggles with his reluctant bride, Baby Doll Meighan (Caroll Baker), in Elia Kazan's controversial *Baby Doll* (1954). (Copyright 1954 Newton Productions)

until she turns twenty. Archie fully intends to bed his young bride, but before he can do so another middle-aged suitor, Silva Vacarro (Eli Wallach), appears on the scene to give him stiff competition for the young lady's attentions.

Baby Doll stimulated an intense struggle, not only from the MPAA but also from conservative Catholics. Kazan based his film on Williams's screenplay about a man marrying a nineteen-year-old girl in the South. The subject of child brides, taboo during the thirties and forties, now appeared less objectionable. The PCA's response to Kazan's film proved true to form. Shurlock found relatively little to protest in the steamy triangle that develops in the film between Archie Lee, Baby Doll, and Vacarro. The scenario is reminiscent of the triangle in *The Moon Is Blue*, which failed to receive a seal, but this time Kazan's film successfully evaded the strict letter of the code, which banned child brides, underage sex, and adultery.

The film titillates audiences as the two men compete for Baby Doll's attentions, and she, despite her actual age, comes across as a child. Vacarro and Archie Lee compete for the childlike, sexual Baby Doll, in what seems dangerously close to pedophilia. During his brief courtship of her Vacarro exclaims, "You're a very delicate woman, Mrs. Meighan. There's not much of you, but what there is is choice. Delectable, I might add." He sits next to her on the swing and begins touching her and sweet-talking her. She begins to respond, telling him, "I feel so weak, my head is fuzzy." He tells her, "Give in, stop fighting it." Their mutual attraction continues to build, but despite their obvious attraction for each other the ultimate consummation remains just ambiguous enough to avoid PCA censure.

Kazan and Warner Brothers blatantly capitalized on the underage sexuality aspect by featuring in trailers an infantile Baby Doll, sleeping in a crib, sucking her thumb, and dressing like a little girl. Vacarro uses a porch swing to seduce Baby Doll, likening it to a baby's crib as he begins slowly and sensuously caressing her. To capitalize on the steamy, virtually taboo sexuality Warner Brothers posted a huge billboard on New York's Broadway featuring Baby Doll lounging sensuously in her crib and hired a young actress dressed like the character to climb the scaffolding and lounge next to Baby Doll's picture. The ad campaign capitalized on Baker's childlike appearance, and Warner Brothers planned for the opening to coincide with Christmas. The events that followed, however, caught Warner Brothers off guard. The Catholic Legion of Decency immediately condemned the film, charging that it was "morally corrupt." On December 16 New York's Cardinal Spellman branded Kazan's film "evil" and "immoral" and forbade Catholics to see it "under pain of sin" in a heated sermon delivered in St. Patrick's Cathedral. This sermon, as well as the Legion of Decency's condemnation, received widespread press coverage, and other religious leaders announced their support for a boycott. This negative publicity caused many theater owners to cancel screenings. Warner Brothers feared that any boycott of *Baby Doll* could spill over to others of its films, and Hollywood feared negative publicity and angry feelings that could alienate Christians from other Hollywood films. Although a religious boycott ensured establishment of the Production Code in 1934, *Baby Doll* became the first film forced from the screen by the threat of a religious boycott.[35] The censorship war over *Baby Doll* further diminished the PCA's authority over motion picture content. If the organization was lax enough to award a seal of approval for such an objectionable film, then what power did it still possess?

Baby Doll may have been a legal adult, but Baker's childlike performance, coupled with her character's fourth-grade education and her youthful appearance and wardrobe, all signaled childhood sexuality. Breen, although criticizing the "legal incest" theme, ultimately awarded Kazan's film a seal of approval.[36] Kazan evaded the prohibition against childhood sexuality by depicting his main character with child-like innocence while depicting Archie Lee's attempts to seduce her as virtual child molestation. Because of the taboo nature of the child-adult relationship themes in Kazan's film, the *New York Times* critic dubbed Kazan's film "possibly the dirtiest

American-made motion picture that was ever legally exhibited."[37] That kind of publicity should have boosted box office sales. However, the child-sex taboo proved too much for Hollywood, and it was forced into retreat for the first time since 1933.

Biblical Evasions

Pioneer director Cecil B. DeMille, who had learned to navigate the relatively safe waters of the pre-code era, effectively circumvented the postwar code by relying on a strategy he first used in the twenties of setting the narrative in biblical times. Biblical films offered abundant historical justifications for presenting steamy sexuality or gladiatorial violence. In *The Ten Commandments* (1956), DeMille returned to the story of Moses, which he had pioneered in 1923. Both films take liberties by depicting orgiastic Oriental debaucheries. In one memorable scene as Moses (Charlton Heston) returns from the mountaintop clutching the Ten Commandments he encounters the Israelites dancing around the famous golden calf, engaging in a full-blown Dionysian orgy. Hays would never have permitted that scene, and others of a nearly naked Adam and Eve, but times had changed, and DeMille relied on that, as well as the historical period, to convince the PCA to grant a seal. Although Breen complained about the orgy scene, DeMille left it in and in the end no one objected.

Stanley Kubrick's *Spartacus* (1960) further challenged the censors. First of all, Kubrick hired Dalton Trumbo, a member of the original Hollywood Ten, to script his film. Instead of the usual practice of using a pseudonym for the blacklisted writer, Kubrick decided to leave Trumbo's name on the credits. In a further affront to the PCA, Kubrick created thinly disguised gay characters, which earlier PCA censors would never have permitted. However, since the subject was historical, Shurlock looked the other way after Kubrick included Crassus (Laurence Olivier), a bisexual Roman commander, despite Shurlock's protestations about the presence of this "sex pervert." Again, since the setting was ancient Rome, Kubrick received his seal. Other filmmakers followed DeMille's and Kubrick's lead in *David and Bathsheba, King of Kings, Ben Hur, The Robe, El Cid,* and *The Greatest Story Ever Told.* Postwar audiences enjoyed these dramas, particularly because many of them depicted situations and characters unavailable in films featuring contemporary settings.

Even mainstream directors like Alfred Hitchcock occasionally defended their films against PCA mandates. *Rear Window* (1954), Hitchcock's voyeuristic exploration of the lives of a New York apartment building's residents, presents an excellent example. Characteristically, the censors objected to the film's sexuality. Breen's office expressed concern regarding "Miss Torso," a buxom young woman who appears at her window wearing nothing but black panties. Breen complained that "the picturization of the young girl as wearing only black panties is unacceptable." Also, Breen objected to the

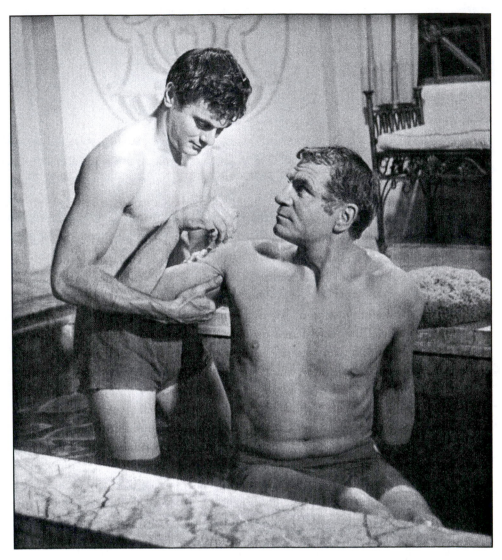

Roman body servant Antonius (Tony Curtis) sensuously massaging Marcus Licinius Crassus (Laurence Olivier) in Stanley Kubrick's *Spartacus* (1960). Censors disliked this scene's homoerotic undertones, yet the scenes of the two remain, disguised and heavily nuanced. (Copyright 1960 Universal Studios)

"newlyweds" sequence, in which the wife appears to demand incessant sex from her husband. Finally, he criticized the display of Lisa Freemont's (Grace Kelly) lingerie. These concerns appear trivial compared with the overwhelming sense of voyeurism that the film exudes. Spying on his neighbors with the assistance of a pair of powerful binoculars and a professional telephoto lens, L. B. Jeffries (James Stewart) appears ignoble and slightly suspicious. Is he a voyeur? The movie never answers that question, and the PCA allowed it to remain unanswered.

Hitchcock's *Psycho* (1960) also proved contentious with the PCA. According to *Alfred Hitchcock and the Making of Psycho,* the film encountered heated opposition from the PCA because some censors insisted they could see one of Janet Leigh's breasts in the famous shower scene. Hitchcock held onto the print for several days, left it untouched, and resubmitted it for approval. Astoundingly, each of the censors reversed their positions—those who had previously seen the breast now did not, and those who had not, now did. They passed the film anyway after the director removed one shot that showed the buttocks of Leigh's stand-in. The board was also upset by the racy opening showing Marian Crane (Janet Leigh) with her lover Sam in a hotel bedroom, so Hitchcock said that if they let him keep the shower scene he would reshoot the opening with them on the set. Since they did not show up for the reshoot, the opening stayed. Another cause of concern for the censors was that Marion was shown flushing a toilet with its contents (torn-up paper) fully visible. In film and TV at that time a toilet was never seen, let alone heard.[38]

During the sixties, as television continued to erode their audiences, filmmakers willingly flouted the censors and explored previously taboo subjects. Seemingly outrageous films like Stanley Kubrick's *Lolita* (1962), a British film that broke new ground in the treatment of child-adult sexual relations, appeared, and Martin Ritt's *Hud* (1963) was filled with steamy sexuality. There were also Mike Nichols's *The Graduate* (1965), featuring the famous seduction of a recent college graduate, Ben (Dustin Hoffman), by a married, middle-aged Mrs. Robinson (Katherine Ross), and a host of others. Finally, Mike Nichols's *Who's Afraid of Virginia Woolf?* (1966) occasioned an abrupt departure from the code. Nichols's film, and recent Supreme Court decisions outlawing prior censorship, ensured the demise of the Hays Code. That demise occurred in 1968 after MPAA president Jack Valenti abandoned the Hays Code and adopted a different system based on age restrictions instead of prior censorship. The Hays era officially ended in 1968 with the adoption of the new code.

Sex

The Hays Code censored sex far more stringently than it curbed violence. The seductive gold diggers and gangsters of pre-code days were replaced by oddly mismatched couples who never engaged in sex openly; yet their actions became laden with underlying sexuality. The screwball comedy genre produced some of Hollywood's all-time classics (*It Happened One Night, My Man Godfrey, Bringing Up Baby, His Girl Friday*). Prohibited from open depictions of sexuality, these films relied instead on subtleties like innuendo and symbolism. Film noirs also relied on innuendo and double entendre, but by the forties Hays censors, distracted by World War II, allowed filmmakers greater leniency. A new femme fatale with modern styles and murderous proclivities arose in movies like *The Maltese Falcon, Double Indemnity, Sunset Boulevard, Gun Crazy*, and dozens of others. Hollywood grew adept at suggesting sex through double entendres, symbols, and innuendo. In fact, as the Hays era waned in the fifties filmmakers increasingly opted out of MPAA censorship, deciding to release their films unrated rather than submit to sexual censorship. Filmmakers increasingly opted to shun censorship in order to create greater sexual realism.

Violence

Interestingly, the Hays Office, especially Joseph Breen, refused to condemn movies because of too much violence. Perhaps relating to feelings of machismo on the part of some directors as well as regulators, Hays censors permitted graphic violence so long as it was directed toward a worthy enemy, including organized crime, Nazi Germany, Fascist Italy, and the Empire of Japan. Hays-era gangster films switched allegiance from bootleggers to gangbusters, but violent scenes remained at approximately the same level as during the pre-code era. The film noir movement of the forties and fifties broke new ground regarding graphic violence, although it was depicted with a degree of subtlety. During the postwar decades film violence increased.

Gender Roles

During the Hays Code, filmmakers adapted to challenging social and political realities. The Depression inaugurated the Hays era, World War II punctuated it, and the cold war witnessed its demise. Gender roles in movies changed rapidly, occasioning intense criticisms. In place of the loose flappers and vamps of the pre-code age were complex females of the screwball comedy genre. Female protagonists of screwball comedies appear as free spirits, with subtle undertones of the seductress. They survive not by beauty alone but through a combination of brains, brashness, and assertiveness. Sporting tailored, manlike suits, Hildy (Rosalind Russell) and the other women from screwball comedy compete well in what was once strictly a man's world. They are not that different from *Gone With the Wind*'s feisty Scarlett O'Hara (Vivien Leigh). These characters emerge as tough and independent, even more so than their flapper and vamp predecessors.

During the forties screwball comedies gave way to film noir, ushering in a new kind of female character: the femme noir. These females contrast with "good girl" characters that support the males, included in many noirs to contrast with femmes fatales. Femmes noir not only compete with men; they engage in life-and-death struggles with their male counterparts, often seducing unsuspecting males first into affairs and later into murder. Barbara Stanwyck's Phyllis Dietrichson in Billy Wilder's *Double Indemnity* (1944), Gilda (Rita Hayworth) in Charles Vidor's *Gilda* (1946), and Lana Turner's Cora in Tay Garnett's *The Postman Always Rings Twice* (1946) exemplify the new, dangerous noir females. During a period that witnessed rapid changes in women's roles, from Rosie the Riveter to Martha (Elizabeth Taylor) in Mike Nichols's *Who's Afraid of Virginia Woolf?* (1966), the Hays Code women turned from wisecracking reporters to seductive, profanity-spewing vixens threatening male domination as never before. Women's roles during the Hays period varied considerably and include good girl roles like Mary (Donna Reed) in Frank Capra's *It's a Wonderful Life* (1946). But for every Mary Harris there are dozens of Coras and Phyllis Dietrichsons.

King's Row depicts women of loose morals and, even though Warner Brothers attempted to sanitize the film of any hint of nymphomania, womanizing, and mercy killings, those elements still remain, delivered indirectly through suggestion and innuendo. Hints of nymphomania also appear in *The Big Sleep, Gilda, The Maltese Falcon, The Strange Love of Martha Ivers, Slightly Scarlet,* and many others. The Hays period witnessed the rise of a new breed of female characters fully capable of dominating males sexually. These femme fatale characters competed with the Hays period's good girls, which often turned out to be actual girls, played by Judy Garland, Shirley Temple, and Haley Mills (*The Wizard of Oz, Heidi, Pollyanna*). Other notable good girls of the Hays period include Mary Hatch Bailey (Donna Reed) in Frank Capra's *It's a Wonderful Life* (1946), Jan Morrow (Doris Day) in Michael Gordon's *Pillow Talk* (1959), and Pollyanna (Mills) in David Swift's movie of the same name (1960). Mills's version of "the glad girl" character harks back to Mary Pickford's performance in the 1920 version. Each of these "family values" characters exhibits positive, supportive, nonthreatening female attributes. They stand in stark contrast with the "bad girls" of film noir.

Film noir influenced all genres, including romantic comedies. *The Moon Is Blue's* (1954) female characters illustrate fifties sexual mores very well. Free-spirited Patty O'Neil's (Maggie McNamara) glib use of terms like *seduce* and *virgin* proved too much for the MPAA, but her basic character appears normal and conventional by today's standards. In the same film, Cynthia Slater's (Dawn Addams) blatant behavior, however, evokes the gold digger seductresses of pre-code films like *Red-Headed Woman* and *She Done Him Wrong*, who employ sex as an instrument for personal enrichment. *High Noon's* Helen Ramirez (Katy Jurado), a single woman who becomes the girlfriend of two male characters, also challenged the code's prejudices against premarital sex. By today's standards, these characters appear tame and conventional.

As female roles changed dramatically during the Hays Code, so did male roles. New male roles include bemused screwball accomplices like *It Happened One Night*'s Peter Warne (Clark Gable), *Bringing Up Baby*'s David Huxley (Cary Grant), and *His Girl Friday*'s Walter Burns (Cary Grant). Unlike the male vamps and swashbuckler heroes like Rudolph Valentino and Douglas Fairbanks Sr. of the pre-code period, men of screwball comedy often function as foils to their more flamboyant better halves. The men of thirties musicals, like *Top Hat*'s Barry Travers (Fred Astaire) and *Gold Diggers of 1935*'s Dick Powell, dance and woo their costars with proper gentlemanly behavior, seemingly oblivious to the withering effects of the Depression. These characters pursue women romantically, never skipping any necessary steps of intimacy, unlike swashbuckling heroes of pre-code days.

World War II ushered in the combat hero, played by John Wayne, Robert Mitchum, Dana Andrews, Montgomery Clift, and Audi Murphy, among many others. These rugged protagonists are above all team players, masters of military discipline and martial arts, fearless in the face of combat, but also loyal to the group and to the organization. If anyone tries to go it alone and be above the group, he is sooner or later made to realize the error of his ways (see *Air Force*). Throughout the forties combat heroes predominated in Hollywood in such classics as *Thirty Seconds Over Tokyo*, *Wake Island*, *Guadalcanal Diary*, *Flying Leathernecks*, *The Sands of Iwo Jima*, *D-Day*, *The Sixth of June*, *The Battle of the Bulge*, and *Sahara*, among many others. These combat heroes embodied bravery, loyalty, and the ability to work with others. That was the primary message of combat films for men.

While one group of film heroes waged war, another group remained on the home front battling the era's dangers, from duplicitous women to shady underworld bosses. Film noir males at times appear as tough as combat heroes, but at best they seem slightly bemused and betrayed. Most often they end up seduced, used, and discarded. *Double Indemnity*'s Walter Neff (Fred MacMurray), *Sunset Boulevard*'s Joe Gillis (William Holden), *The Postman Always Rings Twice* protagonist Frank Chambers (John Garfield), and many others find themselves used and betrayed by their women. In many Hays Code films the female characters, more than the males, emerge as strong, formidable, dominant, and dangerous.

Homosexuality during the Hays Code is conspicuous by its absence, but by the late fifties the subject began to surface in films. Lillian Hellman's provocative novel *The Children's Hour* depicts two teachers accused of lesbianism by one of their students. The novel forms the source for William Wyler's *Three Lives* (1936), but the PCA forced Wyler to change the suggestion of lesbianism to one of adultery. Hellman approached the PCA personally to request an exception to the agency's ironclad rule about depictions of homosexuality of any kind, but Breen reportedly responded, "Lesbianism on the screen? Who ever heard of such a thing? And how could it be done tastefully?"[39] Wyler had to wait until 1961, as the Hays Code continued to unravel, to film Hellman's real story in *The Children's Hour*. Finally, after lengthy negotiations, the MPAA voted to amend the code. On October 3, 1941, Geoff Shurlock announced, "In keeping with the culture, the mores and values of our time, homosexuality and other sexual aberrations may now be handled with care, discretion, and restraint."[40]

Creating the Couple

During the Hays Code the romanticized ideal of marriages made in heaven appeared weak and unrealistic. Often one or more of the romantic partners, usually the female, was a "screwball," an odd duck with definite nonconformist tendencies. Screwball comedies thrived on the sparks that flew between other characters and zanies like Katharine Hepburn's Susan Vance (*Bringing Up Baby*), Rosalind Russell's Hildy Johnson (*His Girl Friday*), and Claudette Colbert's Ellie Andrews (*It Happened One Night*). These sparkling performances showcased a new female model, less bold and overtly sexual than the earlier seductive vamps of the pre-code period but still seething with barely suppressed sexuality. These females, like Hildy Johnson and Susan Vance, epitomize the "fast-talking dames" of Hollywood. Audiences soon learned to decode fast-talking women as women with loose morals.[41] Screwball comedy's males, on the other hand, often appear bumbling and ineffective, like Cary Grant's Professor David Huxley (*Bringing Up Baby*), William Powell's Godfrey Parke (*My Man Godfrey*), and Cary Grant's Walter Burns (*His Girl Friday*). These characters are vastly different from the seductive sheikhs and matadors of the pre-code period. The resulting couples in screwball comedies come across as wacky, mismatched characters that nevertheless usually end up falling in love with each other.

W. S. Van Dyke's *The Thin Man* (1934), later a popular series, features screwball-type characters that are madly in love with each other and, surprisingly, happen to be married to each other. Julie Burchill notes that "one new variation [on the theme of sexuality] was the wife as Vamp, mockingly vamping only one man. Myrna Loy as Nora Charles made a great and graceful living vamping William Powell as Nick Charles." The result was a variation on the themes of the pre-code period that satisfied Joseph Breen and the Hays Code.[42] The couple appeared made for each other, despite their bantering. Nick's excessive drinking, in one scene downing a dozen martinis, argues today for a diagnosis of alcoholism. Even more recent James Bond heroes imbibe an occasional dry martini "shaken not stirred," but few heroes can match the Thin Man's drinking stamina.

In sharp contrast to *The Thin Man's* alcohol-abusing but happily married pair, noir couples function more as horrible mismatches, whose characters appear fatally attracted to each other, ultimately causing their downfall. From Bogart's Sam Spade and Astor's Brigid O'Shaughnessy in *The Maltese Falcon*, to Fred MacMurray's

Walter Neff and Barbara Stanwyck's Phyllis Dietrichson in *Double Indemnity*, to Lana Turner's Cora Smith and John Garfield's Frank Chambers in *The Postman Always Rings Twice,* noir couples risk seduction, duplicity, manipulation, and even death from their partners. These films reveal striking tensions between the sexes during the forties and fifties. The film noir cycle, revived today in the form of "neonoir," catalogues the failures of romantic love.

Hays Code Westerns also feature mismatched couples, although the genre always focused more sharply on male roles than on female ones. In fact, in Westerns, the emphasis is on the male characters and the issue of masculinity. Robert Lang, in *Masculine Interests: Homoeroticism in Hollywood Film,* notes that the real issue in Westerns turns out not to be violence but *style.* Western audiences stare at male characters, as do other male characters. Lang argues that this focus on masculinity in Westerns constitutes homoeroticism.[43] This gay subtext became more openly associated with homosexuality during the later Valenti Code (see *Midnight Cowboy,* 1968). Couples that survive in the Hays Code often do so at great cost to themselves and to others, like *High Noon*'s Marshal Will Kane (Gary Cooper), who epitomizes the warrior archetype, and his bride Amy (Grace Kelly), who begins the film as a moralistic "librarian" archetype. Most often, the outlaw heroes ride off into the sunset, leaving behind any entangling alliances with local women, like Alan Ladd's Shane. In fact, Western relationships often prove ephemeral at best, leaving the distinct impression that the settling of the West had little to do with the family and more to do with individual deeds of violence performed by men.

Deviant couples pop up frequently in the fifties, especially those based on Tennessee Williams's and Eugene O'Neil's scripts. The most socially sensitive turns out to be between Caroll Baker's Baby Doll Meighan and Karl Malden's Archie Lee Meighan, a bond that barely avoids the issue of underage sexuality. Although the PCA awarded this film a seal of approval, the Legion of Decency and other conservative groups quickly forced the film from theaters, and only recently, with the advent of video and DVD versions, has this classic become available for viewing.

The Hays period, born out of the threat of a religious boycott, encompassed Hollywood's golden age. It produced some of the industry's most enduring classics, but it also engendered some of its bitterest censorship. Hollywood continued its experiments with industry-dominated self-censorship, which worked out fairly well sometimes but completely failed at other times, eventually leaving filmmakers with no choice but to defy the system and release their films unrated. Ultimately, the system proved unconstitutional and unworkable and was finally abandoned. Today it is remembered not only for the classics it produced but also for the censorship controversies it invoked and engendered.

CHAPTER FOUR

The McCarthy Code

McCarthyism fostered the most powerful unofficial Production Code in film history. In its heyday, from 1947 through 1957, McCarthyism wielded a profound influence on cinema, both directly and indirectly. No other social or political movement exercised so much power and control over movie form and content. Soon after it arose, McCarthyism, a product of postwar conservatism and cold war paranoia, immediately targeted Hollywood. Its impact reverberated throughout the film industry for decades, suppressing leftist, liberal, and at times centrist political expression. Even today producers avoid films with obviously political themes, a residual effect of McCarthyism, named after Wisconsin Republican senator Joseph McCarthy. Its adherents banished or deported hundreds of liberal and left-leaning filmmakers from the industry and sent ten filmmakers to prison in a sensational sedition trial. Eventually, the movement stimulated a new genre of propagandistic anticommunist films as well as a spate of sci-fi invasion thrillers. Its influence extended to a wide variety of mainstream, nonpolitical films as well.

McCarthyism opposed leftist political thought, popular during the thirties and forties with U.S. intellectuals. The movement abhorred film noir and social problem films, both popular World War II genres. McCarthyism ended the careers of many filmmakers by silencing popular writers, directors, producers, and actors for decades. It left its mark on an entire generation, and it continues to affect filmmakers today through its modern religious incarnation: evangelicalism (see chapter 6). In fact, McCarthyism profoundly impacted movies as no other political movement before or since.

The Depression and communism's Popular Front lured many intellectuals into communist and related organizations. John P. Diggins notes that communism appealed to left-of-center groups during the thirties and forties after the movement embraced centrists and liberals. Liberals were especially vulnerable to the Communist Party USA's (CPUSA) influence because they "had always urged a common front against fascism." In addition, liberals "found themselves in the mid-thirties without a viable ideology."[1] For these reasons, many intellectuals and creative people, including filmmakers, embraced communism or joined CPUSA-sponsored organizations. Progressive political views grew in popularity during the thirties, which witnessed Franklin D. Roosevelt's New Deal, giving the decade a leftist tinge. Diggins and others now label this period the "Old Left," which formed the foundation for the "New Left" of the sixties and seventies.

Isolationism

As World War II ignited, Americans found themselves immersed in a great debate about the efficacy of involvement in another world war. U.S. experiences during World War I, culminating in critical reaction to the punitive Treaty of Versailles in 1919, caused many to advocate neutrality in the thirties as Europe erupted into another war. Roosevelt, wishing to assist Britain and other U.S. allies attacked by the Axis powers, privately encouraged prowar sentiment by quietly supporting patriotic motion pictures like *Pastor Hall* (1940) and *Sergeant York* (1941) while urging Congress to pass the Lend-Lease Act (1941). A debate over U.S. involvement in the rapidly widening conflict erupted in Congress in 1941 during the Senate Subcommittee Hearings on Motion Picture and Radio Propaganda. Senator Gerald Nye (R-ND), the most vociferous proponent of neutrality, warned the motion picture industry against producing prowar films. "I have no desire for moving-picture censorship," Nye asserted in the hearings. However, "I do hope," he warned, "that the industry will largely recognize the obligation it owes to our country and its people."[2] Thus, the first clash between political conservatives and Hollywood in the forties occurred over the issue of U.S. neutrality, with prominent conservatives opposed to U.S. participation in the war and deeply suspicious of Roosevelt's influence on Hollywood.

Why We Fight

After Japan attacked Pearl Harbor on December 7, 1941, few, including Senator Nye, dared call for neutrality. Instead, the Japanese attack unified the country and inspired millions of Americans with a desire to assist the war effort. In 1942, in order to counter German propaganda films like Leni Riefenstahl's *Triumph of the Will,* Army chief of staff George Marshall ordered the creation of a set of training films to teach Americans "why we fight." He asked popular director Frank Capra to produce a series of seven training films covering that subject. At first Capra refused, stating that as a feature film director he had no experience creating documentaries. Marshall appealed to his patriotism, and Capra eventually agreed to the task. His first act was to hire seven writers and direct them to write seven possible scenarios or treatments for the film series. When the writers submitted their work he rejected their scenarios and fired them all because he found their submissions "larded with communist propaganda" and promptly hired seven new, more conservative writers.[3] The first installment arrived in 1942, just five years before the first House Un-American Activities

Committee (HUAC) hearings in Hollywood, yet it presaged later cold war battles. It also occurred four years before Will Hays decided to retire from the presidency of the MPAA to devote his time to voluntary efforts to combat communism in Hollywood. One would suppose that Hays, with his superb connections as "Mr. Hollywood," functioned effectively in laying the groundwork for the congressional hearings that began just two years later. Capra's staff cleansing foreshadowed McCarthy-era blacklisting. After wartime hostilities ceased, a struggle between the Old Left and the anticommunists that had been simmering for years escalated into a bitter culture war.

During World War II U.S. support for the Union of Soviet Socialist Republics (USSR), a crucial ally in the war against Nazi Germany, surged. However, after the Allied victory many refocused suspicions on the USSR, which competed with the United States for global influence even before hostilities ceased. By 1947 the wartime alliance disintegrated, and the new threat posed by the USSR transformed film villains from Nazis, Italians, and Japanese into communists. Public concerns over Russian intentions intensified after the USSR successfully tested a thermonuclear bomb in 1953. By that time, the cold war was already well established.

Social Problems

Audiences sided with Hollywood by demanding more of the new, profoundly disturbing films exposing long-festering social problems, including post-traumatic stress syndrome (William Wyler's *The Best Years of Our Lives* [1946]; Edward Dmytryk's *Till the End of Time,* also in 1946) and anti-Semitism (Edward Dmytryk's *Crossfire* [1947] and Elia Kazan's *Gentleman's Agreement* [1947]). *Crossfire,* though widely acclaimed by critics, failed to receive any Academy Awards despite nominations, perhaps in part because Dmytryk and producer Adrian Scott were both blacklisted. A few years later Otto Preminger's *The Man with the Golden Arm* (1955) explored drug addiction, but by then the social problem genre had disappeared, the victim of McCarthyism. These problem films proved popular with postwar audiences and shared many stylistic and thematic commonalities with the film noir movement.

William Wyler's *The Best Years of Our Lives* (1946) plumbed the depths of the hardships facing returning veterans unused to life in a peacetime society. Wyler's film shocked many by its frank depiction of philandering, drinking society. One of Wyler's characters, Fred Derry (Dana Andrews), recently an army lieutenant, finds no professional work and settles for a job as a soda jerk. Another, Al Stephenson (Fredric March), who served in the war as an army sergeant, assumes a position as an official at a local bank. In a common scenario reflecting real life, instead of the loving spouse he left behind, Derry encounters an estranged, unfaithful wife, Marie (Virginia Mayo). A third man, Homer Parish (Harold Russell), returns handless, representing millions of disabled veterans. These damaged ex-soldiers attempt to cope with a world greatly changed since they went to war. By 1947, as the U.S. Congress began investigating alleged subversion in Hollywood, social problem films like *The Best Years of Our Lives* withered and soon disappeared. With anticommunism in ascendancy, Wyler realized that he would likely never be allowed to make another film like *The Best Years of Our Lives* again.[4]

After the war the FBI began investigating mainstream filmmakers. In the increasingly threatening postwar political climate even Frank Capra's *It's a Wonderful Life* (1946), the perennial Christmas movie, came under FBI surveillance. Capra's film raised FBI suspicions because the villain, Mr. Potter (Lionel Barrymore), is a wealthy capitalist. While Capra shot the film FBI agent D. M. Ladd wrote to J. Edgar Hoover regarding Capra's treatment of the struggle between big banks and small savings and loans, as represented by Mr. Potter's bank and George Bailey's (James Stewart) savings and loan. The use of a banker as villain aroused Agent Ladd's suspicions. Capra's film, according to Ladd, "represented rather obvious attempts to discredit bankers by casting Lionel Barrymore as a 'Scrooge type' so that he would be the most hated man in the picture. This, according to these sources, is a common trick used by communists."[5] The bureau took no action on the film, perhaps due to its popularity at the box office and with the critics. In fact, Capra's film received an Academy Award nomination for Best Picture, and Capra received a nomination for Best Director. James Stewart also received a nomination for Best Actor. However, Capra's film garnered no Oscars. Instead, Wyler's *The Best Years of Our Lives* won Best Picture, Best Director, Best Actor (Fredric March), and Best Supporting Actor (Harold Russell). Ironically, Capra's film is still viewed by millions each year, whereas Wyler's film circulates primarily among a small audience of aficionados.

Film noir often challenged conventional wisdom and often contained hidden political messages that raised censors' concerns. Joseph Breen became much more incensed by the political implications of *The Maltese Falcon*'s Sam Spade's (Humphrey Bogart) speech about the ambitions of the district attorney than about the film's sexuality. The speech, Breen said, "should be rewritten to get away from characterizing most district attorneys as men who will do anything to further their careers." In realization of the changing political climate, Breen added, "This is important."[6] Even before McCarthyism appeared, the MPAA had revealed itself as politically and socially conservative, favoring films that presented no challenges to the status quo. Unfortunately for Hollywood, the film noir movement proved deeply vulnerable to PCA attack.

World War II conservatism, fueled by rising patriotism spawned by the war and the rapidly approaching cold war, captured the public imagination. Xenophobia and super patriotism became the hallmarks of the movement, labeled "McCarthyism" for its chief proponent, Wisconsin senator Joseph McCarthy, who captured headlines by claiming that the United States faced grave dangers from hundreds of subversive agents employed by the State Department who were actually clandestine communist agents who were disloyal to the United States. Although several other politicians, including Parnell Thomas and Richard Nixon, sought to capitalize on fears of Soviet subversion, McCarthy's irascible personality and aggressive speeches thrust him into the forefront of the conservative movement that still bears his name.

The McCarthy Code

The informal but powerful McCarthy Code that emerged threatened filmmakers who probed too deeply into social problems, assuming that these films were tainted by liberalism, socialism, or communism. The code forbade:

1. Depictions of U.S. social problems, including anti-Semitism, alcoholism, battle fatigue, and corruption in U.S. institutions.
2. Strikes and union-organized boycotts. Any prounion sentiment was viewed with alarm.
3. Criticism of the United States and any of its policies.
4. Condemnation or exposure of witch-hunts or blacklisting.
5. Undermining capitalism and big business.

These tenets matched nicely with the Hays Code, which similarly prohibited condemnation of the government just as it discouraged criticism of capitalism and business interests.

With the advent of McCarthyism, all liberal politics became taboo, and filmmakers eschewed all overtly political films, as well as social problem films, to focus on musicals, Westerns, and sci-fi. The film noir movement, too, gradually faded as many of its adherents, including Abraham Polonsky, Edward Dmytryk, Clifford Odets, and Dashiell Hammett, among dozens of others, found themselves deported, blacklisted, or imprisoned. McCarthyism, allegedly an anticommunist movement, was at that point functioning as an antiliberal movement as well.

The House Un-American Activities Committee

McCarthyism captured international attention in the fall of 1947 when the House Un-American Activities Committee (HUAC) began conducting a series of sensational hearings on alleged communist infiltration of the Hollywood film industry. The committee's three general goals included (1) to prove that the Screen Actor's Guild harbored communist members; (2) to show that those writers inserted subversive materials into films; and (3) to prove that Roosevelt had encouraged pro-Soviet films. During the initial hearings, which grew increasingly raucous and contentious, prominent Hollywood conservatives like Clark Gable, John Wayne, Gary Cooper, Ginger Rogers, and Adolph Menjou lent credence to allegations of communist influences in the film industry, further fueling demands to "clean up Hollywood."

The forties witnessed the formation of the Motion Picture Alliance for the Preservation of American Values (MPA), a powerful conservative lobby. Several notable writers, including Morrie Ryskind, Robert Hughes, and Jim McGuinness, joined the alliance, along with actors John Wayne and Clark Gable, as well as philosopher Ayn Rand, all prominent conservatives. The organization lamented what it perceived as a dangerous trend toward collectivism and communism among filmmakers, particularly those producing social problem films and film noirs, and pledged to combat that trend with the values of patriotism, freedom, and individualism. The Screen Actors Guild, under the direction of Ronald Reagan, proved a close ally, as was a craft union, the International Alliance of Theatrical Stage Employees (IA) under the leadership of Roy Brewer. The trade journal *Counterattack* sided with these conservative elements and began publishing a regular feature called "Red Currents" exposing communist-front organizations as well as left-leaning "fellow travelers." Each of these organizations represented Hollywood anticommunists, and their presence reveals a fierce struggle between left and right that quickly engulfed Hollywood.[7]

In the spring of 1947 the HUAC, in the midst of a massive investigation into an alleged communist infiltration into several U.S. industries, began holding "friendly" hearings in Hollywood, allegedly at the request of anticommunist filmmakers. Several friendly witnesses appeared, including Adolph Menjou and Gary Cooper, who read prepared statements expressing concerns about communist infiltration into Hollywood. In October 1947, five months after conducting preliminary hearings, Congressman J. Parnell Thomas (R-NJ), chair of HUAC, opened the first public hearings on alleged communist infiltration and subversion of the motion picture industry. Thomas subpoenaed a group of writers and producers to answer questions regarding "the extent of Communist infiltration in the Hollywood motion picture industry."

The Hollywood Ten

Thomas and his staff eventually subpoenaed nineteen "unfriendly" witnesses, all of whom had been identified by "friendly" conservative witnesses as possibly belonging to the Communist Party. They grilled each witness with the question, "Are you now, or have you ever been, a member of the Communist Party?" Eventually, after summoning dozens of witnesses, ten filmmakers, including producer/director Herbert Biberman, director Edward Dmytryk, producer/writer Adrian Scott, and screenwriters Alvah Bessie, Lester Cole, Ring Lardner, Jr., John Howard Lawson, Albert Maltz, Samuel Ornitz, and Dalton Trumbo, received contempt of Congress citations for refusing to provide direct answers to the questions or to divulge their past and present political affiliations. The contempt citations constituted a criminal charge, and in April, federal prosecutors tried the group in federal court in Washington, D.C. The court found the "Hollywood Ten," as they were dubbed in the press, guilty of contempt of Congress and gave them each the maximum sentence, one year in jail and a $1,000 fine. The highly publicized Hollywood Ten trials, and the efforts of supporters of the accused to keep the fate of the ten in public awareness, was one of the most sensational spectacles of the postwar period. The trials catapulted Thomas into celebrity status, just as it made the Hollywood Ten famous. Later Thomas, like McCarthy himself, experienced a precipitous fall from grace after he was tried, convicted, and sent to prison for financial corruption. Ironically, he shared the same prison with some of the Hollywood Ten, men he had hounded out of Hollywood and into jail.

The studio heads cooperated fully with the McCarthy-era investigations by reorienting their productions to conform to the movement's values. In late 1947 the major producers met at New York's Waldorf-Astoria Hotel to consider what Hollywood should do about the alleged communist menace. They issued a news release, since labeled the Waldorf Statement, supporting HUAC and condemning the Hollywood Ten.[8]

The Hollywood moguls had taken a stand for compulsory loyalty oaths with the threat of being blacklisted as enforcement. Hollywood had officially come under the influence of McCarthyism.

Blacklisted

On November 25, 1947, one day after Congress issued citations to the Hollywood Ten, studios immediately authorized a blacklist consisting of names of Hollywood professionals who were or had ever been members of the Communist Party or numerous other "fellow traveler" or liberal organizations. The studios made their statement during a meeting at the Waldorf Hotel in New York. The Waldorf Statement served notice that the studios would no longer employ any persons who were currently or formerly members of the Communist Party or affiliated groups. Adding insult to injury was the fact that the Hollywood Ten found their names added to the blacklist. Inclusion on that list meant unemployment. Although Hollywood denied its existence at the time, the blacklist served notice to all studios not to hire any of the listed individuals. The list included some of Hollywood's most talented professionals, including actors Lloyd Bridges and Sterling Hayden; director Elia Kazan; writers Ring Lardner, Jr., John Howard Lawson, Clifford Odets, Larry Parks, Budd Schulberg, and Dalton Trumbo; and director Abraham Polonsky. Even those who had not been investigated by HUAC found themselves on the list, including actor

Dorothy Comingore, director Jules Dassin, actor Will Geer, and writers Dashiell Hammett, Lillian Hellman, and Dorothy Parker. For them, being blacklisted meant selling their homes and attempting to find different work, no matter how menial. Others turned in desperation to alcohol and drugs.

The Left Strikes Back

McCarthyism affected filmmakers not only through congressional committees, but also through wiretaps and other forms of harassment. After World War II the FBI began investigating some of Hollywood's most influential leftists, including writer/director Abraham Polonsky. Polonsky was widely admired as the most talented of Hollywood's leftist directors. He remembers, "I was a left winger. I supported the Soviet Union. In the middle 1940s we'd have meetings at my house to raise money for strikers and radical newspapers."[9] In 1948 the FBI, growing increasingly suspicious of Polonsky, ordered a wiretap on his telephone as he worked on *Force of Evil*, one of the most pessimistic and most enduring of the film noir classics. The government tapped Polonsky's conversation with novelist Ira Wolfert, whose work he was adapting for the film. However, their efforts failed to prevent Polonsky from releasing *Force of Evil* in 1948. Polonsky's noir-style drama stars John Garfield (later blacklisted) as Joe Morse, a slick gangster's lawyer who wrestles with his conscience while being exploited by racketeers. Polonsky chose New York, at that time hopelessly corrupted by racketeering, as his setting. Polonsky and Wolfert strongly suspected that they were breaking strong taboos about depictions of official corruption. Deep into their tapped conversation both men referred to the likelihood that federal agents were eavesdropping.[10]

Polonsky's film depicts a world of corruption in which two brothers, Joe Morse (Garfield) and his older brother, Leo (Thomas Gomez), who runs a small-time numbers office in New York, become enveloped in a criminal conspiracy, catapulting crime boss Ben Tucker (Roy Roberts) to master of the entire city. Rival gangster Fico (Paul Fix) attempts to muscle into the operation. In a move possibly inspired by the FBI wiretap of Polonsky, a special prosecutor appointed by the New York governor taps Tucker's and Joe's phones and uses this information to break the numbers racket. Most film noirs up to that time depicted corrupt individuals and institutions, but *Force of Evil* departs from the norm by showing complete social breakdown, driven by greed and cupidity. Joe, who admits to being in Tucker's "hip pocket," explains Tucker's power. "I will tell you . . . how the boom was on, and I could feel money spread all over the city like air." *Force of Evil* depicts an entire city in the hands of gangsters. Polonsky's film, even more than films like *Crossfire, Asphalt Jungle,* and *Clash by Night,* presented unflattering views of the criminal justice system and, ultimately, of capitalism itself. Paul Buhle and Dave Wagner observe that as the

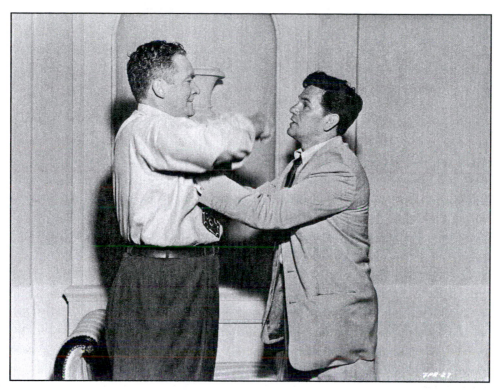

Abraham Polonsky's classic film noir *Force of Evil* (1948) was the subject of an FBI investigation because of Polonsky's communist ties. Although the agency never acted against the film, Polonsky became one of the famous Hollywood Ten filmmakers who received prison sentences for refusing to cooperate with the House Un-American Activities Committee. (Copyright 1948 Enterprise Productions)

characters "go down" the movie's message is that the ultimate crime "is capitalism, and capitalism, crime."[11]

Critics rank *Force of Evil* as a seminal film noir. One year earlier Polonsky had achieved acclaim for his script for *Body and Soul* (1947). Today critics, including director Martin Scorsese, consider *Body and Soul* as one of the finest noir boxing films of all time. In part because of the controversies surrounding *Force of Evil,* a surprising number of the cast and crew of *Body and Soul,* including Polonsky, actors John Garfield, Anne Revere, Lloyd Gough, Canada Lee, Art Smith, Shimen Ruskin, producer Bob Roberts, and cinematographer James Wong Howe, ended up either blacklisted or gray-listed during the HUAC hearings, while director Robert Rossen saved himself by naming names. After his encounter with HUAC, Polonsky never again directed a film despite his obvious talents. He soon joined actor John Garfield and a number of other friends and acquaintances on the blacklist, and eventually became a member of the Hollywood Ten.

Hollywood progressives soon organized a response to the HUAC hearings and the convictions of the Hollywood Ten. In an event billed as "Hollywood Fights Back," thousands gathered in Hollywood's Gilmore Stadium in 1947 to hear Katherine Hepburn and Vice President Henry Wallace speak out against McCarthyism's attacks on Hollywood. "Silence the artist," Hepburn warned, "and you silence the most articulate voice the people have." Dalton Trumbo, one of the Ten, reportedly ghost-wrote her speech.[12] In response to the prison sentences meted out to the Hollywood Ten, 204 Hollywood professionals signed an amicus curiae brief in support of them, but the Supreme Court declined to hear their appeal. Of the 204 signers, 84 soon found themselves blacklisted. Was it payback? During the McCarthy period any opposition to the movement resulted in blacklisting, deportation, or prison.

American Legion Blacklist

In 1949 the powerful American Legion founded its own blacklist, initially consisting of 128 names of people it claimed were active members of the "communist conspiracy." Writer Lillian Hellman appeared on the legion's list, along with other prominent intellectuals. As a result of the listing, Hellman suddenly found herself unemployed, even though she had earned credits on ten films and was widely recognized as one of Hollywood's best and most prolific writers. She would not work again until 1966. The legion had a long history of activism against liberals and progressives. During the bitterly fought labor disputes of the period legion volunteers kidnapped union organizers, beat them, and dropped them far from the town's borders. They had to make their way back to their base as best they could. Few troubled themselves to return and face the legion again.

The blacklists fostered familial breakups, alcoholism, drug addiction, bankruptcy, and mental breakdowns. Foreign-born directors Jules Dassin and Joseph Losey found themselves deported. Others became demoralized after HUAC's J. Parnell Thomas compelled them to testify against friends, revealing memberships in forbidden organizations in exchange for immunity from prosecution. A few of Hollywood's most talented writers managed to obtain a little work by writing under pseudonyms. The most famous example is the "Robert Rich" who won an Academy Award in 1954 for Best Screenplay. Rich turned out to be none other than Dalton Trumbo. The fact that so many of Hollywood's most gifted individuals were silenced or forced underground no doubt contributed to a noticeable decline in the quality of both writing and production throughout the fifties.

The blacklist remained a secret document, never officially acknowledged by Hollywood, thereby adding the shame of silence to Hollywood's efforts to suppress leftist ideas and talents. Not until June 22, 1950, when the *Counterattack* pamphlet titled

Red Channels appeared and named 151 entertainment industry officials as "Red Fascists and their sympathizers," did anything like an official list materialize. Although it remained hidden, however, the blacklist destroyed many promising careers. Hollywood's failure to provide openness in its treatment of its leftist and progressive members remained unbroken until 1960 when Dalton Trumbo, one of the Hollywood Ten, acknowledged authorship of *Spartacus* and *Exodus*, two of Hollywood's most successful films.

Witch-Hunts and Loyalty Oaths

McCarthy and his supporters eagerly sought to ferret out communists and fellow travelers in every profession. Government and academe also proved vulnerable to frenzied hunts for undercover agents operating secretly from within. Outspoken university professors were fired or discovered their contracts were not renewed. During this period agitation arose for "loyalty oaths," in which employees and officials swore loyalty to the United States. In 1950, in response to the HUAC hearings, conservative directors Leo McCrary and Cecil B. DeMille urged all members of the director's guild to take loyalty oaths. That way, they could also demonstrate their own loyalty.[13]

In 1951 HUAC opened its second investigation into alleged communist influences on Hollywood films. Witnesses abandoned their earlier strategy of evoking the First Amendment freedom of speech argument, choosing instead to invoke the Fifth Amendment's right not to self-incriminate. These hearings did not result in congressional citations as the first ones had, but as a result the blacklist grew to include many more names. The subcommittee appeared relentless in its drive to uncover subversives in Hollywood, but its real purpose, as with other McCarthy-era organizations, was to attack and banish liberals and progressives, not communists or subversives.

Anticommunist Films

McCarthyism also inspired several anticommunist movies, tapping into a new market for cinematic subversion. Between 1947 and 1954 nearly forty explicitly anticommunist films appeared, despite the fact that nearly all of them lost money. Hollywood continued to turn out anticommunist films despite their failures at the box office in order to assure everyone, particularly the federal government, of their staunchly anticommunist credentials. After 1947 few in Hollywood wished for any kind of association, however remote, with communism. Exhibitors, too, continued screening anticommunist films like *I Was a Communist for the F.B.I.* and *I Married a Communist* for the same reason: to demonstrate their patriotism and loyalty during a changing, uncertain, dangerous period.

By the late forties the first blatantly anticommunist films appeared, including *Despotism* (1946), *Don't Be a Sucker* (1947), *Behind the Iron Curtain* (1948; Canadian), *Guilty of Treason* (1949), *Conspirator* (1949), *The Red Menace* (1949), and *Walk a Crooked Mile* (1949). In 1950 Robert Stevenson's *I Married a Communist* enjoyed success at the box office. In it Robert Ryan plays a shipping executive with a radical past that comes back to haunt him. Thomas Gomez, who played a supporting role in *Force of Evil,* plays the head of the communists, who are portrayed as a gang of thugs. In 1951 Gordon Douglas's *I Was a Communist for the F.B.I.* also screened in theaters across the country. These films feature anticommunist, "better dead than red" themes underscoring the evils and dangers of communism. In 1952, Leo McCrary's *My Son John* premiered, a film in which two parents, played by Helen Hayes and Dean Jagger, discover to their horror that their son, played by Robert Walker, is secretly a communist agent. They treat the event with the same fears and hysteria that they might display if they had discovered that he was a heroin addict. Also in 1952 Edward Ludwig's *Big Jim McClain* appeared, starring John Wayne and James Arness as HUAC investigators who travel to Hawaii to ferret out communist agents. A staple during the late forties through the late fifties, the first cold war cycle of anticommunist films ceased in 1957, coinciding with the death of Joseph McCarthy. Before the McCarthy Code ended, Hollywood had produced over forty anticommunist films. Television producers followed Hollywood's lead by launching the popular *I Led Three Lives,* featuring a U.S. double agent posing as a suburban citizen. All of these films and television shows contributed to an air of suspicion regarding communist subversion. At times, it almost seemed that communists lurked around every corner.

R. G. Springsteen's *The Red Menace* (1949) exemplifies the anticommunist genre. Springsteen's film stars Robert Rockwell as Bill Jones, a distinguished war veteran who is recruited by the Communist Party after an operative overhears Jones's complaint against a real estate company that specializes in duping veterans into buying worthless homesites. Soon, he finds himself embroiled in a communist cell after being seduced by Mollie Flaherty (Barbara Fuller). He attends a class on Marxism run by the party and given by another party member, Yvonne Kraus (Betty Lou Geison), where he learns that "there's only one kind of truth, and that is the communist truth as seen by Marx, Lenin, and Stalin." Evil communists in this film abhor decent people, especially a Catholic priest who informs Jones that communism is atheistic and leads to innumerable sins. "God isn't very popular in some circles today," he explains. "The atheistic systems are always founded on hatred."

The communists in this film appear as one-dimensional proponents of such dubious sentiments. Except for Nina Petrova (Harrne Axman), the female communists behave licentiously and libidinously, eager to seduce any men who come their way. Nina, however, begins to doubt the party line, particularly after communists murder her father in Europe. She befriends Jones, and the pair eventually turns its back on the party and flees to Texas. There they encounter a kindly rural sheriff known locally as Uncle Sam. Sam assures the young couple that they need fear nothing from the communists, who can never hurt good Americans. "What you kids want to do," explains Sam, "is get yourselves hitched and raise a couple of real American kids." The anticommunist films often promote marriage and parenthood against perceived communist promiscuity.

The Red Menace illustrates the central theme of anticommunist films, namely, "beware of communist subversion." In this film, subversion surfaces in labor disputes and in organized protests against crooked businessmen. Eventually, however, marriage, family values, and Christianity in the film trump communism's atheistic, humanistic philosophy. In this film the "subversive" characters Yvonne and Mollie seduce and occasionally murder men who fall under their power, like mythological sirens. Only by renouncing communism and embracing Christianity and Americanism do communists like Nina possess any hope for the future.

During the fifties more anticommunist films appeared, though none were as successful as *I Was a Communist for the F.B.I.* and *Red Menace*. With the McCarthy Code's prohibition against depicting political subjects, filmmakers substituted symbolism, innuendo, and other evasions for overt political content. One of the most popular and effective genres proved to be sci-fi, which reframed widespread fears of communist subversion into paranoia about alien invasions. Sci-fi's dramatic moments turned on deep anxieties regarding U.S. vulnerability to clandestine subversion from within, or "the red menace."

Backlash

McCarthyism immediately encountered heated opposition. First Lady Eleanor Roosevelt blasted the government for its harassment of the filmmaking industry. She questioned the entire notion of an Un-American Activities Committee, stating that such a committee, in itself, was un-American. She argued that "in our country we must trust the people to hear and see both the good and the bad and to choose the good." Roosevelt believed that HUAC had no legitimate role in a democratic society. "The Un-American Activities Committee," she concluded, "seems to me to be better for a police state than for the U.S.A."[14]

Eventually, the Hollywood Ten themselves decided to take their case directly to movie audiences, their only recourse against the government's case against them. The defendants hastily crafted a twenty-minute film promoting their cause and denouncing the government's censorship efforts. We will never know how general audiences might have responded to *The Hollywood Ten* (1949), one of the earliest controversial political documentaries produced. It was immediately banned, and, given the climate of the day, no mainstream theaters dared show it. Instead, it played to small audiences at union halls, community meeting rooms, and private homes. Slowly, the account of the Hollywood Ten became better known because of this film. It is now available in public libraries and specialized video rental outlets. It marked one of the first attempts to use the film medium to disseminate unpopular social and political views. World War II had already stimulated the creation of the handheld movie camera, and audiences had grown accustomed to short documentaries in the form of newsreels that brought the latest footage from the battlefields. Without the new war-inspired technology it is doubtful whether the Hollywood Ten could have made their own motion picture, but the small, inexpensive handheld cameras of the era allowed groups and even individuals access for the first time to the film medium. This film would prove to be only the forerunner of an entirely new film political genre, operating for the most part under the MPAA radar.

In 1952, during the height of McCarthyism, the U.S. Supreme Court suddenly cut the ground from under movie censors, both official and unofficial, in the so-called *Miracle* case, or *Burstyn v. Wilson* (1952), in which the Court ruled that motion pictures, like periodicals, are protected under the First Amendment against attempts to suppress their content. This ruling meant that film was finally considered "free speech" instead of "entertainment." The Court overturned the venerable *Mutual Film Corp. v. Ohio Industrial Commission* (1915), in which it had affirmed four decades earlier that motion pictures were not a form of free expression but a form of entertainment, and as such were subject to prior censorship. The 1952 decision called into question the legal foundation for the Hays Code as well as the efforts of McCarthyism to limit and control political and social film content. Although the Hays Code persisted until 1968, *Burstyn v. Wilson* foreshadowed the end of both the Hays Code and the unofficial McCarthy code.

By 1951 suppression of leftist films, especially the blacklist of many of the industry's most talented professionals, achieved full strength. Hollywood filmmakers not on a list acquiesced to McCarthyism and, with a few exceptions, focused on safe genres like family melodramas, Broadway musicals, and romantic comedies (*Picnic, Guys and Dolls, Breakfast at Tiffany's*). Some good film noirs appeared, but by the end of the decade no A-budget noirs were produced. Fifties audiences, made up primarily of members of the postwar "Silent Generation," grew accustomed to films that openly expressed no controversial issues. The major exception to the wholesale repression of liberal and progressive views is *Salt of the Earth* (1954), by Hollywood Ten director Herbert Biberman and blacklisted producer Paul Jarrico. This film documents a contentious strike by New Mexican Latino mine workers against the Delaware Zinc Company. Set in the mythical village of Zinc Town, formerly the peaceful Hispanic community of San Marcos, the film relates the history of a long struggle against a racist corporation that forced Hispanic miners to work singly, exposing them to much greater danger than Anglos, but deployed Anglo miners in pairs, a far less hazardous practice. The workers' wives eventually force the men to demand better sanitation because, although company houses rented to Anglos contain bathrooms and hot running water, those rented to Latino families lacked those basics.

Throughout production the filmmakers faced powerful harassment. Trade presses denounced the project as subversive. *The Hollywood Reporter* warned of "Hollywood Reds" embarked on "an un-American racial issue propaganda movie" in New Mexico. Perhaps because of this publicity, mysterious vigilantes fired shots occasionally at the crew during filming. After filming, prominent unions refused to work on the project, which by then had become extremely controversial. The filmmakers resorted to subterfuge in order to complete the editing process, which takes weeks but in this case stretched to one year. Throughout it all conservatives wrote angry letters to HUAC, the MPAA, and the Screen Actors Guild demanding action to halt production on the film.[15]

Once the film was finally completed, the filmmakers encountered a growing number of theater owners who suddenly declined to screen the film. California congressman Donald Jackson (R) denounced the film from the floor of the House of Representatives, and the FBI began an investigation into its financing. The American Legion called for a nationwide boycott. Union projectionists received orders not to touch it, and so it opened in only a few theaters. The film proved successful abroad, however, winning several awards in Eastern Europe. It remains one of only a few prostrike films in existence (see also *The Milagro Beanfield War*). Jarrico, an early name on the blacklist, enlisted Michael Wilson, another blacklisted writer, to create the screenplay. Delays occurred, allegedly due to a government conspiracy against the film. Eventually, the three principals filed a lawsuit against the government, causing it to retreat from its alleged harassment of the filmmakers. Finally, the film appeared in 1953 in a handful of theaters. Long a union favorite, today it remains an early indie classic.[16]

Otto Preminger played one final role in ending the McCarthy Code when, in 1960, more than a dozen years after the HUAC hearings, he openly hired Dalton Trumbo, one of the Hollywood Ten, to script *Exodus*. Trumbo, of course, as a member of the Hollywood Ten, was also blacklisted. Prior to 1960, blacklisted individuals had not been able to work on motion pictures without relying on "fronts" to take official credit. By hiring Trumbo, Preminger effectively sounded the death knell for the McCarthy Code.

Mainstream Influence

Will Hays and Joseph Breen labored for decades to free films of progressive, liberal, or radical issues. When Hays retired in 1945 he devoted his energies to combating communism, thereby adding his voice to a movement that would soon result in the blacklist. In addition to that imposed by the MPAA, McCarthyism imposed its own code, enforced by fear, blacklists, and witch-hunts. The movement drove liberal and leftist filmmakers underground and imposed a pall on realistic depictions of political and social issues that still remains powerful today.

Both the Hays Code and the McCarthy Code relied on prior censorship. While the Hays Office wielded the threat of a stiff fine and exclusion from the MPAA, McCarthyists censored movies through witch-hunts and blacklists. Both of these codes focused efforts on censorship before films were even produced by elimination of progressive writers and directors through blacklists and fear. Hollywood generally took on a conservative tone during the McCarthy era, but individual filmmakers like Otto Preminger and Stanley Kramer tested the increasingly outmoded code. McCarthyism's influence on film content lingered throughout the cold war, and today progressive filmmakers like Michael Moore still encounter obstacles in attempting to express progressive or even liberal political values.

Bad Cop Noir

The early fifties spawned a spate of film noirs featuring crooked, devious, or rogue policemen, including Otto Preminger's *Where the Sidewalk Ends* (1950), Joseph Losey's *The Prowler* (1951), William Wyler's *Detective Story* (1951), Nicholas Ray's *On Dangerous Ground* (1952), Fritz Lang's *The Big Heat* (1953), Roy Rowland's *Rogue Cop* (1954), Richard Quine's *Pushover* (1954), Don Siegel's *Private Hell 36* (1954), and Orson Welles's *Touch of Evil* (1958). Each of these films features cops who go wrong for various reasons, from falling in love with beautiful, dangerous women to keeping recovered loot for themselves, planting evidence on suspected criminals, or exhibiting other criminal traits. These films paid homage to the Hays Code by including suitable punishment for the rogue cops' misdeeds, but as time passed the Hays Office was forced to loosen up a few of its standards.

Preminger hired Ben Hecht to write the script for *Where the Sidewalk Ends*, which sizzles with ironic twists and turns. The film features Detective Mark Dixon (Dana Andrews), a cop with a bad reputation for strong-arming suspects. Dixon tracks small-time hood Tommy Scalise (Gary Merrill) through the dark streets of New York, but while on the hunt he loses his temper once again, killing a suspect, then disposes of the corpse to avoid detection. Soon, Dixon falls in love with the suspect's widow, played by Gene Tierney. Before it is over Dixon succeeds in collaring Scalise, who, police conclude, is responsible for the murder committed by Dixon. In a final scene designed to bring the film under Hays Code compliance, Dixon confesses to his chief and his girlfriend, whose father, played by Tom Tully, had been wrongfully accused of the crime. However, Dixon's confession comes too late to save him from a probable criminal conviction, although audiences might imagine a judge doling out a light sentence to a man who had become a hero in the department.

Orson Welles's *Touch of Evil* (1958) provided a dramatic end to the classic noir genre. Welles's film features the ultimate bad cop, police captain Hank Quinlan (Welles), who has a reputation for planting evidence to secure convictions. Welles pits Quinlan against Ramon Vargas (Charlton Heston), a Mexican police detective who embodies all of the qualities of a "good cop." Quinlan quickly spins out of control in pursuing a case against the Grandie family, a drug ring. At one point Vargas discusses the difficulties with police work: "A policeman's job is only easy in a police state," he warns in a thinly veiled reference to McCarthyism, which by 1957 was in eclipse.

McCarthyism can be blamed for the demise of classic film noir. In its place films depicting corrupt law enforcers served as indirect symbols for McCarthyism, with its seemingly noble goals pursued through extralegal means like witch-hunts and blacklists. If the police cannot be trusted, who can be? These films strongly indict local law enforcement officers for corruption and abuse of power, but the real targets are McCarthyism and the Red Scare movement. Hollywood had been burned enough by McCarthyism to be extremely wary about attacking the movement directly, but filmmakers had a field day attacking local government officials as corrupt and even criminal, with the bad cop noirs sending a cynical message regarding the intentions of those who were supposed to be protecting the citizens.

Anti-McCarthy Westerns

Fear of McCarthyism and the blacklist kept most filmmakers from releasing progressive or leftist films. What political elements remain in the films of the period appear indirect, obscured by symbolism and innuendo, time-honored tools of the filmmaker's craft. Howard Hawks's *Red River* (1948) was one of the first Westerns with anti-McCarthy overtones. Hawks's film plumbs the depths of Tom Dunson (John Wayne), who starts out admirably by wrestling a cattle ranch from the barren Texas plains. Later, when facing obstacles during an epic cattle drive, Dunson hardens, and he turns into an unjust leader. His best friend, Groot Nadine (Walter Brennan), observes in a voice-over that "Tom had changed. He'd always been a hard man. Now he was harder." Dunson's protégé and unofficial adopted son Matt Garth (Montgomery Clift), who represents a post-McCarthy perspective, wrestles command of the cattle drive from Dunson, then heads for the new railroad town of Abilene, Kansas, leaving Dunson behind vowing revenge. Eventually, Dunson and Garth reconcile after engaging in an old-fashioned Western street fight. Dunson finally transforms from an arrogant, dictatorial trail boss by rediscovering his humanity. In the process, he must have reminded many in the audience about the excesses of anticommunism readily apparent in 1948.

One of the most highly esteemed Westerns, Fred Zinneman's *High Noon* (1951), makes a strong but subtle statement about Hollywood, McCarthyism, and middle-class complacency. Scriptwriter Carl Foreman coded the film's political messages using symbolism and innuendo. The dramatic tension revolves around the return of outlaw Frank Miller (Ian MacDonald) to the small Western town of Hadleyville, presided over by Marshal Will Kane (Gary Cooper), just married to Amy, a Quaker pacifist (Grace Kelly). Miller's mission involves revenge against Kane for having arrested him and helped in his conviction for murder. When Kane learns of Miller's impending return by train, he initially takes the townspeople's advice, and his wife's, and decides to flee to another town. Soon, however, guilt at his cowardice causes him to reconsider and return to Hadleyville to face Miller and his gang. "I think I ought to stay" is his laconic comment signaling his commitment to fight Miller's gang. Kane soon learns that none will help him fight Miller, including his deputy, Harvey Pell (Lloyd Bridges). The townspeople close their businesses and retreat into the safety of their homes out of cowardice, leaving only Kane, an elderly retired sheriff, and later Amy to face the vicious outlaw gang. Finally, Kane outguns Miller's gang, leaving only Miller himself, whom Amy kills to save Kane. Kane celebrates his victory by flinging his badge to the ground in disgust. What upset him is not so much Hadleyville, described in the film as "a dirty little town in the middle of nowhere," as it is his discovery of the abjectness of most people. Where are the brave citizens willing to fight for peace and justice? It takes very little imagination to equate Zinneman's fictional town with the United States, which was behaving just as cowardly in the face of McCarthyism. Hadleyville symbolizes not just the United States but also Hollywood, which was cooperating fully at that time with McCarthyism. Foreman acknowledged that he had intended *High Noon* to be "a parable about Hollywood and McCarthyism." While writing the script, he watched "a community beginning to crumble around the edges as these high-powered politicians came in." McCarthyism, Foreman observed, involved "putting this community [the United States] through an inquisition that was getting more and more painful for a lot of people, and people were falling to the wayside one way or another." Shortly thereafter Foreman received a subpoena by HUAC while on the set of *High Noon*. After he pleaded the Fifth Amendment to avoid answering questions about his previous or current association with communism, he discovered that he, too, had been blacklisted. Unable to find work in Hollywood, he moved to England. There he wrote scripts anonymously or wrote under pseudonyms. Foreman continued his career in England but was unable to find work in Hollywood until 1975, twenty-four years after being blacklisted.[17]

Preminger, Losey, Lang, Hawks, Zinneman, Foreman, Welles, and many other directors of Westerns and film noirs attacked McCarthyism indirectly in their films, minimizing their risks of being blacklisted. Although they were unable to attack McCarthy or any of his supporters directly they attacked indirectly, by presenting intolerant, duplicitous, egotistical protagonists occupying positions of leadership. Viewers easily connected the intolerance and abuses of these protagonists with acts of intolerance and abuse by McCarthyists. Many filmmakers involved in film noir and Westerns found themselves silenced, but not before assisting in the creation of some of the most memorable films of all time.

Alien Subversion

Robert Wise's science fiction thriller *The Day the Earth Stood Still* (1951) turned the era's widespread fears of communist subversion and a coming nuclear war into audience paranoia over invasions of aliens from outer space. Klaatu (Michael Rennie), the gentlemanly alien in Wise's film, comes to Earth with a pacifistic message. Klaatu warns a gathering of earth's leaders about an impending nuclear war unless they renounce conflict in favor of peace. "Your choice is simple: join us and live in peace or pursue your present course and face oblivion." His advice comes from an advanced civilization that long ago renounced war. "We shall be waiting for your answer," he warns. "The decision rests with you." Klaatu's pacifist sentiments coming from a human would not have gone over well during McCarthyism, so Wise chose an alien from outer space as his pacifist. Surprisingly, this film escaped attack by McCarthy's supporters, probably due to its fantastic plot. Still, Wise's film served as a model for other sci-fi films that followed. By 1954 the messages contained in sci-fi films changed from pleas for peaceful coexistence to dire warnings to be vigilant against hidden enemies that were eating at the heart of America.

Gordon Douglas's *Them* (1954) admirably captures the era's paranoia regarding subversives "burrowing from within," to use a popular McCarthy-era phrase. In Douglas's film, however, the aliens burrowing underneath Los Angeles are not communists but giant ants, eight to twelve feet long, preying upon human beings and multiplying at alarming rates. Distinguished etymologists, played by Edward Gwenn and Joan Weldon, join with police and military officers, played by James Whitmore and James Arness, to combat the giant ant infestation. The ants mutated due to radiation from the atomic bombing of Hiroshima, although the film leaves vague why they appeared in the United States, unless it was symbolic payback for the destruction of that city by atomic bombs. Efforts to eradicate the giant insects, which pose an imminent danger of annihilating the human race in less than one year, partially succeed, until investigators discover a large nest in an unfinished tunnel system under the city. The savage insects, which strike at night and return to the safety of their nests during daylight, embody fears of evil subversives burrowing deep into the government and, especially, Hollywood. Savage monsters breeding in underground Los Angeles suggest McCarthy-era fears of traitorous communist agents subverting Hollywood.

Dr. Miles Bennell (Kevin McCarthy) carries his girlfriend Becky Driscoll (Dana Wynter) so that she will not wake up and turn into one of the "pod people" aliens in Don Siegel's *Invasion of the Body Snatchers* (1956). The pod people resemble popular conceptions of clandestine communist agents subverting U.S. society. (Copyright 1956 Republic Pictures)

The scenario of monsters burrowing into society struck a chord, and soon other filmmakers followed with their own sci-fi films. In 1956 Don Siegel's classic *Invasion of the Body Snatchers* depicted an infestation of aliens intent on murdering every earthling. Siegel's villains, extraterrestrial "pod people," assume the physical appearance and identities of humans before they murder them in a small California town. The aliens, blending perfectly with society, provide convincing proxies for subversive communist agents widely believed to lurk in every institution as part of a global conspiracy for world domination. In the film's dramatic prologue, Dr. Miles Bennell (Kevin McCarthy), the film's physician protagonist, after being picked up on the highway trying to warn motorists of the invasion of the evil doppelgangers, pleads hysterically with the doctors and nurses in the hospital, "Make them listen before it's too late!" Similar hysteria promoted the witch-hunts ruthlessly ferreting out communists, leftists, and even outspoken liberals during the fifties.

Sci-fi films proliferated during the fifties and early sixties, often characterized as "the Golden Age of Science Fiction." Some of the more memorable include Jack Arnold's *Creature from the Black Lagoon* (1954), in which a prehistoric-like humanoid surfaces in the Amazon River; Irwin S. Yayworth's *The Blob* (1958), about a growing mass of protoplasm that threatens humanity, which launched Steve McQueen's acting career; and Stephen Sekely's *The Day of the Triffids* (1963), in which intelligent plants attack humanity. The McCarthy-era sci-fi films always reflected paranoia about aliens of one kind or another invading the United States. Sometimes, the aliens blend in with the citizenry like subversive terrorist cells, burrowing deep underground or hiding in large greenhouses. At other times, they emerge from the distant past, perhaps awakened by atomic testing, and confront humanity with primordial terrors. On a subliminal level, they represent deep-seated fears and anxieties of the McCarthy period.

Anti-McCarthy Costume Drama

Opposition to McCarthyism found new expression in Stanley Kubrick's 1960 gladiatorial classic *Spartacus.* Hollywood Ten writer Dalton Trumbo scripted Kubrick's film based on Howard Fast's best-selling novel. Kubrick cast Kirk Douglas as Spartacus, a Roman slave who shines in the gladiator ring and as a political organizer. Spartacus survives in the harsh gladiatorial world, but he becomes increasingly bitter about his slavery. He ignites a revolt of gladiators and slaves, explaining to his fellow gladiators, "An army of gladiators. There's never been an army like that!"

Soon, Spartacus succeeds in raising a massive army of slaves dissatisfied with their lowly status under Roman rule. While exhorting his followers to revolt, he tells them, "I do know that we're brothers, and I know that we're free. We march tonight." The idea of a vast group of people subjugated by corrupt overlords corresponds to filmmakers' feelings of persecution in the McCarthy era. Throughout the early cold war, filmmakers faced blacklists and other repression that certainly felt like a form of slavery. To reinforce his points about official corruption's stifling freedom, Kubrick made his Romans less than heroic. He characterized the corrupt Roman official Crassus (Laurence Olivier) as bisexual, despite PCA Geoffrey Shurlock's threatening letter to Universal Studios warning of several "unacceptable elements" in the script, the chief among them being Crassus's bisexuality.[18] With perverted Roman noblemen like Crassus and noble slaves like Spartacus, Kubrick made his film a powerful political allegory of slavery versus freedom. Many in the audience must have realized that beneath the surface McCarthyism, not the Roman Empire, served as Kubrick's ultimate villain.

Neo-McCarthyism

Although McCarthyism ended officially with Joe McCarthy's own demise in 1957, its influence in films continues even today. Hollywood's renowned phobia against films with political messages stems from the McCarthy period. In Robert Altman's *The Player* (1994), director Martin Scorsese, playing himself, pitches a political film to Hollywood producer Griffin Mill (Tim Robbins). Scorsese asks Mill, "Does political scare you?" Mill replies, "No, political doesn't scare me. Radical political scares me. Political political scares me." This obviously refers to the lingering effects of McCarthyism on political films. As long as the memory of HUAC hearings, the Hollywood Ten, and the blacklist linger, the fact that moguls fear political films should not surprise us. Therefore, a large part of McCarthy's legacy consists of its effective banning of leftist or progressive films. However, another important part of that legacy remains the symbolic, coded Westerns, film noirs, and sci-fi that speak for the artistic successes achieved only after filmmakers learned to disguise their politics by expressing it in coded, subtle form.

Despite pronouncements on the death of McCarthyism, however, the movement ultimately refused to remain moribund. Adherents awaited more favorable reception. Today, few of the old players still live, but a new generation claims the mantle of Joe McCarthy. Labeled New McCarthyism, this movement includes neoconservatives and political evangelicals. Neo-McCarthyism now makes its presence known on college campuses, on talk radio shows, and on conservative television channels, particularly Fox News. Writers David Horowitz and Ann Coulter apologize for McCarthy while recycling the senator's views. Coulter praised McCarthy for correctly identifying the dangers of subversion while castigating liberals for opposing him in *Treason: Liberal Treachery from the Cold War to the War on Terrorism* (Crown Books, 2003). Coulter also attacked liberals and exonerated McCarthy in 2003 in her nationally syndicated column, in which she charged, "[Liberals] were systematically undermining the nation's ability to defend itself, while waging a bellicose campaign of lies to blacken McCarthy's name."[19]

The conflicts between neo-McCarthyists, evangelicals, and other conservatives on the one hand and progressives, liberals, and moderates on the other constitute some of the most recent battles in the culture wars. Neoconservatives and evangelical Christians find themselves united against progressives, feminists, multiculturalists, and peace activists. Although the neoconservative movement shares many of the values of McCarthyism, it has yet to stimulate congressional hearings about film ratings. However, in 2001 Senators Joe Lieberman and John McCain proposed a federal ratings system to correct the "failures" of the Motion Picture Association of America. On April 24, the Federal Trade Commission issued a report on the state of the industry, which was immediately greeted by a statement signed by senators from both parties, including McCain. They criticized self-regulation on the part of the recording, movie, and video game industries, threatening, "If anyone believes that our concerns and the concerns of American parents can be eliminated simply with opportunistic pledges, they are sorely mistaken."[20]

Instead of banning films and blacklisting filmmakers, some of today's conservatives employ documentaries to promulgate their ideas. Today's political documentaries provide abundant information on the rise of New McCarthyism. Low production costs (compared with other media) and abundant venues available for low-budget documentaries provide compelling reasons for selecting that medium. Neoconservatives and evangelicals should thank Michael Moore and his documentaries for the current crop of conservative docs. Moore's films take aim at sacred conservative shibboleths like gun ownership and George W. Bush's potential complicity in the 9/11 attacks, along with his shadowy ties to the Saudi royal family. Moore's films, like *Fahrenheit 9/11* and *Sicko,* evoked outrage from conservatives and stimulated a number of counterdocumentaries with conservative biases.

On September 16, 2004, the "first-ever conservative film festival" occurred outside Dallas, Texas. Twenty-four films screened at the American Renaissance Festival, including *The Peace Commies* (2004), which attacks antiwar protestors by likening them to communists. One of the chief leftist filmmakers, Michael Moore, found himself under attack during that festival in the world premier of *Michael Moore Hates America* (2004). Filmmaker Michael Wilson, creator of *Michael Moore Hates America,* traveled around the country filming Americans enjoying success stories while attempting to obtain an interview with Moore, which never occurred. This scenario refers to Moore's *Roger and Me,* in which he attempts unsuccessfully to have a meeting with Roger Smith, General Motors' CEO. The popularity of Wilson's film within the ideological confines of a conservative film festival suggests the extent to which Michael Moore has become a demon to those in the neoconservative movement. It also demonstrates the increasing cultural esteem of documentary films.

Another notable film screened at the festival was *George W. Bush: Faith in the White House* (2004). This pro-Bush propaganda film provided yet another answer to Moore's *Fahrenheit 9/11*.

Among the array of conservative films at the festival, the most controversial offering turned out to be Evan Maloney's *Brainwashing 101* (2004). Maloney's film, along with its sequels, *Brainwashing 201: The Second Semester* (2005) and *Indoctrinating U* (2006), charges that many university professors are using their classrooms as political forums to inculcate progressive ideology. In these films Maloney echoes charges made earlier by neoconservative writer David Horowitz that liberal college professors indoctrinate their students with left-wing political ideology. Maloney's film alleges the existence of "speech codes," elaborate though unstated rules mandating political correctness in speech. This film aired on college campuses throughout the United States and at conservative film festivals. During the Liberty Festival in Los Angeles (October 2005), Maloney's *Brainwashing 201: The Second Semester* garnered a prize for Best Short. Maloney's sequel also reflects David Horowitz's neoconservative thesis. In fact, Horowitz himself introduced the film at the festival, braving hecklers who reportedly ran onstage screaming, "Fascists have no right to speak!"[21]

In response to the charges of liberal bias leveled in Maloney's film, the Bruin Alumni Association, a small, short-lived group of UCLA alumni, formed with the avowed purpose of challenging political correctness at UCLA. Spokesperson Andrew Jones explained to the media, "I'm very concerned about the level of professional teaching at UCLA." For the next few weeks the Bruin Alumni Association attempted to monitor political comments from UCLA professors, but their attempts have so far proved ineffective. Two UCLA professors, historian Ellen DuBois and education professor Peter McLaren, who were listed along with twenty-eight others as the "dirty thirty," spoke out against Maloney's film, expressing outrage at its message of intolerance. DuBois stated that the film "is a totally abhorrent invitation to students to participate in a witch-hunt . . . against their professors." McLaren labeled the film "a reactionary form of McCarthyism. Any decent American," he added, "is going to see through this kind of right-wing propaganda."[22] Maloney responded to these charges of McCarthyism and to allegations that the Bruin Alumni Association engaged in witch-hunts. In an online article he defended himself from charges of McCarthyism by claiming that UCLA and other universities constitute "an environment where professors overwhelmingly hold one worldview." Therefore, his film and the various groups formed around its issues are, he feels, "relevant," because a lack of intellectual diversity means that students are being shortchanged.[23] The controversy surrounding Maloney's films, and Horowitz's writing, shows little signs of abating, and it has had a profound impact on college campuses and conservative film festivals. The attempted suppression of the liberal political views of college professors evokes frightening accounts of McCarthyism's witch-hunts against liberal professors fifty years earlier.

In 2005 George Clooney released *Good Night and Good Luck*. Clooney's docudrama chronicles television commentator Edward R. Murrow's famous clash with Joseph McCarthy. Clooney cast David Strathairn as Murrow, the muckraking television commentator who finally tired of McCarthyism and decided to attack it where it was most vulnerable: in McCarthy's ill-advised speech charging the army with being soft on communism. Murrow exposes this attack as demagoguery, drawing McCarthy's ire. As a result, McCarthy is finished, his career as an anticommunist warrior comes to an end, and Murrow and the courageous forces of journalism triumph. To conservative reviewers, however, Clooney's film was anathema. *Movieguide* awarded it a −3 rating, their second-worst classification. The reviewer dismissed Clooney's film as demonstrating a "humanist, politically correct, liberal worldview about TV commentator Edward R. Murrow. Murrow's pseudojournalistic hatchet job on Senator Joseph McCarthy, which distorts history, including the radical antidemocratic aims of the American Civil Liberties Union, fails to honestly deal with the facts which do not fit its worldview while downgrading the dangers of Communism."[24]

This critic evokes the conservative view that Senator McCarthy deserves to be remembered as a courageous anticommunist crusader instead of the dangerous demagogue he appears to be to those on the left. Today's conservatives continue to revere McCarthy as an icon, just as liberals stereotype him as a would-be dictator. Therefore, a film excoriating the late senator was bound to evoke attacks from conservative reviewers. Clooney's film earned favorable reviews in a large number of liberal periodicals, including *The Boston Herald, New York Magazine,* and the *L.A. Weekly.* Generally, the more liberal the press, the more likely it was to praise Clooney's film in its review. Conservatives tended to echo the *Movieguide* reviewer.

Gender Roles

Although women's roles changed profoundly during the McCarthy era, females assumed supportive roles as nurturers and crusaders in the anticommunist dramas of the early 1950s. In anticommunist films the role of seductress is reserved for communist female characters who behave like godless nymphomaniacs. Anticommunist female characters function more as loyal wives and mothers and as helpmates to crusading men. The problem with glamorizing "good girls," though, has always been how to keep audiences interested. Pollyanna-like characters are not known to inspire huge box office sales. The evangelical movement of past decades also encounters this problem. Seductresses and zany screwballs seem more attractive.

During McCarthyism filmmakers learned to express liberal and progressive views through innuendo. A few films, including *High Noon, The Searchers,* and *Spartacus,* presented subtle critiques of McCarthyism and its excesses. In these films male protagonists come off as corrupt, authoritarian, and racist. Also, the bad cop noir cycle of the fifties depicts authoritarian cops as flawed, corrupt, weak, and undeserving of support. Although McCarthy-era censorship doomed blatantly political movies, it encouraged a deeper, subtler discourse about authoritarianism.

McCarthyism promoted good girl characters as opposed to the femme noir seductresses with which they competed for audiences. Conventional females feature not only in anticommunist films like *Red Menace* but also in more mainstream movies that bear the influences of McCarthyism, like Becky Driscoll (Dana Wynter) in Don Siegel's *Invasion of the Body Snatchers*. Fred Zinneman's *High Noon*, a veiled attack on McCarthyism, significantly features not only good girl Amy Kane (Grace Kelly) but also bad girl Helen Ramirez (Katy Jurado). In addition, Amy Kane kills a man to save her husband, certainly not conventional behavior for good girl characters.

Once seduced by communist women and ideology, male characters in anticommunist films transform into robotic, ruthless ideologues willing to sell their own relatives for the good of the revolution. The vixens in *The Red Menace* enjoy seducing males and then indoctrinating them into the party line. Once inside, many find it difficult if not impossible to escape from the tentacles of the international communist conspiracy. These films were intended as urgent wake-up calls desperately needed in order to forestall a complete takeover of the United States by the international communist conspiracy, not as dramatic vehicles containing well-rounded characters.

Creating the Couple

Typical anticommunist films end with a couple pledging or uniting in marriage. The marriage institution, like the family, provides potent strategies to combat the supposed permissiveness of communist relationships, as in *The Red Menace*, which ends with the betrothal of Nina (Hanne Axman) and Bill Jones (Robert Rockwell). In Don Siegel's *Invasion of the Body Snatchers*, Miles (Kevin McCarthy) and Becky Driscoll (Dana Wynter), his lovely ex-girlfriend, find themselves falling in love all over again, but this time they are older, and, like a growing number of Americans in the McCarthy period, both have had failed marriages in the past. Aside from their former relationships, Miles and Becky appear as an ideal couple. He has a successful small-town medical practice, and she is a beautiful college graduate who fills the role of upper-middle-class wife and potential mother in small-town America. The idyllic life Siegel depicts is nothing less than the American Dream, threatened to its core by alien doppelgangers, or "pod people," who subvert the political and economic life of the small California town of Santa Mira.

Miles and Becky represent the antithesis of what the pod people offer, security in a collectivist society. Although they appear identical to humans, the pod people lack human emotions, corresponding to the period's stereotypes of godless, emotionless subversives undermining America. Of the pod people, one of the humans, Don Kaufman (Larry Gates), observes, "Desire, ambition, faith—without them life is so simple." If the pod people lack emotions, Siegel takes pains to present Miles and Becky as brimming with emotions—love for each other, disgust for the pod people, and compassion for fellow humans. Therefore, the McCarthy-era couple endorses the ideal of young lovers from the same ethnic group and social class coupling.

In 1997 Hollywood celebrated the fifty-year anniversary of the blacklist by hosting a large retrospective of the period at the Motion Picture Academy. Abraham Polonsky, one of the few survivors, shared the stage with actress Marsha Hunt and writer/producer Paul Jarrico of *Salt of the Earth*. Thus, two of the most hated and feared of the Hollywood leftists received the applause of an appreciative crowd, an award that would not have been possible during the McCarthy period. Jarrico's film continues to receive critical praise, and Polonsky's has undergone a revival, with Martin Scorsese praising the film lavishly in a special feature added to the DVD version.

McCarthyism impacted an entire generation of films, and those who came of age during the fifties became known as the Silent Generation primarily because the most vocal social critics found themselves muted, blacklisted, or imprisoned. The remaining talents, and some of the blacklisted ones under assumed aliases, managed to create a number of outstanding films that carried deeply symbolic political messages. Would these films have been as great if they had emerged during a time of more laissez-faire Production Codes? As is often the case, when filmmakers are forced to abandon realism, a few talented individuals create understated, symbolic, and nuanced motion pictures.

CHAPTER FIVE

The Valenti Code

Throughout the long tenure of the Hays Code a major problem gradually revealed itself to censors. They labored under the notion that "correct standards of life" referred to immutable moral precepts somewhat akin to Victorianism. However, over time correct standards appeared to change while the code remained static. Profanity that shocked one generation, like Rhett Butler's admonition to Scarlett O'Hara, "Frankly, my dear, I don't give a damn" in Victor Fleming's *Gone With the Wind* (1939), seemed naive during World War II when U.S. soldiers and sailors gave profanity new panache. With the arrival of the postwar period U.S. families experienced rising affluence and an increased birthrate. The decade witnessed profound social changes, including the Civil Rights Movement and the eventual rise of feminism. As the cold war erupted on the Korean Peninsula and in Southeast Asia, Americans confided to Kinsey pollsters about their shocking lack of sexual fidelity and unconventional sexual diversity. Divorce rates accelerated and intergenerational conflict became commonplace. Although vestiges of Victorian morality lingered well beyond the thirties, its influence greatly diminished as the twentieth century advanced.

The rise of television during the fifties also profoundly affected Hollywood studios, creating even more competition than radio had in the twenties and thirties. Producer Samuel Goldwyn warned in 1949 that "the future of motion pictures, conditioned as it will be by the competition of television, is going to have no room for the deadwood of the present or the faded glories of the past." He predicted that "as it was in the early days of motion picture history, . . . it will take brains instead of just money to make pictures." Goldwyn foresaw that the entire nation would eventually be connected via coaxial cables, providing television with even greater advantages over movies.[1] By 1953, four years after Goldwyn's warning, movie attendance plunged from a high of 76 million per week in 1947 to only 50 million, a decline of over one-third.[2] Clearly, filmmakers would need to invent some creative strategies for dealing with these new conditions.

During the late fifties and sixties foreign films presented yet another challenge to Hollywood as the European filmmaking industry rapidly recovered from the devastations of World War II. U.S. directors competed with Ingmar Bergman, Federico Fellini, and Jean-Luc Godard for increasingly scarcer audiences. During the following decades foreign films, with their greater freedom to depict sexuality, made inroads into Hollywood markets already buffeted by television. Not since the onslaught of the Great Depression had Hollywood faced such a dire threat to its economic vitality. Hollywood fought back with Technicolor, 3-D, wide screens, and enhanced sound systems. If audiences preferred to view movies and programming in the comfort of their homes, perhaps they could be lured to the theaters by intriguing technology?

In addition to technology, filmmakers began experimenting with a variety of thematic strategies designed to woo audiences from TV, including the time-honored lures of sex, spectacle, and violence. Filmmakers pushed the boundaries of acceptable themes early in the fifties by depicting such previously taboo issues as prostitution, nymphomania, adultery, childhood sexuality, and graphic violence. Films featuring these devices increasingly challenged the Production Code, which gradually compromised, weakened, and eventually died.

Cracks in the Code

By the late fifties the bottom had dropped out of already weak box office sales, and movie attendance totaled only 35 million tickets a week, the lowest since the Great Depression.[3] By the sixties, Hollywood faced stiff competition from independents as well as European filmmakers. By 1960 Hollywood had produced 141 films whereas foreign producers had released 361 films.[4] The situation called for a solution, but it was not until 1968 that the MPAA finally jettisoned the old Hays Code and adopted a completely new concept in motion picture ratings.

In 1965 the U.S. Supreme Court, in *Freedman v. Maryland,* dramatically restricted the use of prior censorship of films, throwing out Maryland's censorship laws in the process. This decision undermined all state and local censorship boards. After this ruling, opponents successfully challenged censorship laws in New York, Virginia, Kansas, and Memphis, Tennessee. Although the Supreme Court had yet to rule on other censorship laws, legislators read the handwriting on the wall, and all censorship bodies, state and local, quickly faded from the scene. The case of *Interstate Circuit v. Dallas* (1968) put the final nails in the old code's coffin. Soon, the entire Hays Production Code itself disappeared in favor of a new rating system. The turbulent sixties proved to be the last decade for the old, badly weakened Hays Code.

Jack Valenti

After MPAA president Eric Johnson's death in 1963 Hollywood began a search for a worthy replacement. Louis Wasserman, president of Universal-International, surveyed Lyndon Johnson's and John F. Kennedy's staffs, hoping to discover a replacement among those ranks to serve Hollywood as well as Will Hays had done. Wasserman eventually settled upon influential Texan Jack Valenti, who had headed a large public relations firm in Houston until tapped by President Johnson to serve as a special adviser. During his tenure as presidential adviser Valenti garnered a reputation for loyalty, diligence, and hard work, as well as for the ease with which he formed relationships with influential individuals worldwide. Valenti proved so loyal that one contemporary observed, "If LBJ dropped the H-bomb, Valenti would call it an urban renewal project."[5] He seemed the perfect choice to fill Hays's shoes.

In 1966 Mike Nichols vigorously opposed the MPAA's attempt to censor the dialogue of his film *Who's Afraid of Virginia Woolf?*, which was rife with risqué lines. Nichols's film explored the marital strife between George (Richard Burton), a college professor, and Martha (Elizabeth Taylor), his wife. The film script faithfully recreates Edward Albee's stage script with racy epithets like "Jesus H. Christ," "screw!" "angel tits," "monkey nipples," and the now-famous "hump the hostess." Nichols, backed by Warner Brothers, staunchly refused to cut the dialogue. As a result, the Production Code Administration (PCA) decided to deny the film a seal of approval, and Warner Brothers appealed to the MPAA. The MPAA Board under Jack Valenti met at the St. Regis Hotel in New York and eventually decided to issue a PCA seal because "the film was not designed to be prurient. This film document, dealing with the tragic realism of life, is largely a reproduction of the Edward Albee play." The MPAA acknowledged that Albee's play had received critical acclaim, including the prestigious New York Drama Critics Award. Eventually the board granted Nichols's film an exception to the normal code requirement for clean dialogue and pristine sexual situations. The board accepted Warner Brothers' pledge to limit audiences to eighteen or older. After the film's release, with brilliant performances by Richard Burton and Elizabeth Taylor, the MPAA's decision to issue a seal of approval seemed vindicated, especially after it earned five Academy Awards. Warner Brothers agreed to film the $73-million feature without purging the "profanity and . . . blunt dialogue" that the PCA demanded. Valenti therefore agreed to grant Nichols's film an exception to the normal rating system and allow it to be screened in theaters with the warning "Suggested for Mature Audiences."[6]

The Valenti Code

Following closely upon *Freedman v. Maryland*, *Who's Afraid of Virginia Woolf?* seemed the final straw for the Hays Code. At this juncture, several compelling reasons existed for jettisoning the entire Hays Code and replacing it with something completely different. Jack Valenti, who proved more liberal than Hays and his successors, played a crucial role in that change. The final transformation occurred in 1968 when Valenti scrapped the old code altogether and substituted a new rating system designed to avoid prior censorship completely. The new code substituted an age-based system regulating audience age, not film content. Films under the new system received an MPAA rating, thereby avoiding prior subject matter restraint. The PCA, the enforcement arm of the MPAA, substituted age-based categories, including G for general admission, R for restricted to those over sixteen (later seventeen and then eighteen) unless accompanied by an adult, and X for allowing no one under eighteen. This system appeared to turn the old Hays Code on its head. From then on, the MPAA only regulated audience age rather than film content.

The stated objectives of the new code included:

1. To encourage artistic expression by expanding creative freedom.
2. To assure that the freedom which encourages the artist remains responsible and sensitive to the standards of the larger society. Valenti desired that the new code "keep in close harmony with the mores, the culture, the moral sense, and the expectation of society."[7]

Thus, the MPAA evoked the perennial "freedom versus responsibility" dichotomy, implying that freedoms are limited and filmmakers bear responsibility to present socially acceptable images and dialogue. However, "artistic expression" and "freedom" never appeared in the Hays Code. How could they, when that code functioned by controlling subject matter? By contrast, the Valenti Code focused on "the artist" and on his or her needs. In theory, the new code transformed the MPAA and the film industry from adversaries to allies, which caused unforeseen consequences for decades.

In response to *Freedman v. Maryland*'s limits on prior censorship, the Valenti Code states unequivocally that "censorship is an odious enterprise. We oppose censorship and classification governments because they are alien to the American tradition of freedom." Accordingly, the new code took pains to distance itself from any association with censorship, which had formed the dynamics of the Hays Code. By 1968 censorship had gone out of fashion, along with racial discrimination and the Vietnam War. New times demanded a new approach and a new code. The new code reflected a more liberal, less conservative approach to Production Codes. Its effects, however, have not always matched its appearance or its promise.

G: General Audiences

In fact the Valenti Code substitutes postcensorship for prior censorship. For example, to receive a G rating films must not encourage sex, nudity, or drugs. Violence may exist, but it must be exaggerated, cartoonish, and unrealistic. There may be instances in which language transcends the conventions of polite conversations, but none of the most sensitive Anglo-Saxon expletives can appear. This proscription amounts to a de facto code by forcing filmmakers wishing to make films for general audiences into complying with specific criteria. The rating designated family-oriented films and films that appealed to teenagers and preteens, including animated films like the Disney organization's classics (*Snow White and the Seven Dwarfs, Pinocchio,* and *Bambi*), as well as family-oriented features like *Old Yeller, Sounder,* and *Swiss Family Robinson.* G ratings served as the entry level, guaranteeing sentimental, innocuous, uncontroversial, and largely unrealistic subject matter. Even today, the G rating designates films designed for family viewing. Audiences interested in adult situations and realistic relationships will normally find little of interest in G-rated films.

PG: Parental Guidance

The next category of film ratings often proves the most profitable for filmmakers. PG ratings mean the films contain adult subject matter or language. PG films bear a warning that "some material may be inappropriate for children under 13." Parents are "strongly cautioned." They may possess some "strong language," including Anglo-Saxon words like "shit," "ass," and "fuck," but usually only once. As Kirby Dick's documentary on the MPAA system, *This Film Is Net Yet Rated* (2006), warns that filmmakers should "choose your 'fuck' carefully." A simple "fuck you" may be permissible, but filmmakers may never use the word to refer to the sex act.[8] One aspect of the PG rating that proved especially egregious to the evangelical community was the tendency to rate any film with a religious theme as PG rather than G. Evangelicals fought this unspoken edict and eventually succeeded in reversing it in 2006.

R: No Children Seventeen or Younger without Parent or Guardian

R-rated films may contain sexual themes, frank sex talk, nudity, rough language, and violence. Sexuality may be depicted, but only heterosexual couples assuming the traditional "missionary position" with the man in the dominant (top) position. Other forms of lovemaking, including homosexuality, ménage a trois, bestiality, and pedophilia, receive an automatic NC-17 rating. In practice, however, this rating proves difficult to define. Often, producers cut, trim, and modify films that are in danger of receiving NC-17 ratings to secure the much more desirable R rating. In fact, the R rating now serves as a benchmark beyond which few filmmakers venture to tread. Producers are willing to do almost anything to secure R ratings instead of NC-17 ones, from hiring the finest lawyers to threatening directors with breach of contract lawsuits, since most contracts call for the director to deliver films with no more stringent ratings than R.

Parental Control

Valenti also relied on the venerable principle of parental control. The preamble reads, "In our society parents are the arbiters of family conduct. Parents have the primary responsibility to guide their children in the kinds of lives they lead, the character they build, the books they read, and the movies and other entertainment to which they are exposed." Accordingly, the review board established by Valenti was supposed to be composed of parents, and the code purported to represent the interest of parents in the films their children viewed. The new code made children, through various age categories, the sole arbiter of motion picture ratings, and protecting children the mandate under which the new code operated. However, although the Valenti Code was designed to regulate audiences, not content, as the Hays Code had done, it quickly became clear that in order to regulate audiences the MPAA must provide de facto regulation of film content, since most filmmakers avoided the consequences of NC-17 ratings.

Pornography

The U.S. Supreme Court for decades struggled with the issue of what constitutes "pornography." In *Roth v. United States* (1957) the Court defined it as a violation of "community standards taken as a whole." However, that definition proved difficult to define in practice, and in 1973 the Court again attempted a definition by abandoning "community standards," which vary considerably according to locality, and substituting instead the principle that the "average person" would find that a work "taken as a whole" appeals to the "prurient interest." That definition, too, proved slippery to enforce in practice, although it remains in force today. In *New York v. Ferber* (1982) the Court decided that "the States are entitled to greater leniency in the regulation of pornographic depictions of children." The principle of protecting children against sexual abuse proved less contentious than the earlier prohibitions against adult pornography.

Valenti intended the new system to completely replace the Hays Code, focusing on audience age instead of film content. In that sense, it would not be a Production Code as the term has been used. Despite this intention, however, the new regulatory guidelines contain a de facto Production Code, encouraging certain kinds of films while discouraging others. The Valenti Code clearly mandates that "the basic dignity and value of human life shall be respected and upheld." Furthermore, it demands that "restraint shall be exercised in portraying the taking of life; evil, sin, crime, and wrong-doing shall not be justified." That appears nearly identical to the Hays Code's rule that all criminals must pay for their crimes. Additionally, the code admonishes that "special restraint shall be exercised in portraying criminals or antisocial activities in which minors participate or are involved." This harks back to the original Don'ts and Be Carefuls of 1927, despite Valenti's alleged abhorrence of the old proscriptions. It appears that the new code duplicates many of the central principles of earlier codes.

Evolving Code

In the original Valenti Code of 1968 G meant "Suggested for general audiences. All ages admitted." M meant "Suggested for mature audiences. Parental discretion advised." Many expressed confusion over the M label, especially as it differed from the G designation. In 1970 Valenti replaced M with GP, meaning "All ages admitted (parental guidance advised)." Eventually, other ratings also transformed with changing demands. In 1970 the age restriction for R films increased from sixteen to seventeen, effectively barring thousands of teenagers from attendance. However, these changes failed to quell a rising chorus of grumbling from critics and filmmakers about the code.

In 1972 continuing problems with the GP rating motivated Valenti to throw it out completely and replace it with a new PG rating that carried the warning "Parental Guidance Suggested. Some material may not be suitable for Pre-Teenagers." This rating remained in effect throughout the seventies and continues in force today, although currently the warning states, "Some material may not be suitable for children." Robert Wise's *Star Trek—the Motion Picture* (1979) closed the book on G ratings for the major studios. In fact, filmmakers no longer desire G ratings for films destined for wide audiences that include adults. Wise reedited his film for DVD release, adding enough adult material to earn a PG rating. No doubt he hoped that the more restrictive rating would lure adults to the movie. Later 1970s family films received PG ratings, including Disney productions like *The Black Hole* (1979), *The Watcher in the Woods* (1980), and *The Devil and Max Devlin* (1981). Filmmakers discovered that PG films attracted children like the earlier G films, but they also appealed to adults.

By the mid-1970s Hollywood moguls faced declining box office revenues, as audiences increasingly opted to watch television rather than attend movies. At first, filmmakers appeared at a loss as to how to regain their audiences. Pauline Kael, the decade's most prominent critic, pondered this disturbing trend, which, she says, began around 1973. Kael charges that "a number of the most devoted movie fans stopped going to the movies." This lost audience consisted of young people in their twenties and thirties, including college students. This group had earlier embraced counterculture movies like *Easy Rider, Five Easy Pieces, M*A*S*H*, Little Big Man, Midnight Cowboy,* and *They Shoot Horses Don't They?* These films all appeared in the late sixties and early seventies, early products of the Valenti Code. By 1973, however, Kael observed sadly that "the interest in pictures has left these people." Why?

Primarily because the film industry was focused on turning out blockbusters with big stars and even bigger budgets instead of interesting, complex movies for adults. The industry gradually abandoned adult audiences in favor of teenagers, offering blockbusters like *Magnum Force, Dirty Harry, The French Connection,* and *Walking Tall* that rely on graphic violence for box office success, eschewing substance and adult relationship themes because of fears of negative ratings. Forgotten by audiences, according to Kael, were more excellent films with smaller budgets like *The Conversation, Mean Streets,* and *Loving.*[9] Those films differed from the blockbusters panned by Kael because of their character-driven nature and because they are well written and acted, and above all well directed. Also, they feature less graphic violence than the more popular blockbusters, but, because audiences were either bored or turned off by Hollywood's mainstream fare, these films were also not well attended.

PG-13

The 1980s witnessed increasing conflicts between filmmakers and the MPAA over the boundary between PG and R ratings. In 1982 two films, *Poltergeist* (coproduced by Steven Spielberg) and Disney's *Dragonslayer,* received R ratings that ultimately changed to PG upon appeal. However, some parents objected to *Dragonslayer's* explicit scenes featuring violence and gore. Other more adult-oriented films, including *Terms of Endearment* (1983), *Sixteen Candles* (1984), and *Footloose* (1984), which might have received R ratings a decade earlier, also received PG ratings. Finally, 1984 witnessed two violent films, Spielberg's *Indiana Jones and the Temple of Doom* and *Gremlins,* that also received PG ratings. In response to intense criticism from parental groups, Spielberg suggested a new rating, PG-13, issued with the warning, "Parents are strongly cautioned to give special guidance for attendance of children under 13." The rating provides filmmakers with cover from enraged parents. Valenti conferred with theater owners about Spielberg's proposal before deciding to institute the new rating on July 1, 1984.[10] John Milius's *Red Dawn* (1984) became the first PG-13 film. Milius's film depicts a band of small-town teens turned guerrilla warriors combating a communist invasion. *Red Dawn* resonates with elements of McCarthyism and, like many films of its time, features graphic violence, so its PG-13 rating seems appropriate.

X to NC-17

Originally, X ratings signified films containing adult subject matter, not pornographic films. In fact, several screen classics began with X ratings, or at least their threat. In 1972 the MPAA threatened to give Martin Scorsese's stylish neo-noir thriller *Taxi Driver* an X. Columbia, the producer, sided with the censors and informed Scorsese that if he did not cut offensive scenes, they would do it for him. To comply, Scorsese removed some offensive footage of spurting blood and also suggested desaturating the color in the film's gory shoot-out finale. The MPAA agreed, eventually awarding *Taxi Driver* the desired R rating.[11] This pattern quickly repeated itself as studios negotiated with the Valenti office to avoid X ratings. R ratings allowed Hollywood to appeal to younger audiences, often providing the necessary and desired profit margin.

The first two films to receive X ratings under the Valenti Code are Robert Aldrich's *The Killing of Sister George* (1968) and James Schlesinger's *Midnight Cowboy* (1968). Aldrich's film depicts lesbian relationships, a taboo subject in 1968. Schlesinger's film features some gay encounters by the central character, played by John Voigt. In classic examples of "ratings creep," both films now receive R ratings on the DVD versions. As a result, what was once completely forbidden to all those under eighteen became merely restricted. During the "sexy seventies" movies continued to explore the sexual revolution that began in the "swinging sixties." Over time, X ratings proved unexpectedly popular with pornographers, who eagerly flouted them on marquees and ads. Some proudly advertised their porn features as XX and even XXX. Even today some pornography is still marketed as "X rated." This unintentional outcome of the rating system disturbed Valenti, and in 1990 he moved to eliminate X altogether and replace it with NC-17. At a news conference held to announce the new categories, Valenti stated, "We have concluded that over the years some people have come to endow the X film rating with meaning it does not have, never had had, and was not intended by founders of the rating system."[12] However, despite Valenti's desire to rid the MPAA of any association with X-rated pornography, NC-17 films quickly became identified as the "new X" in the minds of many. Newspapers, video rental outlets, and video sales outlets routinely treat NC-17 films like X-rated films. Most newspapers and television stations refuse to advertise NC-17 films, and neighborhood video rental outlets like Blockbuster also avoid NC-17 films. Wal-Mart and Target routinely refuse to stock NC-17 films, thereby depriving the filmmakers of substantial revenue. Because of these restrictions, filmmakers usually agree to excise or obscure offending scenes to secure R ratings. In fact, usually they are willing to do anything rather than receive NC-17 ratings. The difference between NC-17 and R spells success or failure at the box office.

Philip Kaufman's *Henry and June* (1990) received the first NC-17 rating for its rendition of Anais Nin's sensational diary about Henry Miller's (Fred Ward) unconventional relationships with his wife June (Marina de Madeiros) and fellow author Nin (Uma Thurman) in Paris during 1931. Kaufman's frank portrayal of this ménage a trois immediately enveloped the film in controversy. Valenti reputedly created the NC-17 ruling to accommodate the daring (for its day) film.

Nevertheless, the film was soon banned in a Boston suburb by officials from Dedham, Massachusetts, because local theaters had agreed not to show X-rated films, and the new NC-17 category, they argued, meant nothing less than disguised X films.[13] Apparently, the NC-17 rating failed to silence all of the voices calling for censorship of sexually explicit themes. In fact, today's video sales industry still adheres to the "anti-X" mentality by refusing to stock NC-17 films. This situation prompts many producers into reediting their films for the video market. John Waters, for example, released his NC-17-rated *A Dirty Shame* (2005) in an R-rated DVD version that allows him to sell his film in Blockbusters, Targets, and Wal-Marts. In a stab at the MPAA Waters labeled his R-rated film the "neutered version."

Code Explanations

Beginning in 1990 Valenti directed the Classification and Rating Administration (CARA) to include a brief explanation for its NC-17 ratings and, more recently, for all of its ratings. The reasons for NC-17 ratings most often involve "sexuality," "nudity," or occasionally "sensuality." Other reasons submitted include "violence," "language," and "drug use." Often, CARA further explains its ratings with qualifying words like "strong sexuality," "graphic sexuality," "explicit sexual content," "some explicit sexuality," "graphic nudity," "strong violence," "an intense brutal rape scene," "brief drug use," and other descriptive statements. For example, Adrian Lyne's *Unfaithful* (2002) received an R rating with the descriptive "sexuality, language, a scene of violence." However, producers print these sentences in tiny type, so don't expect to read the descriptions on DVD labels without the use of a powerful magnifying glass.

Sex

The Valenti Code, like all codes, focuses on sexuality more than any other activity. Therefore, sex plays a paramount role in contemporary film ratings. The code warns that "indecent or undue exposure of the human body shall not be presented" and "illicit sex relationships shall not be justified. Intimate sex scenes violating common standards of decency shall not be portrayed." These warnings evoke earlier codes, particularly the Hays Code but also the venerable Don'ts and Be Carefuls of pre-code days. The Hays Code prohibition against depictions of "impure love," including premarital sex and adultery, comes to mind. Other Valenti Code admonitions include "Restraint and care shall be exercised in presentations dealing with sexual aberrations." Furthermore, the code warns, "Obscene speech, gestures, or movements shall not be presented. Undue profanity shall not be permitted." In practice, this code, like the phrase "undue profanity," proves difficult to define. The Valenti Code also fails to define "illicit sex relationships" and "common standards of decency." These concepts always prove elusive. What appears "illicit" today may not seem so tomorrow. And the term *common standards* does not appear to accurately describe today's culturally divided society. What might be considered obscene in red states and cities might not be so considered in blue localities, and what might be permissible in cities might be condemned in rural areas. These slippery issues, and the basic concept of film ratings itself, confuse filmmakers as well as the general public.

The list of films that precipitated censorship controversies from the Valenti period is substantial, and it includes some of the period's most memorable movies. *Behind the Green Door* (1972) became the first blatantly pornographic film to appear during the Valenti Code. Artie and Jim Mitchell, owners of an X-rated cabaret in San Francisco, directed this openly pornographic indie about a hapless woman, played by porn star Marilyn Chambers. She is kidnapped by theater owners, played by the Mitchell brothers, and forced to perform lewd sexual acts with a variety of partners live in front of a studio audience. The low-budget indie, which depicted miscegenation, lesbianism, and masturbation, became an underground blockbuster hit, grossing more than ten times what it cost to make. This event started a trend toward indie porn films exhibited in X-rated theaters. Features included *Deep Throat* (1972), *The Devil in Miss Jones* (1973), *Emmanuelle* (1974, French), and a variety of other imitators. The success of these indie films further supported the growing practice in Hollywood of leaving sex to the indies.

By the seventies a values revolution created an ideal climate for films that frankly and relatively realistically explored sexual relationships. Mike Nichols's *Carnal Knowledge* (1971) explores the sexual history of two college roommates, Jonathan (Jack Nicholson) and Sandy (Art Garfunkel), and their sexual experiences with various women over a period of decades. Nichols's film explores men's sexual relationships with women and finds them very inadequate and dysfunctional. Because of frank dialogue and implied fellatio, Nichols's film received an R rating from CARA, not an X. That did not prevent a local court in Albany, Georgia, from arresting a theater owner for showing the film. The case wound up before the U.S. Supreme Court, which ruled unanimously that the film was not obscene, reversing the lower court's decision.[14] This case demonstrates that even with R ratings, films that frankly explore sexual themes may evoke censorship on a local level.

Bernardo Bertolucci's *Last Tango in Paris* (1972) stars Marlon Brando as an aging expatriate in mourning after his wife's recent suicide. While shopping for an apartment in Paris he encounters a young, beautiful bride-to-be named Jeanne (Maria Schneider). The two begin an impassioned sexual relationship in which they promise not to reveal personal information about themselves because Jeanne will soon marry her fiancé. Due to its frankly sexual nature, especially in its positive treatment of premarital sexuality, the MPAA awarded it an X rating. Prominent critics like Roger Ebert and Pauline Kael gave the film rave reviews and predicted it would inaugurate a new era in serious, X-rated features. Instead, disappointing sales at the box office quickly taught filmmakers to avoid frank sexual depictions in the future.[15]

Louis Malle's *Pretty Baby* (1978) exemplifies the open attitudes toward sexuality during this period. Malle's film stars Brooke Shields, who was then twelve years old, as a child prostitute in 1917 Storyville. In addition to the subject of child prostitution, censors objected to scenes of twelve-year-old Shields appearing nude. Because of this, censors demanded cutting 3 minutes from the 109-minute film. The unedited version now appears on the DVD. Because of tightening sexual standards, Malle's film in its present form appears a better candidate for an NC-17 ruling than an R rating. Today, teenage nudity would doom this film to financial oblivion.

Thus by the seventies the pattern was set. Films that violated the MPAA's standards for nudity, language, and sexual depictions invariably received X ratings. Once so rated, mainstream theaters refused to screen them and periodicals refused to advertise them. As a result, Hollywood learned that it could not afford to devote A-budget films to sexuality because of the great financial risks involved. Independent filmmakers quickly stepped into the breach and produced X-rated features screened in alternative theaters. This established a two-tiered system of indie filmmakers making low-budget pornographic films while the majors increasingly bet their money on sensationalism and violence. This two-tiered situation still exists, with only independent films depicting sexuality realistically. Today's R-rated films tend to avoid the subject of sexuality as their main themes.

Starting in 1974 a few filmmakers began crafting a reprisal of the classic film noir genre of the forties and fifties. They realized that the Valenti Code allowed filmmakers enough freedom to treat sexual subjects more directly than at any time since the pre-code era. Just as Hollywood appeared nearly creatively and financially bankrupt, the relative freedom of the Valenti Code allowed filmmakers to reprise one of their most successful genres—film noir. The relative freedom of the Valenti period fostered the creation of new genres, particularly one bold new thriller genre that fused elements of violent noir films of the past and raunchy, sexually explicit melodramas and sultry comedies of pre-code days. Sexually charged thrillers heralded a new erotic melodrama genre, descending from film noir. The genre appeared in 1974, only one year after Kael's bleak assessment of the state of the art. Because of this vibrant new genre, it appears that her pessimism may have been premature.

Early neo-noirs include Roman Polanski's *Chinatown* (1974), Dick Richards's *Farewell My Lovely* (1974, British), and Ridley Scott's *Blade Runner* (1982). They each featured weak, confused males much like those in the classic noir genre. These characters confront seductive, often murderous femmes fatales straight out of the classic period. In fact, Richards's film marks a reprisal of the Raymond Chandler novel first picturized by Edward Dmytryk as *Murder My Sweet* (1944). Both depict private investigator Philip Marlowe, played by Dick Powell and Robert Mitchum. As in the classic film noir genre, sexy, violent films attracted audiences and critics alike, who increasingly found themselves drawn to these depictions of gender wars. The Valenti Code allowed these sexy thrillers, as long as they did not become too explicit in either nudity or dialogue.

During the late eighties and early nineties the neo-noir genre presented even more daring depictions of seductive femmes fatales. Bob Rafelson's *Black Widow* (1987) introduced audiences to a deadly femme fatale named Catherine Petersen (Theresa Russell), nicknamed the Black Widow, who seduces wealthy men into marriage, then murders them for their money. Critics described her as a gold digger, a modern adaptation of the pre-code icon. Only now the femme noir wants not only to seduce men but to murder them as well. Thus was born the neo–femme noir that remains popular with audiences even today.

During the nineties the neo-noir genre, which by then might be labeled "sexual film noir," was crafted in large part by scriptwriter Joe Eszterhas, who wrote some of its most significant scripts, including Paul Verhoeven's popular *Basic Instinct* (1992). Verhoeven and Eszterhas's film focuses on a police search for an ice-pick murderer in San Francisco. Michael Douglas plays Nick, a police detective who finds himself strongly attracted to the chief suspect in the case, a bisexual crime novelist named Catherine Tramell (Sharon Stone). Eszterhas embellished the film with sexy copulation/bondage scenes, explicit dialogue, and lesbian lovemaking. One notorious example of controversial footage comes as Verhoeven's camera travels up Sharon Stone's miniskirt, revealing her seemingly naked crotch, which she uses to unnerve her interrogators.

The combination of a weak male character and a strong, sexual, even bisexual female character proved too much for CARA, which forced the filmmakers to soften the film's sexual edges. Clearly, these kinds of characters involved in a seemingly self-destructive relationship would not be permitted by CARA unless handled discreetly, with blurred details and innuendos substituted for more direct forms of depiction. Eventually, the film received an R rating after TriStar Pictures/Columbia agreed to cut a scant forty-two seconds from key sex scenes, including the deletion of three indirect references to oral sex. One deletion occurs in a love scene between Nick and a former girlfriend and department-appointed psychologist, Dr. Elizabeth (Beth) Garner (Jeanne Tripplehorn), in which their sex act strongly implies that Nick has raped her. The film's mixture of violence, murder (five altogether), and steamy sexuality, toned down slightly to avoid an NC-17 rating, along with superb performances by Stone and Douglas, makes *Basic Instinct* one of the best examples of the sexual thriller genre. In 1993 the film was rereleased for video distribution in an "unrated director's cut" version with the excised scenes restored.

Stone's Catherine Tramell, like femmes fatales from the classic period, reverses the usual gender roles and transforms into a cunning, violent antagonist. Like *Black Widow*'s Catherine Peterson, she serves as the film's villain as well as its female lead. She is duplicitous, promiscuous, irreverent, hedonistic, egotistical, bisexual, and murderous, shocking and titillating audiences expecting more traditional feminine roles from Hollywood. Both Nick and Catherine represent characters from the film noir genre, star-crossed lovers heading for destruction. Nick functions as the helpless lost soul who finds himself unable to fend off the advances of Catherine, a quintessential seductress who uses her sexuality and intellect to ensnare her victims.

Basic Instinct generated public relations problems, most of which surrounded the characterization of Catherine as a psychotic bisexual. San Francisco–based gay pride organizations blasted the film and picketed its theatrical release in San Francisco. The fatal attraction of the lost soul detective and the murderous novelist remains a shocking example of a seductress/murderous archetype with an impulsive "lost soul" victim. The combination portends gender and sexual conflict, to say the least. The film proved controversial with both gay and feminist groups. Members of Queer Nation and ACT UP threw paint bombs on the set in San Francisco, blew whistles, and urged motorists to honk their horns to disrupt shooting because of alleged "homophobia" and "gay bashing." Queer Nation and the National Organization for Women (NOW) announced plans to disrupt the Academy Award ceremonies because Michael Douglas and Sharon Stone were officiating. In Toronto, activists shouted the name of the killer to moviegoers standing in line to purchase tickets. The resulting controversies and media attention led scriptwriter Joe Eszterhas to withdraw his name from the film, even though he had received a record fee of $3.3 million for the script.[16]

In addition to *Black Widow* and *Basic Instinct,* other neo-noir thrillers, including *Disclosure* (1994), *The Last Seduction* (1994), and *Dream Lover* (1994), depict femmes fatales that rely on seduction to undermine and threaten to destroy their male counterparts. The femmes noir of these films, including Meredith Johnson (Demi Moore), Wendy Kroy (Linda Fiorentino), and Lena Mathers (Madchen Amick), represent the "do-me feminism" then in vogue, in which female characters apply lipstick, open their blouses, and allow full reign to their libidos. Unlike their classic film noir predecessors, these characters appear physically and emotionally equal if not superior to their male counterparts. These ultrastrong women confront hollow, shell-like males, like *Disclosure*'s Tom Sanders (Michael Douglas), *The Last Seduction*'s Clay Gregory (Bill Pullman), and *Dream Lover*'s Ray Reardon (James Spader), who appear weak, confused, and easily duped in their encounters with these newly emboldened archetypes. These characters exemplify perceptions of male impotence during this period. The formula of ultrastrong females confronting and besting weak males speaks volumes about male perceptions of inadequacy and fears of female

Femme fatale Briget Gregory/Wendy Kroy (Linda Fiorentino) seducing Mike Swale (Peter Berg) in John Dahl's neo-noir thriller *The Last Seduction* (1994). (Copyright 1994 October Films)

competition. The MPAA censors endorsed this formula, one that demonstrated consistently high box office receipts. Studios negotiated for and received R ratings for these films, each one slightly sanitized in the process.

Neo-noir seductresses continue to provide a reliable revenue stream for producers. They also discovered other lucrative formulas tolerated by censors. Many R-rated films of the nineties also focused on previously taboo subjects, including Steven Soderbergh's 1989 *Sex, Lies, and Videotape,* exploring voyeurism and adultery, and Woody Allen's *Husbands and Wives,* depicting adultery and divorce. David Lynch's *Blue Velvet* (1986) features male violence through Frank (Dennis Hopper) and his gang and *Wild at Heart* (1990) also revels in southern gothic violence. Hollywood continues to create violent thrillers that avoid NC-17 ratings.

Violence

Like earlier codes, the Valenti Code focuses much more on sexuality and related issues than on violence. Although the code warns that films should affirm "the basic dignity of human life," it fails to prohibit brutality or graphic violence, except with regard to animals. Why did Valenti avoid the issue of violence? Perhaps the reason is that violence is not taboo, whereas many forms of sexuality are. Some argue that film violence stems from the general violence in society—social violence engenders violent entertainment. Wars in Iraq and Afghanistan, terrorism, and counterterrorism contribute to the overall levels of violence in society. High crime rates desensitize people to violence.

The Valenti Code not only tolerates violence; it has unleashed it upon the public as never before. Soon after the code went into effect in the late sixties Arthur Penn's *Bonnie and Clyde* (1968), George Roy Hill's *Butch Cassidy and the Sundance Kid* (1969), and Sam Peckinpah's *The Wild Bunch* (1969) appeared with higher levels of violence than any previous films. They include graphic scenes, filmed in slow motion, of bullets raking bodies, blood spurting from wounds, and other violent images. Penn, Hill, and Peckinpah realized that while the new ratings system discouraged realistic depictions of sexuality, it allowed depictions of graphic violence. Although the trend toward violent films actually began during the film noir and classic Western periods of the forties and fifties, the Valenti Code greatly accelerated that trend. From that point until today, Hollywood studios rely on graphic images of violence to attract audiences. In fact, the industry's proviolence reputation stems from its efforts to avoid the more controversial sexual allures while relying on the safer (from the MPAA's perspective) allure of violence. Cinematic violence, though commonplace, is rarely boring, and it is not prohibited by the Valenti Code, whereas most serious sex is. In that sense, the current code harks back to the Hays Code's tolerance of violence, particularly in relation to its policies regarding sex.

This deep-seated attraction to violence appalls many. In the aftermath of the 1999 Columbine High School killings President Bill Clinton met with studio moguls to urge them to curb film violence. His concerns and the concerns of other officials led to stricter policing of the sales of films and video games. Ultimately, theaters began requiring identification at all R movies. Although Hollywood promised to reduce film violence, violence in the years following the massacre proved little different from earlier reliance on violence in films. After the 2007 Virginia Tech killings, studios grew concerned that the massacre would once again stimulate calls for film censorship. Eli Roth's *Hostel II,* a 2007 sequel to Roth's 2005 indie hit about college students being tortured and murdered in a remote hostel in Slovakia by a crazed serial killer, was slated for release around the time of the Virginia Tech shootings, but some in the industry worried that the film might seem insensitive in light of the killings and thereby provoke a backlash against Hollywood and the MPAA. Despite this, Lionsgate Films, a studio known for its violent offerings, proceeded with the film's release as scheduled. The ultimate fate of other violent films, however, has been clouded by the poor performances of several recent films featuring graphic violence, including *Dead Silence, The Hills Have Eyes 2, Grindhouse,* and *The Reaping.* All of these R-rated violent films experienced poor box office returns, causing some analysts to wonder if the demand for extreme violence might be slackening.

When *Hostel II* arrived in 2007 it immediately sparked controversy for its R rating. The film contains graphic scenes of someone severing the penis and testicles from a bound man and then giving them to a dog to eat. Another scene features a nude woman suspended upside down, her throat cut, while another nude woman writhes in orgiastic pleasure in her blood. Mark Harris, incensed at the level of violence in films, charges the MPAA with violating its duty to protect children from violent images. First, he cites the usual litany of criticism of the Production Code: "Indies have it harder than studio films, naked men are naughtier than naked women, and almost any sex is worse than almost all violence." However, to Harris, the problem runs deeper. "The MPAA has never decided whether its job is guidance or rule making. As a result, four ratings—G, PG, PG-13, and R—are merely advisory." It leads to leniency with regard to violence. "The raters tell parents what's in a movie and let them decide whether to take their kids," explains Harris. "But the fifth rating—NC-17—carries the force of law: It's the only stage at which raters decide their judgment should overrule yours."[17]

Today, movie violence permeates even family films. Examinations of recent G-rated films by Kimberly M. Thompson and Fumie Yokota in "Violence, Sex, and Profanity in Films: Correlation of Movie Ratings with Content" revealed a high correlation between violent depictions and films made for children. Disturbingly, Thompson and Yokota discovered that animated movies aimed at children contain significantly more violence than nonanimated features. Animated films rated G by the MPAA received a significantly higher content-based score for violence on average than nonanimated films rated G. Firearms also appeared in a large number of G films, and in a surprising discovery the authors found significantly higher gross revenues for PG-13 and R-rated films that received MPAA warnings for violence compared with those films that did not.[18] Clearly, violence permeates movies at all levels because violence attracts large audiences.

Animated features for children also contain increasing amounts of violence. Fumie Yokota and Kimberly Thompson analyzed seventy-four G-rated animated films, from *Snow White* (1937) to *The King and I* (1999). The films they surveyed include the earliest animated children's features, starting with *Snow White and the Seven Dwarfs* (1937), *Fantasia* (1940), *Pinocchio* (1940), *Dumbo* (1941), and *Bambi* (1942). They compared them with other animated features, the most recent being *The Swan Princess 2* (1997), *A Bug's Life* (1998), and *Mulan* (1998). They found that the average children's animated feature film, approximately eighty minutes long, contains nine and a half minutes of violence, 11.8 percent of the average film's length. Surprisingly, the authors found that the average amount of time depicting acts of violence in children's animated films has increased from approximately six minutes in 1940 to nine and a half minutes in 1999, an increase of over 50 percent. The increase is even greater when one compares the levels of violence in the original Disney animated features with the Pixar features (also owned by Disney). *A Bug's Life* and *Mulan* each contain more than twice as much violent content as *Snow White, Pinocchio,* and *Bambi.* The acceleration of violence in these animated films presents a disturbing aspect of these popular features. As the authors explain, "our study reveals a striking behavioral message implied by many of the G-rated animated films that the good guys triumph over the bad through the use of physical force."[19] Perhaps children inured to movie violence may tolerate greater levels of it as adults?

Although G-rated features became more violent, the same scenario held true for PG-13 films. A 2004 study revealed that nearly all of the PG-13 movies marketed to children contained significant levels of violence, posing a significant emotional health risk for adolescent children. In the study published by *Pediatrics, the Official Journal of the Society of Pediatrics,* Theresa Webb, Lucille Jenkins, and colleagues concluded that "a vast and robust body of empirical research shows that exposure to media violence poses a significant risk to the health of children and adolescents." "This is especially true in contemporary American society," they argue, "wherein the average young person's engagement with visual media in all its formats can run to as many as 8 hours a day." In addition, the group found that the three most pervasive and detrimental effects of exposure to media violence include increased aggression, a heightened sense of fear for one's own safety, and desensitization toward the pain and suffering of others. After an exhaustive content analysis of hundreds of PG-13 films released between 1999 and 2000, the authors discovered that of the seventy-seven top-grossing PG-13 films they analyzed, nearly 90 percent were "permeated with violence."[20] The situation stimulated two Congressmembers to introduce the "Family Friendly Flights Act" on September 25, 2007. Should we find it disturbing that nearly all PG-13 films contain significant amounts of violence? Should we find it disturbing that Hollywood deliberately targets teenagers with violence-laden films? To what extent can youth violence be blamed on Hollywood models?

Today's movie rating system increasingly inspires attacks from some high-profile critics. Roger Ebert argues that the system places too much emphasis on suppressing sex while allowing the portrayal of horrific violence. In addition, Ebert charges that the rating system focuses upon trivial details, including the number of times a profane word appears, rather than on films' general content. To address these issues Ebert advocates the creation of an A (adults only) rating to designate films high in violence or mature content that should not be marketed to teenagers, but that lack NC-17 levels of sex. Such a rating, Ebert believes, might encourage the production of nonviolent adult-themed films.[21] Given the oft-cited problems with the NC-17 rating, Ebert's suggestion surely merits further consideration.

The MPAA's reputation has now become so tarnished that the online *Urban Dictionary* defines it as "a great moral teacher, proving to everyone that nudity and sexuality are more harmful to young people than depictions of graphic violence. A beating, beheading, disembowelment, immolation, crucifixion, dismemberment? No problem! But catch a brief glimpse of a breast or a patch of pubic hair? Pornography!"[22] As this excerpt suggests, criticism of the MPAA has become fashionable. The first attack in a motion picture occurred in 1999 in Trey Parker's *South Park: Bigger, Longer, and Uncut* (1999). Parker harbored a grudge against the MPAA for awarding his 1997 animated feature *Orgazmo* an NC-17 rating. In *South Park,* one of the animated characters comments scornfully, "Remember what the MPAA says; Horrific, deplorable violence is okay, as long as people don't say any naughty words!"

As if the attacks by Trey Parker and Roger Ebert weren't enough, in 2006 Kirby Dick's documentary *This Film Is Not Yet Rated* also dealt a powerful blow to the organization's prestige. Dick's film exposes the Ratings Board as consisting mostly of people with children over the age of eighteen or who have no children, a contradiction of official MPAA statements that board members are selected from those who have children between the ages of fifteen and seventeen, peak audiences for Hollywood films. The film also charges that the board treats homosexual material much more harshly than heterosexual material. An MPAA spokesperson responded to this charge by stating, "We don't create standards; we just follow them." Dick's film also discovered that the board's raters receive no training and are deliberately chosen because of their lack of expertise in media literacy or child development. He learned that senior raters have direct contact in the form of required meetings with studio personnel after movie screenings. Dick's film also reveals that the MPAA's appeals board consists mostly of movie theater chain and studio executives. Finally, the film reveals that two members of the clergy (one Catholic and one Episcopalian) also sit on the appeals board and probably wield considerable influence, a situation that was unknown prior to the film. It raises some disturbing questions about the role of organized religion in motion picture ratings.[23] Along with Roger Ebert and Trey Parker, Kirby Dick has emerged as one of the most prominent of the growing number of MPAA critics.

In addition to critics and directors, some industry veterans provide disturbing insights into Hollywood's current culture of violence. Audrey Totter, who acted in such film noir classics as *Lady in the Lake* and *The Postman Always Rings Twice,* charges that addiction to violence saps Hollywood creativity and robs movies of much of their power. She believes that "Hollywood should police itself, but there's too much money to be made." Audience demand for violence drives producers to turn out more violent movies. "As long as people go to see the violent movies . . . Hollywood will keep churning them out." The problem is that "there is always a new youth market that hasn't been initiated yet to the violence."[24] As long as new markets continue appearing, expect Hollywood to continue old patterns and habits. In today's ratings climate, filmmakers need powerful incentives to produce nonviolent films.

Those who remember earlier periods bemoan the current dearth of thought-provoking films. Veteran actor Evelyn Keyes (*Union Pacific, Gone With the Wind, The Adventures of Martin Eden, A Thousand and One Nights*) admires the freedom that today's filmmakers have, except in one very important area. "People are still hung up about sex," she explains, "whispering about it, keeping secrets from children. Making it dark and dirty." Finally, she notes sadly, "women are still depicted as sex objects."[25] Part of the blame for the objectification of women lies with the current rating system, which places insurmountable obstacles in front of filmmakers who wish to address sexuality with any degree of realism.

Some observers dispute any causal link between violent films and social violence. Although some cite studies to support such a link, Jonathan L. Freedman in his book *Media Violence and Its Effect on Aggression*, assesses the scientific evidence. He notes that "the results of the research generally do not demonstrate that exposure to media violence causes agression."[26] These results, with roughly half of the studies supporting a causal link while the other half found no evidence for such a link, suggest the complexity of this issue. Albert Bandura's study revealed that exposure to TV violence can produce at least four effects on children: it teaches aggressive behavior; it weakens restraints against aggression by glamorizing violence; it habituates and desensitizes reactions to cruelty; and it shapes public images of reality. Bandura learned that although only 10 percent of major crimes in society are violent, 77 percent of major crimes depicted on TV are violent, which has the effect of making people more fearful of becoming crime victims. "Children and adults today have unlimited opportunities to learn the whole gamut of homicidal conduct from TV within the comfort of their homes," Bandura said.[27] Bandura's findings also apply to violent movies. To what extent do movies contribute to the culture of violence? Some research suggests that they contribute quite a lot. If so, the fault rests indirectly with the Valenti Code.

The NC-17 category is certainly the most problematic of the various ratings, and critics agree that it must be rethought, reconfigured, or abandoned entirely. Many observers, including Roger Ebert, Trey Parker, and Kirby Dick, advocate jettisoning the NC-17 rating altogether. However, research indicates that increased violence also taints other ratings, even G. The situation has become opposite from what the Valenti Code intended. According to the MPAA, "A G-rated motion picture contains nothing in theme, language, nudity, sex, violence or other matters that, in the view of the Rating Board, would offend parents."[28] Although G-rated films may be devoid of sex and nudity, they contain increasingly high levels of violence. In fact, violent films now predominate in each rating category. It appears likely that a thorough revision of the entire code, not only NC-17, is needed. A code as rigorous at restricting violence as the current one is in restricting sex would reverse the current powerful incentives to include violent content. Or, would restricting screen violence result in more underground violent features? One problem with applying the same restrictions against violence as are currently in place regarding sex is that the latter appear arbitrary and puritanical. Would similar restrictions against depictions of violence also become arbitrary, restrictive, and puritanical? Perhaps we need to rethink the entire method of rating films for audience ages. New categories could be created that would convey more information about violent content as well as sexuality. Parents could decide to limit their children's attendance at violent films as they now do with films containing sexual material.

In 2006, in response to some of the charges leveled at the MPAA rating system by Kirby Dick, Roger Ebert, Trey Parker, and others, the MPAA announced some minor changes in the current system:

1. For the first time, CARA will post the ratings rules on the MPAA website, describing the standards for each rating. The ratings and appeal processes also will be described in detail, along with a link to paperwork needed to submit a film for a rating.
2. Most members of the ratings board will remain anonymous, although CARA will describe the demographic makeup of the board, which is composed of parents. The names of the three senior raters have always been public; now, they will be posted online.
3. A filmmaker who appeals a rating can reference similar scenes in other movies, although the appeals board still will focus heavily on context.
4. CARA will formalize its rule that a member of the ratings board doesn't stay on the board after his or her children are grown.
5. CARA also will formalize its educational training system for raters.

When the CARA rules were implemented later that year, the MPAA and National Association of Theater Owners (NATO) designated additional members to the appeals board who don't come from the MPAA or NATO fold. (Indie filmmakers might be one possibility.) "NATO and MPAA will occasionally be able to designate additional observers from different backgrounds to the appeals board." In addition, the MPAA vowed to increase its efforts to educate parents, including circulating a poster and video that will advertise a new Red Carpet Ratings Service, a weekly e-mail alert that gives the parents the ratings for new releases.[29]

These reforms will likely result in more transparency in the rating process and more flexibility at the appeals level. However, reforms alone accomplish little to reduce the industry's reliance on violence to attract audiences. They also leave intact the virtual prohibition against depictions of adult relationships. Although Joan Graves, chair of the MPAA's Classification and Rating Administration (CARA), recently announced what amounts to a public relations campaign surrounding the NC-17 rating, little has changed substantially with regard to the rating. Graves admitted that ever since its inauguration in 1990, NC-17 has been associated with soft-core porn. And although the National Association of Theatre Owners says there is no written policy on banning NC-17 films, it acknowledges that some exhibitors won't show the movies. "It's not an effort to have more NC-17 [films] necessarily," Graves says. "It's an effort to discard the myths around that rating. An NC-17 doesn't mean the movie is a bad movie, and it doesn't mean it's pornographic. It simply means that there are elements in it that we believe most American parents think are out of bounds for children."[30]

Unfortunately, though the proposed changes may result in greater openness, they fail to address the vexing issue of film violence, to say nothing of the thorny issue of movie sexuality. Code reform must address the iniquities associated with the NC-17 rating and deal with the consequences of decades of indirect promotion of violence while still supplying parents and other interested parties with relevant information about film content. One suggestion would be to rate all films for violence as well as sex. Of course, CARA does provide a brief synopsis explaining its ratings, but perhaps it should create separate ratings for both of these issues. Films would carry a rating for V (violence) and S (sex). Age limits could still be used, but there should be much greater consistency between sex and violence, unlike the current system in which sex trumps violence every time. Studios would no longer receive an automatic pass on violent films from the MPAA, so they would be forced to rethink their policy regarding this issue. Also, if violent content were held to the same standard as sexual content, filmmakers who wished to do so would be empowered to create films exploring adult relationships. Without the kiss of death of an automatic NC-17 ruling, mainstream filmmakers might be tempted to tackle issues relating to relationships for a change.

Evasion

Normally, profit motives compel studios to comply with CARA. By rating films NC-17 CARA captures producers' attention and ensures compliance with its dictates. The list of NC-17 films that later earned R ratings on appeal grows annually. Recent and significant films such as *The 40-Year-Old Virgin* (2004), *American Psycho* (2000), *Bad Education* (2004), *Clerks* (1994), *The Cooler* (2003), *A Dirty Shame* (2004), *Eyes Wide Shut* (1999), *Pulp Fiction* (1994), *Showgirls* (1995), *Starship Troopers* (1997), *The Dreamers* (2003), and *Team America: World Police* (2004) appear in edited

Members of *The Wild Bunch* gang (Ernest Borgnine, Robert Ryan, William Holden) being disarmed by Mexican soldiers in Sam Peckinpah's *The Wild Bunch* (1969). Mexican military later ambush and kill all gang members in one of the most violent scenes at the time. (Copyright 1969 Warner Bros.–Seven Arts Pictures)

versions after being resubmitted to the MPAA. The producers of each of these films cut out offending scenes or won a reversal of their original rating on appeal. In nearly all of these cases, the offending material turned out to involve sexuality, although violence was also noted. Sam Peckinpah's *The Wild Bunch* (1969), for example, one of the most violent films of its day, originally earned an R rating. Warner Brothers resubmitted it in 1993 for video release, only to discover, to their surprise and dismay, that the MPAA decided to award it an NC-17 this time around, presumably because of the presence of graphic violence. Warner Brothers appealed this ruling, arguing that the original R rating should still apply. The studio won the appeal, and the rereleased film received an R rating.

At times, producers may decide to surrender their ratings and release films unrated. Usually, they do so to avoid the stigma of the NC-17 rating. Examples of films that have surrendered their ratings include *Kids* (1995), *Kika* (1993), *Requiem for a Dream* (2000), *The Story of O* (rated in 2000), *This Film Is Not Yet Rated*

(2006), and *Tie Me Up, Tie Me Down* (1990, originally rated X, rerated NC-17, then surrendered). *The Ugly* (1998), a small independent film, originally received an R rating, but surrendered it.

Larry Clark's *Kids*, for example, earned an NC-17 rating for depicting New York City teenage street culture in realistic detail, focusing on a twenty-four-hour period in the lives of four teenagers. Telly (Leo Fitzpatrick), a hedonistic slacker, sets off to seduce as many virgin girls as he can. However, he fails to realize that he carries HIV and unwittingly infects an anonymous teenage virgin (Sarah Henderson) with the deadly virus, then sets out to deflower another young virgin. After girl number one tests positive she attempts to prevent Telly from infecting other young virgins but arrives too late to a raucous party to prevent his next seduction. Emotionally and physically exhausted, she falls into a deep sleep, and Telly's friend Casper (Justin Pierce), taking advantage of the situation, rapes her. Clark's film focuses on a segment of contemporary youth culture and delivers a strong safe sex message, yet the MPAA awarded it an NC-17 rating, thereby barring the very audiences that needed to watch it. Since most video rental and sales outlets refuse to stock unrated movies, Clark's film, like other unrated features, remains unavailable to younger teenagers. By surrendering their ratings, filmmakers like Clark signaled that they preferred no rating, with all of the accompanying economic problems, to the ratings they received from the MPAA.

As we see from the numerous examples of filmmakers' resubmitting their films or appealing their rulings, and in some cases opting to surrender their ratings, the ratings issue continues to be vexatious, sensitive, and expensive. That is because the NC-17 rating constitutes the financial kiss of death for filmmakers, who rely on teenage audiences for their bread and butter. Deprived of their main markets, filmmakers, particularly independent ones, face financial failure. Therefore, the Production Code, although severely altered from what it was under Hays, still carries with it overwhelming financial implications for filmmakers. We also see that the Valenti Code failed in its efforts to eliminate prior censorship.

Censorship

Valenti promised to abandon subject matter censorship, outlawed by the Supreme Court, but over time this promise proved empty. Although producers no longer submit scripts to censors for prior censorship, movies still receive ratings, currently defined by age, not content. However, as Hollywood struggles to compete with television, the Internet, and other technological challenges, audience age proves critical. With average audiences still largely composed of teenagers, a film receiving an NC-17 ruling, for example, may not repay production costs, let alone turn a profit, because teenagers are unable to view it, newspapers are unwilling to advertise it, and video rental outlets are unwilling to stock it. Also, the MPAA continues to examine "thematic elements" and to raise the age limits for any elements it deems inappropriate for young audiences. So it turns out that the age-based ratings still effectively restrict and inhibit films at the political margins. The Valenti Code only changed the rationale for prior restraint of material deemed offensive from protection of all audiences to protection of sensitive young audiences, which now account for the bulk of Hollywood revenue. Under the Valenti Code, producers still face de facto prior censorship, but now they must guess what censors will do instead of receiving written reactions from them prior to production.

Today's producers have little incentive to make films for which most of their audiences would be excluded under MPAA restrictions (like NC-17 and even PG-13), even though they can now produce such films freely. Valenti intended to use the new system solely to provide information to parents regarding the suitability of motion pictures for children. That, at least, provides the official justification for the current rating system. He argued that the system assisted parents during the troubled times of the late sixties, which were marked by "insurrection on the campuses, riots in the streets, rise in woman's liberation, protests of the young, doubts about the institution of marriage, abandonment of old guiding slogans, and the crumbling of social traditions."[31] The system still functions to assist parents, although the ramifications of CARA ratings go far beyond mere parental information.

Although *Freedman v. Maryland* outlawed prior censorship, it took many subsequent court decisions to finally eradicate the censorship boards. However, many argue that the MPAA ratings system even today continues the practice of censorship under the guise of providing information to parents. Even though some critics use the term *Production Code* to mean only the rules and regulations employed by the Hays Office and Hays's successors, a more accurate usage of *Production Code* would certainly include the current age-based system. In theory, the code created by Valenti avoided prior censorship. However, in statement and in practice the Valenti Code profoundly affects film content. Almost immediately, filmmakers learn the limits of sensitive scenes and dialogue. Afterward, they actively limit projects that are likely to receive NC-17 or R ratings. That alone constitutes a powerful form of censorship. And, even if this dynamic proved insufficient, studios routinely remove or otherwise obscure scenes and passages deemed offensive to CARA. Once these scenes are identified, studios cut and resubmit their altered films. This, of course, constitutes another form of censorship.

Today's producers no longer submit scripts to the MPAA during the production phase, but they submit their finished films for ratings, which often spell financial success or failure. Today's filmmakers feel compelled to omit or alter any scenes that the MPAA finds objectionable, willingly taking any steps necessary to conform to the MPAA's perspective by excising and sanitizing films to meet code objections.

Although the Court outlawed prior censorship of film content, in practice the Valenti Code forced filmmakers to alter their finished productions significantly to avoid financially devastating ratings. In practice, filmmakers reject controversial images and themes, particularly sexual ones, in their films for fear of receiving a dreaded NC-17 rating.

For a variety of reasons, including the MPAA's close connections with Hollywood and the reluctance of major studios to risk producing films doomed to financial failure, few of the films receiving NC-17 ratings originate in the major studios, all charter members of the MPAA. Instead, this harsh rating traditionally falls on indies willing to buck conventional sexual mores. Important independent films that garnered NC-17 ratings included Peter Greenaway's *The Cook, the Thief, His Wife, and Her Lover* (1989), which received high critical acclaim as a parable of sex and greed. Pedro Almodovar's *Tie Me Up, Tie Me Down* (1990) also received critical acclaim for its story of a mental patient (Antonio Banderas) who kidnaps and binds a dope-addicted former porn star, played by Victoria Abril. It turns out that he was only interested in settling down with her, not in terrorizing or killing her. Despite this gesture toward the MPAA, though, Almodovar's film failed to receive an R rating. One explosive sex scene placed this film in the NC-17 category. The MPAA continues to rate the DVD as NC-17. This case illustrates once again the fact that adult sexuality fares poorly at the hands of CARA.

During the past decade the struggles over film censorship reveal a society confronting previously taboo issues like homosexuality, rape, and oral sex, often hindered by censors adhering to an obsolete code. In fact, Valenti Code censorship has noticeably weakened several recent films. Stanley Kubrick's final film, *Eyes Wide Shut* (1999), serves as a potent example of heavy-handed censorship. In Kubrick's film an affluent, happily married physician (Tom Cruise) explores a steamy, surreal sexual underworld after learning from his wife (Nicole Kidman) about her powerful fantasies about sex with a stranger. One key scene in which several people enjoy an orgy originally showed thrusting, erect penises, giving it a strong sexual aura. This scene, included in the "European version," was screened initially by critics, who expressed outrage when they subsequently learned that the studio had omitted the depictions of erect penises in the orgy scene by superimposing mysterious hooded figures in front of them to secure an R rating. In response, Roger Ebert charged that greed motivated the rating system and prevented CARA from adopting a workable adults-only rating because of industry reluctance to turn anyone away. "Thus movies are crammed into the R category, sometimes having to be edited to qualify," he noted. "We need an A-for-adult rating *between* the R and the NC-17 (a.k.a. X), to separate nonporn adult films from pornography. . . . Terrified of outside censorship, the MPAA is more sensitive to content involving language, mild sexuality, and subtle drug references than the average American moviegoer."[32]

Kramer's *The Cooler* (2003) exemplifies the current policy of negotiating ratings. Kramer's erotic thriller received the dreaded NC-17 rating initially, but the producers ultimately negotiated an R rating after appealing to the MPAA. The Valenti Office especially disliked a scene featuring William H. Macy performing cunnilingus on nubile Maria Bello. After hearing the studio's appeal, the MPAA finally decided to allow the scene. By contrast, Jane Campion's R-rated *In the Cut* (2003) graphically depicts an act of fellatio in which a woman pleasures a man orally. To avoid the NC-17 rating Campion only needed to blur some details. The protagonist, played by Meg Ryan, witnesses and becomes eroticized by an act of fellatio, in which a male receives oral sexual pleasure from a female. The remade scene allows the audience to see a blurred point of view shot that nonetheless clearly evokes the taboo act. This situation harks back to Hollywood's notorious gender bias against females. Receiving sexual pleasure is much more permissible for males than females. Similarly, in 1998 the MPAA forced Troy Beyer to excise a scene from *Let's Talk About Sex* that employed a peach to demonstrate the art of fellatio on a woman. To Mary Ann Johanson, "The MPAA has subjectively decided that the depiction of male sexual pleasure is more important than that of women." In addition, she charges that, in terms of the disparity between being able to depict nudity of women and being unable to depict the same nudity of men, and in the freedom directors have to depict violence toward women, "men deserve a measure of dignity when it comes to nudity that women do not merit, that watching a woman being murdered is less objectionable than watching a woman have an orgasm."[33]

Under the current rating system filmmakers choose whether to risk their investment, amounting to tens of millions of dollars, to retain their film's original vision and integrity. In 2004, for example, after prolonged negotiations, Fox Searchlight released Bernardo Bertolucci's sexually explicit *The Dreamers* in the director's original NC-17 version rather than editing out enough to earn the milder R designation. Bertolucci claimed that his film would be severely harmed by Fox if they tried to secure the R rating. Disputed scenes depict masturbation as well as close-ups of genitalia. *The Dreamers* illustrates the constant tension between filmmakers and censors over sexual material. If Bertolucci had chosen to emphasize violence instead of sex, his films would have automatically received an R rating.[34] Fox Searchlight later released an "R" rated version on DVD.

Today, standards for depicting sexual activities continue to drift in the direction of greater permissiveness and increased realism. A 2004 study undertaken by the Harvard School of Public Health and examining the sexual and violent content of 1,906 feature films released between 1992 and 2003 found evidence for "ratings creep" and concluded that "the MPAA appears to tolerate increasingly more extreme content in any given age-based rating categories over time." Kimberly

Thompson and Fumie Yokoto concluded that "when you look at the average, today's PG-13 movies are approaching what the R movies looked like in 1992." Furthermore, noted Thompson, "Today's PG is approaching what PG-13 looked like a decade ago."[35]

Retirement

In 2004, at age eighty-two, Jack Valenti retired after thirty-eight years in office. He was succeeded as MPAA president by Dan Glickman. At present, he appears to be following Valenti's policies faithfully. It may take a few years, but the MPAA is now in the throes of a crisis similar to the one that greeted Valenti at the start of his career. A chorus of conservative voices now demand greater MPAA oversight of the films and stricter enforcement of the Production Code. Liberals and progressives like Kirby Dick and Roger Ebert have also called for a new, fairer rating system. Glickman now finds himself caught between those two forces, one advocating for a stricter code, the other advocating for a more lenient, less biased code. Glickman will need some of the resilience of his predecessors, particularly Will Hays and Jack Valenti, to ensure the MPAA's health and survival.

On April 26, 2007, Valenti died at age eighty-five, the victim of complications from an earlier stroke. He bequeathed a legacy at once monumental and, increasingly, controversial. Will history remember him as the one who finally abolished prior censorship of films, or will it recall him as the one who created a new method of prior censorship through film ratings? History is already forming the answer to that question. Valenti's legacy will, in the long run, prove as powerful as those of Will Hays and Joseph Breen, his two most famous predecessors. He found himself befriended by politicians and movie stars, as well as the all-powerful moguls, while at the same time berated and condemned by those wanting someone to blame for loosening moral standards. Valenti presided over the MPAA for nearly forty years. During that period the United States witnessed profound social changes, some of which are still in the process of unfolding.

Gender Roles

The Valenti Code focuses primarily on restricting sexuality, particularly nudity, profanity, and graphic and erotic scenes. The rise of the code corresponded with a rise in feminism, and the male backlash against it, which attempted to redefine traditional sex roles and media stereotypes. Notable female characters of the Valenti period reflect "third-wave feminists" no longer content to remain subservient and also increasingly expressing themselves sexually and often violently. These neo–femmes fatales arrived in the eighties and nineties. They surpass the behavior of classic film noir seductresses from the Hays period, epitomizing the "fatal attraction" syndrome evident in today's sexual neo-noirs. Today, the older seductress archetypes transformed into warriors, labeled as "pummel-me feminism" for their violence.[36]

Today's seductresses continue to escalate their violence. Quentin Tarantino's *Kill Bill Volume 1* (2003) and *Kill Bill Volume 2* (2004) feature a superhero known only as The Bride (Uma Thurman), who combines the martial arts skills of a dozen old-fashioned film noir heroes. A highly trained assassin, The Bride combines the characteristics of a male action hero with the aggression of a male warrior. She enacts vengeance on treacherous former colleagues and single-handedly defeats entire armies of samurai warriors. Her ultimate goal: to enact terrible punishment against Bill (David Carradine), her former teacher. To do so she must defeat her former fellow assassins and all of their confederates. She functions as a kind of superwoman, part warrior, part bad girl, a beauty with the strength of ten who can tear any man apart with her bare hands. No longer do today's femmes noir need to resort to seduction in order to prevail, although The Bride is quite capable of that as well. They are now able to go toe-to-toe with male warriors. Clearly, this is a new and dangerous kind of archetype with many negative characteristics.

Though banned during the Hays era, popular archetypes of the Valenti period include the "virgin prostitute." Vivian Ward (Julia Roberts) in Garry Marshal's *Pretty Woman* (1990) expresses the modern appearance of this venerable archetype. Vivian appears smart, determined, and ultimately enduring, despite the fact that she is a prostitute. Her mark, wealthy businessman Edward Lewis (Richard Gere), also strains credibility as he negotiates for the services of a female companion. The virginal prostitute harks back to the gold diggers of pre-code Hollywood, who plied their wares in a ruthless, competitive society. Like today's third-wave "do-me" feminists, femme fatale characters of the past two decades often behave like virgin prostitutes (*Pretty Woman, Kill Bill I and II*), and their sexuality is rarely depicted realistically.

Although female characters have become increasingly more formidable, and certainly more dangerous, Valenti-era males, particularly in the neo-noir genre, display serious, even fatal weaknesses. The rise in strength and power of neo-noir heroines has come at the expense of the power of male characters. Male characters in neo-noirs fall into the lost soul archetypes; they are invariably weak, venal, easily manipulated, spineless, and thoughtless. *Body Heat*'s Ned Racine (William Hurt) all too easily falls for Matty Walker and the triangle murder of her husband. Walker tells him approvingly, "You're not too smart, are you? I like that in a man." *The Grifters*' Roy Dillon (John Cusack) ultimately succumbs to his mother Lily's (Anjelica Huston) wiles and brazen attack on his head with a heavy tumbler. Roy ends up dead and Lily walks free, or rather runs free. There is no true freedom for the femmes noir, nor is there rest for the male noir heroes. Both genders appear doomed to turmoil.

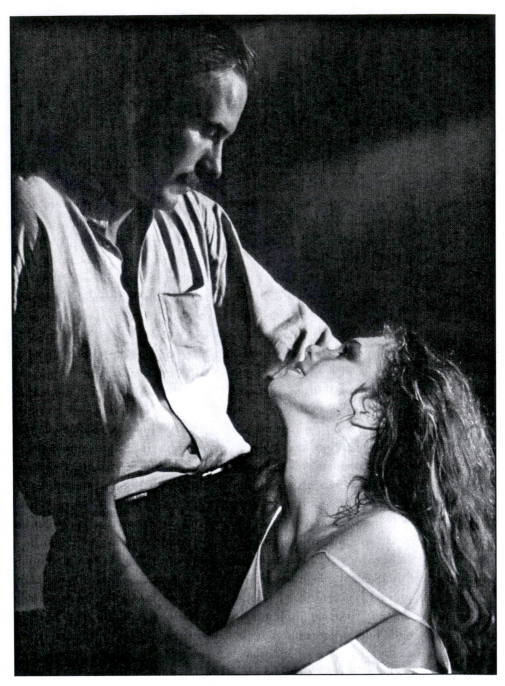

Femme fatale Matty Walker (Kathleen Turner) seduces Ned Racine (William Hurt) in Lawrence Kasdan's influential neo-noir thriller *Body Heat* (1981). (Copyright 1981 Warner Bros.)

The Valenti Code's greater lenience regarding sexual behavior allowed filmmakers to avoid splitting heroes into two characters, a common practice during the Hays era. With the demise of restrictions regarding payment for crimes committed filmmakers were free to present flawed male characters who, nevertheless, functioned as film protagonists. These new male heroes may embody antihero characteristics, or they may even be outright criminals. *Who's Afraid of Virginia Woolf?*'s George (Richard Burton) does not need a double. He can come across as a pitiable specimen of manhood who suggests playing "hump the hostess" with his own wife as hostess and the "humper" their own dinner guest. He can come across as *Basic Instinct*'s Nick Curran (Michael Douglas), who suffers from various neuroses and who manages to select a murderer as his mate, promising a danger-filled and probably short life. The Valenti Code also permits outright criminals as heroes, as in *Match Point*'s Chris Wilton (Jonathan Rhys Meyers), who murders Lola, his mistress (Scarlett Johansson), and gets away with it while remaining married to the boss's daughter. With characters like these, hero doubles become superfluous.

Creating the Couple

The Valenti period witnessed dramatic changes in traditional families. Neo-noir relationships like the ones in *Chinatown, Fatal Attraction, Body Heat, The Last Seduction, Dream Lover, A Perfect Murder, American Beauty, Match Point, Unfaithful,* and numerous others present classic examples of aggressive, dangerous femmes fatales. They encounter weak, indecisive, confused males. These males confront seductive, dangerous females. These characters often deceive and even murder each other. The gender conflict in these films obviously reflects deep-seated social conflicts. The union of warrior/seductress with lost-soul males often proves contentious and, at times, explosive.

In neo-noir, monogamy often equates with monotony. Couples frequently cheat on each other, reflecting Kinsey's observations. Or, they may fight each other in court for custody of their children, as in *Kramer vs. Kramer.* In response to the Valenti Code, Hollywood filmmakers prefer violence over sex. At times, the violence appears gratuitous. Films provide ample evidence for the existence of a culture of movie violence, and, as a result, Valenti-era characters rarely shrink from attacking each other or doing each other in. These films appear to overrepresent dysfunctional couples and nontraditional families, from dangerous neo-noir relationships to dysfunctional *Kramer vs. Kramer*–type families. With the advent of the Valenti Code, it seems, courtship turned hazardous and often fatal.

Oliver Stone's *Natural Born Killers* (1994) introduced Mickey (Woody Harrelson) and Mallory (Juliette Lewis) Knox, a husband and wife couple from hell. The couple begins by killing Mallory's father, Ed (Rodney Dangerfield), who openly molests his daughter and threatens to rape her. After dispatching both of Mallory's parents the couple goes on a killing spree, outing any who become seduced by Mallory's beauty and seeming openness to sex. Eventually, the two are interviewed by pompous television reporter Wayne Gayle (Robert Downey, Jr.), who ignores the obvious risks involved in interviewing the two killers, much to his horror as he becomes another victim. Stone's attempt at black humor succeeded with critics and audiences, but the MPAA threatened to award it an NC-17 rating. Stone vitiated their concerns by obscuring any graphic sex or violence through loud music, bright lights, and shifting perspectives.[37] The film stimulated a spate of copycat murders, with killers revealing that Stone's film played a major role in their psychological development. Even worse, the two Columbine High School killers, Eric Harris and Dylan Klebold, possessed a copy of the movie that they viewed on several occasions and mentioned specifically in the audiotapes they prepared prior to the massacre. Other killers later revealed their affection for Stone's film, making it the one film that stimulated more copycat killings than any other in history.

The Valenti era's contentious family films reflect growing pressures on relationships in contemporary society. Promiscuity, adultery, prostitution, AIDS, and homosexuality reflect deep social changes, including immigration, urbanization, secularization, computerization, and globalization. The era's wars, including Vietnam, the Gulf War, the Balkan wars, and the current wars in Iraq and Afghanistan, also affect film ratings and content. In addition, the Civil Rights Movement, the rise of feminism, and antiwar movements also resulted in ratings disputes. The Valenti Code, designed to defuse code wars, actually stimulated quite a few of its own.

Presently, flaws in the code that once appeared minor inconveniences gape like open wounds. The problems besetting young directors, especially of indie films, have intensified as they struggle to produce cutting-edge, alternative films. However, if they attempt to depict sexual relationships realistically they run the risk of earning NC-17 ratings. When established filmmakers like Bernardo Bertolucci, Jane Campion, John Waters, Trey Parker, Kevin Smith, and Ang Lee routinely encounter ratings problems and pressures to cut and alter, less-established filmmakers may bear even greater burdens. This pressure may partially explain the strange absence of younger directors making films. Sharon Waxman observes that filmmakers who showed promise in the 1990s, including Kimberly Pierce, Darren Aronofsky, David O. Russell, Baz Luhrmann, David Fincher, and Cameron Crowe, experience greater difficulties getting their projects made than filmmakers of previous generations.[38] The absence of an antagonistic outside force, like McCarthyism or "the establishment," may account for the lack of cohesiveness that today's filmmakers have, even for others of their generation. Instead of cohesiveness, today's filmmakers experience intense scrutiny in every part of the filmmaking process. The price of a mistake is oblivion, at least for the foreseeable future, despite their previous track records.

Kirby Dick's *This Film Is Not Yet Rated* levels the now-familiar charges that the MPAA code is inconsistent, biased against indies, and promotes violence over sex. Recently, MPAA officials have gone out of their way to address some of the issues raised in Dick's film. CARA administrator Joan Graves announced in January 2007 that CARA was reviewing its standards regarding violence and might rule that "slasher movies," which routinely receive R ratings, be placed in the NC-17 category. Graves also disclosed CARA's intention to further modify the ratings to make NC-17 less of a "kiss of death" to filmmakers.[39] As yet no specific plans have been announced, but the fact that the MPAA is aware of these issues and is tinkering with the system proves that the code is in a transition stage, with future changes forthcoming.

The Valenti Code, like any code, requires periodic overhauls and mechanisms to facilitate necessary changes. The current secret process appears exceedingly slow and cumbersome. For example, after years of culture wars fought over depicting smoking tobacco, the MPAA announced in 2007 that it would take instances of smoking into consideration. CARA's ratings board, chaired by Joan Graves, announced in May 2007 that teen smoking would be a factor in film ratings alongside sex, violence, and adult language.[40] Under pressure from the antismoking lobby, some studios pledged to eliminate smoking from all films rated G, PG, or PG-13. Some in the industry worry that the smoking situation will embolden other groups to pressure Hollywood to ban guns, trans fats, or other disputed items.[41]

The MPAA rating process, with its tendency toward compromise and its willingness, in the long run, to allow filmmakers to address contemporary issues, provides the necessary moral structure to allow Hollywood to continue offering audiences what they want to view. As Jon Lewis remarks, "the rating system is there to help everyone involved in the project to make money."[42] Jack Valenti himself downgraded the importance of film ratings conflicts, holding that fine films always attract audiences, regardless of the ratings. On the contrary, poorly made films never find audiences, no matter what their ratings. He said, "If you make a movie that a lot of people want to see, no rating will hurt you. If you make a movie that few people will want to see, no rating will help you. Ratings have nothing to do with box office."[43] However, as Mark Harris notes, the NC-17 rating—unlike the other categories— "carries the force of law: It's the only stage at which raters decide their judgment should overrule yours." And, the MPAA's recent rating decisions prove "that they're manifestly incompetent to make it." Many filmmakers today agree with Harris's analysis and vehemently refute Valenti's Code from bitter personal experience. Filmmakers discover that an NC-17–rated film may not even be released by the studio, and if it is released, it will never attract huge audiences. Art house theaters and DVD rentals may provide some revenue, but not like mall theaters and Blockbuster rentals. NC-17 ratings preclude major venues like theater chains and video sales and rental outlets, so box office revenues plummet. The examples of filmmakers like John Waters, Trey Parker, Matt Stone, and so many others soundly refute Valenti's Code.

The Valenti Code reflects sensitive issues that prove vexing to society as a whole. Sexism, even today, manifests itself in movie ratings, as it does in society at large. In today's movies, the limits of permissible behavior differ between male and female characters. Under the Valenti Code, females may pleasure men sexually, even with oral sex, while men cannot perform oral sex upon women or give undue consideration to pleasuring them in other ways. The focus on women remains as sex objects, not receivers of sexual pleasure. As women continue to be victims of violence, they are also depicted almost as sexual victims, able to pleasure men but not to receive pleasure from them. Their role is to serve males. In today's films, female characters must conform to an unstated gender code—the protagonists of *Thelma and Louise* and avengers like Wendy Kroy in *The Last Seduction* and *Kill Bill's* The Bride even the score for women. Sexually, the femmes fatales of neo-noirs from the nineties on revel in sex and use their charms to seduce males. Ultimately, they correspond to the "do-me feminism" movement of recent decades that embraces sex instead of viewing it as an instrument of patrimony.

Nudity, too, remains a sensitive issue, with full frontal shots of women preferred by the MPAA over frontal nudity by men. Men, the dominant sex, demand greater sexual privacy. Since the Valenti Code encourages these disparities, which also existed under the Hays Code, it is clear that today's code remains problematic in many areas. The film industry, like the rest of society, has not yet reached gender equality. Vestiges of this inequality are perpetuated in Hollywood films, with the hidden assistance of the Valenti Code.

The Valenti Code, like previous codes, engendered new genres, including the highly sexual neo-noirs and today's sex comedies. Neo-noirs like *Body Heat, The Grifters, The Last Seduction,* and *Kill Bill* depict women as dangerous sexual predators luring unsuspecting, foolishly weak men into becoming willing accomplices as well as victims. One can only conclude that today's audiences desire films depicting antifeminist stereotypes. Sex comedies also thrive under the Valenti Code, including memorable ones by Woody Allen, John Waters, Quentin Tarantino, Mel Brooks, and Trey Parker. Comedies like *Annie Hall, Manhattan, Serial Mom, Pulp Fiction, Young Frankenstein,* and *South Park* lampoon today's sexual myths and double standards, in some cases depicting culture wars between groups of bawdy hipsters and staid neuters. When one compares the types of films inspired by the Valenti Code with those inspired by the Hays Code, it appears that the latter resulted in more interesting and enduring genres. Screwball comedies like *It Happened One Night, My Man Godfrey, Bringing Up Baby,* and *His Girl Friday* are all recognized as classics today. A few of today's comedies also appear to be classics, including *Annie Hall, Serial Mom, A Dirty Shame,* and *South Park*. The double entendre, innuendo, and symbolism developed to evade the Hays Code added a necessary artistic element that was often lacking in precode films facing less stringent regulations and continues to be lacking today.

CHAPTER SIX

The Evangelical Code

Beginning in the late nineties audiences experienced a dramatic revolution in movies. Religious pressure groups lobby Hollywood to avoid prurient or realistic sexuality and, instead, depict traditional "family values." Today's evangelical movement shares many similarities with other rebellions against movies, including the famous 1934 church-led revolt against Hollywood that ushered in Hays Code censorship. Just as religious conservatives effected dramatic change in Hollywood then, today's evangelicals profoundly impact movies now. Today's evangelicals seek an end to depictions of adultery, premarital sex, homosexuality, and drug use and demand more positive depictions of family values, nuclear families, churches, and ministers, as well as more biblical-themed movies. As a result of lobbying, group prayer sessions, and other forms of evangelical pressure, religious-themed movies now appear with increasing frequency, along with large numbers of secular family values films. These dramatic changes have resulted in a new era dominated by a code advocated by evangelicals and conservative Christians and Jews. In fact, the "evangelical code" emerges as one of the most potent unofficial Production Codes in motion picture history.

The deep roots of evangelicalism date to the rise of Puritanism at the end of the seventeenth century, and the Puritan revolution in England, led by Oliver Cromwell in 1658, exemplifies the potential political power of today's evangelical movement. Puritan immigration to American colonies expanded the movement's power to colonial America until late in the seventeenth century, when the religion declined after the Salem Witch Trials of 1688. Even today, evangelicalism owes a debt to seventeenth-century Puritanism in both theology and politics by advocating a new "Godly theocracy" while opposing the separation of church and state enshrined in the First Amendment.

The term "evangelical," meaning "good news," appeared in the nineteenth century when a large missionary outreach arose to convert millions of the newest subjects of European and American colonialism. Then evangelicals consisted primarily of Methodists and Baptists, who competed for converts to their conservative denominations. Now as then, many evangelicals consider themselves "fundamentalists," believing strongly in the inerrancy of the Bible, Jesus' virgin birth, and the imminent return of Christ. Today's evangelicals adhere to a literal interpretation of biblical prophecy, particularly the End of Days as outlined in Revelation. To adherents only divine grace and salvation redeem human sin and depravity, and individuals escape damnation and enjoy eternal life in heaven only through experiencing spiritual rebirth and strictly adhering to biblical law.

Currently the evangelical movement encompasses the Assembly of God, Southern Baptists, Independent Baptists, black Protestants, African Methodist Episcopal, African Methodist Episcopal Zion, Church of Christ, Churches of God in Christ, Lutheran Church–Missouri Synod, National Baptist Church, National Progressive Baptist Church, Pentecostal denominations, and the Latter-Day Saints. Evangelicals also ally with other conservative Christian movements positioned within such mainline denominations as the Episcopal Church, USA; the Presbyterian Church (USA); and the United Methodist Church, although the mainstream members of these denominations no longer identify with evangelicalism. Conservative Catholics and Orthodox Jews also seek common cause with evangelicals on a variety of social issues, including opposition to abortion, homosexuality, and permissiveness.

Patriarchy forms a central theme in evangelicalism and adherents advocate male domination of church, government, and marriage. They advocate a similar patriarchy in movies. In society as in the media, evangelicals demand heterosexuality, chastity, patriarchy, monogamy, and fidelity to church and family. They strongly oppose feminism, homosexuality, multiculturalism, pacifism, profanity, promiscuity, pornography, hedonism, secularism, and environmentalism and abhor their appearance in films. Evangelicals battle gay marriage laws and sex education in public schools and express an antiscientific bias and opposition to stem cell research, the Big Bang theory, the Theory of Evolution, and theories of global climate change. Evangelicals subscribe to a literalist interpretation of the Bible and oppose any manifestation of "social gospel" emphasizing assistance to the poor, although some now advocate greater antipoverty efforts. To evangelicals, God cares little about feeding the hungry or providing shelter to the homeless and places much greater emphasis on strict adherence to the traditional male-dominated heterosexual nuclear family.

To many evangelicals, Hollywood represents nothing less than the embodiment of Satan and the Antichrist, and producers constitute a secret cabal intent on subverting traditional Christian morality, which is why many oppose Hollywood.

Christian Censorship

The first official religious censorship occurred in 1916 when the American Catholic Church banned A. M. Kennelly's *Power of the Cross* from being viewed by the faithful and threatened to excommunicate Kennelly.[1] This censorship set the tone for future interactions between churches and filmmakers. Cecil B. DeMille's pre-code *Sign of the Cross* (1932) outraged religious conservatives by strongly condemning religious intolerance, a veiled attack on Christian bigotry. Officially, however, religious opposition focused on Claudette Colbert's (Poppaea) nudity as she bathes in a supposed bath of ass's milk. One censor condemned the scene, with "her breasts bobbing on the frothy surface like two scoops of vanilla ice cream."[2] During the ensuing decades conservative Christians continued to pressure filmmakers and Production Code administrators through the threat of boycotts and banning, and by forbidding parishioners to view films they deemed objectionable.

Beginning in 1934, the Hays Code mandated positive portrayal of Christians, especially ministers and priests, placating religious conservatives for a time, but by the forties once again religious conservatives vented their outrage about Hollywood's "excesses." In 1942, shortly after the birth of the film noir genre, the chairman of the Christian Newspaper Men's Committee to Investigate the Motion Picture Industry charged in a news release titled "Hell over Hollywood" that "Hollywood is the closest thing to 'hell on earth' that Satan has thus far been able to establish."[3] This diatribe occurred just five years before the House Un-American Activities Committee began its hearings in Hollywood, which resulted in the Hollywood Ten and blacklists and revealed the strong connections between social and political conservatives.

During World War II the rift between Hollywood and the church temporarily subsided under a blanket of patriotism. As prominent filmmakers like Frank Capra and Howard Hawks enlisted to produce wartime documentaries, a truce blossomed between Hollywood and the clergy. After the war, McCarthyism put the brakes on films' social as well as political messages, further placating conservative Christians. By the 1960s, however, the schism between Christians and Hollywood widened as the old prohibitions against attacking or even questioning churches and ministers eroded. Films like Richard Brooks's *Elmer Gantry* (1960) and John Huston's *The Night of the Iguana* (1964) appeared depicting lapsed ministers who refuse to behave with propriety and godliness. That subject, previously taboo under the earlier Hays Code, drove a wedge between Christians and Hollywood. Even today conservative writers from Jerry Falwell to George Will dutifully and routinely condemn "Elmer Gantry"–style hypocrisy in Christians.[4]

After the Hays Code collapsed in 1968 religion lost its former protection. During the ensuing decades gradual erosion of censorship standards led to "ratings creep," permitting ever more permissive movies, which in turn generated increased animosity between religious conservatives and Hollywood. Today more than one-third of all Americans identify themselves as evangelicals, and the movement now wields great influence. Evangelicalism's power has created a new, unofficial Production Code that encourages G- and PG-rated films laden with religious family values while demanding positive depictions of Christians in all movies. The pressure wielded by powerful pressure groups lobbying for Christian-themed and family values films, along with Hollywood's growing desire to supply the evangelical market, promises to affect movies profoundly for the foreseeable future.

The massive evangelical audience tempts producers into expanding their offerings of Christian-friendly films. To satisfy the evangelical market more efficiently, major studios now employ Christian focus groups that provide feedback to producers on all G and PG films. Currently, producers screen films with religious and family focus groups and remove material and scenes they find offensive, realizing evangelicals can prove crucial in box office sales.[5] These developments signal broad changes in Hollywood, for the first time enabling religious conservatives to realize their long-stated goal of reforming Hollywood. The massive resources now pouring into evangelical and related family values films signal the arrival of a new, profoundly conservative era in movie history.

No longer on the fringes, today's evangelical movies appear in mall theaters, airplanes, hotel rooms, video rental outlets, and video stores. The Christian Broadcasting Network, founded by evangelist Pat Robertson, constitutes only one of a number of Christian radio and television stations agitating for more Christian-friendly films. In addition, a growing number of evangelical movie ratings services and periodicals weigh in on most Hollywood films, adding an evangelistic perspective to their reviews. As a result of a massive public relations assault on Hollywood, coupled with their huge numbers, today's religious conservatives find themselves taken more seriously by the media than at any time since the Catholic boycott of 1934. Reasons for evangelicals' recent success include better organization, increasing Internet access, and the strategic placement of evangelicals within the studio system. Today, Hollywood produces a growing number of religious-themed A-budget features and funds many lesser efforts. In addition, the movement now affects even nonreligious films as producers tweak films to make them more evangelical-friendly. As evangelicalism grows in popularity, Hollywood appears more than willing to produce movies the movement finds acceptable.

Kevin Phillips notes that during the seventies, eighties, and nineties three interrelated groups, Protestant fundamentalists, evangelicals, and Pentecostals, experienced "explosive" growth.[6] Today that growth continues at an accelerated rate, and evangelicals now constitute an impressive new audience demanding biblical-related, family values films. Presently, evangelicals constitute 42 percent of the total population of the United States.[7] Producers, desperate to survive challenges ranging from the Internet to pirated copies of movies, pay close attention to this growing market. Of the 43 percent of Americans who attend church weekly, the vast majority fall into the evangelical category.[8] Without a doubt, the evangelicalism movement represents a majority of the Christian population and a substantial percentage of the population as a whole.

Hollywood movies increasingly reflect the End of Days millennialism as prophesied in the Book of Revelation, in which the Antichrist appears and the earth faces seven years of Tribulations, unleashed by the Four Horsemen of the Apocalypse. To evangelicals, the earth has already entered the predicted End of Days period that began, in their view, with the reestablishment of the nation of Israel in 1948. Since Revelation describes Israel's central role in the End of Days, evangelicals overwhelmingly support Israel and its foreign and domestic policies. Since Israel's establishment, each new Middle Eastern conflict renews evangelicals' faith in the approaching Apocalypse, which will culminate in the Battle of Armageddon, in which Jesus will destroy the Antichrist in a final cataclysmic struggle between good and evil. Because of Israel's prominence in the End of Days, and its role in shaping Christianity, evangelicals embrace Israel and Jews in Israel. Politically, the End of Days translates into a war between good and evil in which conservatives identify with the good and associate liberals with evil. As Chris Hedges notes, "Members of the radical Christian End Times movement are being taught to believe that America is ruled by evil, clandestine organizations disguised as liberal groups. As a result, the fearful are hoping for the end."[9] Although evangelicals express great concerns about Satan and the Antichrist, liberals, progressives, and secularists are their real antagonists. To evangelicals, liberalism equates with Satanism and is promulgated secretly by him. For members of the movement, fighting liberalism means engaging in a crucial battle of good versus evil and participating in the End of Days scenarios.

To enhance their films' appeal to evangelical audiences, a growing number of Hollywood filmmakers openly employ the Revelation mythology, including the Four Horsemen of the Apocalypse, the Battle of Armageddon, devastating plagues, and other biblical scourges. Sci-fi films like *Armageddon, Independence Day, War of the Worlds,* and *The Reapers* draw deeply upon biblical iconology for their imagery. In these films the earth faces plagues, pestilence, meteors, and danger from supernatural forces, all central tenets of evangelicalism. For filmmakers, the end of the world presents intriguing dramatic possibilities. Apocalyptic films of the late twentieth and early twenty-first centuries constitute one of the hallmarks of the era and pay a tribute to the power of the evangelical movement.

Family Values

Evangelicalism strongly endorses "family values," by which the movement means paternalism, chastity, and homophobia. Male supremacy remains a movement dictum, relegating women to supportive roles. Because of their adherence to paternalism, evangelicals strongly object to premarital, extramarital, and postmarital sexuality. Members cite the Apostle Paul, who held that sex must only be performed in patriarchal marriages, where it was "better to marry than to burn in hell." For this reason, the movement vehemently opposes any efforts at sex education in schools. In addition, evangelicals support strict laws outlawing pornography, and of course they oppose prostitution. However, the movement reserves its greatest efforts for opposing homosexuality, considered a mortal sin instead of a manifestation of gender diversity. In fact, the movement's perspective on the family reflects fifties movies like Disney's *Davy Crockett, Lassie,* and *Sounder* as well as television series like *Ozzie and Harriet, I Love Lucy,* and *Leave It to Beaver.* Each depicts nuclear families headed by males. Any suggestion that fifties families no longer represent social norms meets with vigorous opposition. Even liberal denominations like the Episcopal Church now include substantial numbers of conservative members deeply concerned about family values. Today they experience a deep division in their ranks, with conservative dioceses severing their relationships with the Archbishop of Canterbury over tolerance of women priests and homosexuality. In 2007 two dissatisfied Anglican priests traveled to Kenya to be ordained in a conservative branch of the church, part of a growing number making that decision.[10] Conservative Anglicans share common values with evangelicals, as do orthodox Catholics like Mel Gibson.

Links to McCarthyism

Evangelicalism today resonates with vestiges of McCarthyism, its political predecessor. During the forties McCarthyism profoundly influenced religions. The year 1948 witnessed the creation of the evangelical Christian Crusade. Its members pledged to oppose communism in all of its forms. In addition, McCarthy enjoyed support from other conservative religious groups, especially fundamentalists. His followers included Father Edmond A. Walsh, a prominent Catholic.[11] This organization provided a strong religious voice that consistently supported McCarthyism until its decline in the sixties. Today's evangelicals receive ideological guidance from neo-McCarthyists like writers Ann Coulter and Lee Kaplan; right-wing pundits like Bill O'Reilly, Rush Limbaugh, and Joe Scarborough; and conservative critics like Michael Medved and Ted Baehr. These conservatives demonstrate the links between political and religious conservatism.

In 1967 the Christian Crusade garnered national headlines by burning copies of Beatles' record albums to protest John Lennon's comparison of his popularity with that of Jesus Christ. That action recalled McCarthy-era banning and book burning. Eventually, the Christian Crusade grew to over 250,000 families, and today it remains a forum for evangelicals, although Focus on the Family and other conservative Christian organizations now compete strongly for fundamentalist support.

James Dobson's Focus on the Family, established in 1977, enjoys continuing popularity due to its profamily mission "to cooperate with the Holy Spirit . . . by nurturing and defending the God-ordained institution of the family and promoting biblical truths worldwide."[12] Clearly, today's evangelical movement owes a strong debt to McCarthyism, Nativism, and other conservative movements of the past.

Evangelicals strongly oppose the liberal "modernist" wing of Christianity as well as mainstream Christianity in general, which they privately equate with evil. They denounce as blatant heresy religious relativism and any suggestion that Christianity is only one of a number of equally valid monotheistic religions, a claim sometimes made by multiculturalists. To evangelicals, the church's main mission consists of frightening members, with warnings about God's vengeance and imminent return, into abstaining from unsanctioned pleasures and activities. As it was for the Puritans, fear of God provides the first step toward salvation for evangelicals. They perceive God's vengeance at work in the forces of nature, and some in the movement, including conservative Robertson, ascribed the 2005 devastation of New Orleans by Hurricane Katrina to God's righteous response to the excesses of its pleasure-loving populace. Others pointed out that the hurricane struck before a major gay convention was about to be held, suggesting that God unleashed the hurricane to thwart the convention and punish its attendees. Evangelicals also believe that natural disasters like hurricanes and earthquakes are signs of the imminence of the End of Days apocalypse.

As Leslie E. Smith observes, evangelicals blame society's ills on "sexualized media images, moral relativism, liberalized education, and the current scourge of abortion and homosexual rights groups that manipulated otherwise wholesome values like equality and justice in order to bolster their positions."[13] Although evangelicals come in all races and skin tones, whites founded evangelicalism and continue to dominate it today. Evangelical films usually feature white protagonists and antagonists, although the popular *Left Behind* series includes a significant African American character in each episode, perhaps out of respect for the movement's African Americans. Despite this, the movement appears strongly oriented toward European American cultural values. Evangelists are super patriotic, and they scornfully label the idea that other cultures are equally valid as "relativism" and "multiculturalism." Minorities may join the movement and play subordinate roles, but it remains a white-led phenomenon.

Sex

Homophobia's roots go back centuries, where it first arose in opposition to paganism, which had tolerated and even encouraged homosexuality. To evangelicals, homosexuality stems not from genetic or hormonal causes but from mortal sin and moral turpitude. Therefore, the movement vigorously opposes gay marriage, anti-hate-speech ordinances, and antidiscrimination laws. Evangelicals oppose homosexuality not only from a religious perspective; they also perceive it to be injurious to health (citing alcoholism and AIDS). Conservative columnist Pat Robertson charged that God created AIDS as a punishment for gays, just as he destroyed Sodom and Gomorrah for the populace's homosexuality. (Actually, biblical scholars agree that the cities faced God's wrath not for sodomy but for wanting to sexually assault God's angels.) Although a few evangelicals acknowledge, in accordance with recent scientific data, that gay brain patterns differ significantly from straight brain patterns, they also argue that the altered brain patterns stem not from genetic differences but from aberrant behavior, which they ultimately blame on Hollywood and liberal permissiveness. They believe that the altered brains of gays can be reversed through Christian redemption, and the observed differences in brain patterns result from "superficial, reversible changes in behavior and/or makeup of a person's genes." Therefore, individuals, not society, should shoulder the guilt.[14] Of course, evangelicals hold no monopoly on homophobia, which permeates the motion picture history.

Surprisingly, the movement's well-known abhorrence of homosexuality did not inspire attempts to ban Ang Lee's *Brokeback Mountain* (2005), even though the film depicts a secret love affair between two male ranch hands, played by Heath Ledger and Jake Gyllenhaal. The movement now realizes that attempts to have films banned may backfire and create interest in those films. The movement satisfied itself with blasting Lee's film with negative reviews and deliberately avoided providing free publicity by picketing or advocating banning.

Instead of Darwinism, which emphasizes scientific rationalism, evangelicals support the Theory of Intelligent Design, which holds that everything in the universe stems from God's plans, not from natural processes. To evangelicals, God created the universe in seven literal days, despite the biblical injunction that a day in God's life is equal to a thousand human years. These beliefs inspired Nathan Frankowski's documentary *Expelled: No Intelligence Allowed* (2008), which charges that Darwinians in colleges, universities, and academic journals and publishing houses routinely discriminate against adherents of Intelligent Design in an effort to suppress that theory. To Frankowski, the media also plays into the conspiracy. Other contentious issues include prayer in public schools and posting the Ten Commandments in government buildings. The movement also opposes the theory of global warming, feminism (blamed for social ills), flag desecration (treasonable), hedonism (social degeneration), adultery (family breakdown), and sexual promiscuity (social chaos).

In 2006 a few prominent evangelicals attempted to broaden the movement's agenda by including social issues like ending poverty and reducing global warming. However, conservative voices within the evangelical community prevailed at that time. For the moment, the movement continues to focus its major efforts on opposition to homosexuality, stem cell research, and abortion, although a significant countermovement among Christians exists. The old and new evangelical movements clashed in 2007 when the Christian Coalition, one of the nation's largest evangelical associations, rebuffed the efforts of the Reverend Joel Hunter, formerly president-elect of the organization, to include global warming and poverty on the organization's agenda. Hunter spoke for a growing number of evangelicals who are uncomfortable with the traditional agenda. The organization's founder, Pat Robertson, may have influenced the decision to forgo global warming in favor of the traditional antihomosexual, antiabortion platform. A disappointed Hunter finally withdrew from the new position. The evangelical movement has yet to cede power to the constituencies that express concerns about these other social problems.

Evangelicals strongly oppose feminism and multiculturalism, castigated as two of contemporary society's most pernicious evils. Evangelicals argue that feminist policies in public schools discriminate against boys. Fox News posted this charge on its website. In response, Becky Ellis argues that girls, not boys, bear the brunt of sexist policies in public schools.[15] Feminism must surely be to blame for this situation. As for multiculturalism, evangelicals charge that emphasizing diverse cultures detracts from a proper respect for European American culture. Evangelicals vehemently support the rights of white males, which they charge are being subordinated to those of women and minorities.

Evangelicals versus Hollywood

At the start of the twenty-first century evangelicals ramped up the pressure on Hollywood through e-mail campaigns, mass prayer meetings, and threatening to boycott Hollywood films. The movement demanded that Hollywood clean up movies, censoring and sanitizing them from promiscuity, profanity, and drug use. The role of older leaders like Pat Robertson and Jerry Falwell has been passed along to younger members like Ted Baehr and Ted Haggard. They blame Hollywood for promulgating a wide array of social ills, resulting in the decline of the traditional male-dominated nuclear family. To evangelicals, movies create instead of reflect society, so they focus a great deal of attention on reforming movies. In 2007 the editors of *Movieguide* claimed that Hollywood moguls intentionally subvert Christian values. "Even Christians are influenced by Hollywood," explains the editors, "because it is Hollywood that has spent 50 years or more persuading children to accept sexual promiscuity, homosexuality, adultery, atheism, violence as a means of solving problems, and last but not least, big government handouts for every conceivable social ill under the sun." They conclude their report by blaming Hollywood for creating "the socialist tyranny in which we now apparently live."[16] For evangelicals, any meaningful social reform begins and ends with Hollywood.

The Evangelical Code

As a result of evangelical successes in lobbying Hollywood for more Christian-friendly films and fewer sexual thrillers, a discernible "evangelical code" for acceptable movies has emerged. Like the McCarthy code of the late forties and early fifties, the evangelical code remains unofficial, although it exerts a powerful influence on Hollywood. This code consists of the following:

1. **Profanity.** Today's standards differ from the Hays Code prohibitions against every expletive from "damn" and "hell" on up. Evangelicals appear just as sensitive about "damn" and "hell," but focus with greater vigilance on banning words involving bodily functions and procreation.

2. **Sexual liberation.** No sex except between married couples, and even that should never be depicted realistically. No glorification of premarital sex, adultery, promiscuity, or homosexuality.

3. **Nudity.** Evangelicals express particular concerns about this issue. Basically, all socially permissible nudity ended with Adam and Eve in the Garden of Eden. They even condem upper-body male nudity.

4. **Violence.** Some evangelicals object to graphic violence, but members view more violent films than nonevangelicals, and significant evangelical films contain graphic violence.

5. **Liberal politics.** Evangelicals object to liberalism and progressivism in any form and in essence equate liberalism with evil.

6. **Negative depictions of Christianity.** Like the Hays Code, the evangelical code prohibits any negative depictions of Christians, particularly lapsed clergy or phony preachers.

7. **Feminism.** No "militant feminism." No equality of genders. Women are seen as God-destined to play subordinate social roles, so films featuring female protagonists do not usually enjoy their approval.

8. **Secularism.** No "radical secularism." Evangelicals discourage films that equate goodness and charity as springing from human nature, not biblical commandments. They demand no depictions of religion as foolish, dangerous, or dogmatic.

Filmmakers have learned that these issues are taken very seriously by evangelicals, and their code is now taken seriously by mainstream filmmakers.

Audience

The evangelical audience, and the box office revenues it represents, continues to gain Hollywood's attention as studios race to fund or produce Christian-friendly productions. Major studios currently hire scores of Christian focus groups for advanced screenings of all films intended for general audiences and even for PG features. The recent increase in Christian-friendly features and the toning down of antireligious sentiment amount to a new Production Code designed by and for evangelicals. This code contains rules and regulations, which, although unwritten, already impact Hollywood. Because of evangelicals' demonstrated box office impact, producers currently devote resources to producing films reflecting their attitudes and beliefs.

Starting around 2004, Christian film rating services and newsletters established themselves as powerful successors of the Catholic Legion of Decency. Christian conservatives quickly focused their growing influence on producers, demanding more films geared for general admission audiences. Currently, several "Pray for Hollywood" associations pressure producers through group prayer. One large prayer meeting devoted to movie transformation captured headlines during the summer of 2005, and the list of prayer groups, including the influential Hollywood Prayer Watch, continues to pressure producers into being more movement-friendly.[17] Apparently their efforts have helped to convince producers to turn out increasing numbers of G and PG films.

Boycott

In a move that harks back to the Catholic Legion of Decency's threatened boycott of Hollywood in 1933, today's evangelicals regularly threaten the major studios with a new religious boycott if they fail to respond to evangelical desires and concerns. Due in part to industry fears of this boycott, filmmakers have begun to make significant concessions to the movement. Officially, Hollywood listens to evangelicals and attempts to allay their concerns while catering to their needs. Unofficially, moguls distrust and fear religious fundamentalists because of bitter past experiences with religious boycotts. Therefore, it becomes expedient to offer more G and PG features and more religious-themed movies.

Evangelicals routinely capture headlines by protesting Hollywood's most provocative films, including *The Last Temptation of Christ, The DaVinci Code, Kinsey, Good Night and Good Luck, Fahrenheit 9/11, An Inconvenient Truth,* and *Sicko.* These films provoked outrage among evangelicals and also inspired some answer films and renewed prayer vigils and e-mail campaigns to studios and the MPAA. The reaction to Martin Scorsese's *The Last Temptation of Christ* (1988) illustrates the movement's power even decades ago, surpassing past Christian efforts to pressure Hollywood.

Scorsese had reputedly sought studio backing for his film version of Nikos Kazantza-kis's controversial 1948 novel, scripted by Paul Schrader, about a decidedly different Jesus (Willem Dafoe) who works as a cross maker for the Romans. Jesus chooses this line of work to spite God, because "God loves me and I can't stand the pain." When Universal Studios committed to Scorsese's project the studio hired Tim Penland, a Christian marketing consultant, to assuage influential Christians about the film, but Penland resigned after the studio ignored his suggestions for improvements and joined a growing group of angry Christians determined to thwart the film. The Reverend Donald Wildmon, head of the evangelical American Family Association, demanded that the studio cease production of a film he judged "is absolutely the most perverted, distorted concept of the historical Jesus I have ever read." Wildmon's organization mailed 2.5 million "action packets" to 170,000 evangelical ministers outlining the film's biblical shortcomings and obtained a commitment from San Antonio, Texas, theater owners not to show Scorsese's film. Finally, two hundred members of the fundamentalist Baptist Tabernacle began picketing outside the studio, and protesters picketed every theater involved in the film's opening. Defying the Supreme Court ban on prior censorship, cities across the nation, including New Orleans, Santa Ana, California, and Salt Lake City, banned the film. Thieves stole a print scheduled to screen in Salt Lake City and slashed theater seats. Vandals also slashed seats in theaters in Los Angeles. One reason for the vehemence of the attacks appears to have been the frustrations of conservative Christians in the wake of the scandals involving televangelists Jimmy Swaggart and Jim Bakker.[18]

In addition to the access to producers by evangelical lobbyists, focus groups, and prayer vigils, the financial success of Christian-themed films caused filmmakers to give the movement a second look. Evangelicals find common cause with orthodox Catholics like filmmaker Mel Gibson as well as with "renewalists," those who speak in tongues, like many Pentecostal denominations, and charismatics, non-Pentecostals who also speak in tongues or engage in other forms of spiritualism. According to a recent report issued by the Pew Forum on Religion and Public Life, renewalists now make up an impressive 23 percent of the total U.S. population.[19] When we add these to self-described evangelicals, orthodox Catholics, and orthodox Jews, we find that conservative religious adherents now account for almost half of the total population and represent an impressive audience for Hollywood films.

Movie Ratings

Ever since the evangelical audience made itself known through its massive support of Mel Gibson's *The Passion of the Christ* (2004), religious movie rating services have enjoyed a rapid increase in subscribers. These new rating services, despite their brief existence, increasingly impact Hollywood. In 2004 *Christianity Today,* which describes itself as "a magazine of evangelical conviction," began an online movie review feature, Christianitytodaymovies.com. The review currently receives 125,000 log-ins per month. HollywoodJesus.com, which devotes itself to "pop culture from a religious point of view," reportedly receives 1 million visitors each month. More than 2 million film viewers receive one of the publications of Focus on the Family, founded by conservative minister Dr. James Dobson. Robert Johnson, from the Fuller Theological Seminary in Pasadena, California, explains that evangelicals have increased their focus on movies because "there's been a recognition within the evangelical community that movies have become a primary means, perhaps the primary means, of telling our children's stories."[20] Evangelical scrutiny of movies translates into power over film language and content, but now the movement prefers to condemn objectionable films in print rather than organize pickets or protests. Stuart Shepard, editor of Focus on the Family's e-mail updates, which go out to 115,000 subscribers, noted that his organization decided against protesting Ang Lee's *Brokeback Mountain* (2005), a film that chronicles the homosexual love between two ranch hands. "We're not going to go out and protest it because it would probably play into the marketing plans of the producers," he noted after the film's release.[21] Currently, evangelicals prefer to use the power of the press (and the Internet) to enforce Christian boycotts against films they dislike. Even Catholics have abandoned direct protest and outright censorship. The U.S. Catholic Bishops' Office for Film and Broadcasting (OFB) provides a comprehensive rating system for orthodox Catholic viewers. The OFB rating system consists of five main designations:

1. A-I (morally unobjectionable for general patronage).
2. A-II (morally unobjectionable for adults and adolescents).
3. A-III (morally unobjectionable for adults).
4. L (limited adult audience—films whose problematic film content many adults would find troubling).
5. O (morally offensive).

The OFB offered a highly critical review of the acclaimed documentary *Fast Food Nation* (2006) by director Richard Linklater about the abuses, both nutritional and humanitarian, in the fast food industry. Linklater's documentary received widespread critical acclaim, yet the OFB reviewer offers the following negative analysis: "Rough and crude language, a couple of briefly intense, if nongraphic, sexual encounters, fleeting partial nudity, innuendo, some gruesome slaughterhouse shots and drug references." The review concludes with an L rating.[22]

Clint Eastwood's *Flags of Our Fathers* (2006) also received a mixed review from the OFB. Eastwood's film depicts the story behind the famous flag-raising at Iwo Jima during World War II. The reviewer warns of "graphic images of combat violence and gore, as well as recurring rough and crude language and profanity." Eastwood's film earned an A-III rating (adults only). *Happy Feet* (2006), a computer-animated story of a tap-dancing penguin in Antarctica who becomes banished by his puritanical elders for his excessive dancing, garnered some rebukes for "too many themes—tolerance, conformity, environmental responsibility." The review concludes with objections to "some mildly rude humor and innuendo, as well as some menace and two frightening sequences that may upset very young viewers." The OFB rates this film A-II, suitable only for adults and adolescents, no younger children.

Sherry McMurray reviewed the film in *Christian Spotlight on Entertainment.* She found problems with "the many sexual references and innuendos (keeping with the penguin's sole purpose in life, which is to mate)." Although awarding the film four stars for quality, McMurray affixed a "morally objectionable" label to warn Christian viewers of the content.[23] Evangelical periodicals such as OFB, *Christian Spotlight on Entertainment,* and *Movieguide* screen out films that their reviewers find objectionable. *Movieguide*'s webpage explains that "these days, even films advertised for families are chock full of embarrassing situations and loaded with false worldviews. That's why we write *MovieGuide®*: so families can know before they go."[24] A growing number of Christian rating services now exist, with new ones popping up on the Internet every year. Behind these services lies an unwritten code demanding family values films and opposing promiscuity, adultery, and homosexuality. Politically, these issues also reflect the neoconservative agenda with an emphasis on patriotism, heterosexual families, and capitalist business interests.

Violence

Conservatives, including evangelicals, display a great appetite for and acceptance of film violence. The Hays Code tolerated all but the most graphically violent scenes, partly because Joseph Breen, the early code administrator, displayed a tolerance for violence perhaps not unrelated to his Irish origins. Irish culture customarily tolerates fist fights and other masculine contests, and the early cinema certainly reflects that bias. *MarketCast*, a market research organization, revealed in 2005 an interesting connection between violence and conservatives. The study discovered that those who identified themselves as religious conservatives were significantly more likely to view films rated R for violence than were those identifying themselves as religious liberals, by 29 percent to 18 percent.[25] This seeming anomaly, according to Dr. Ted Baehr, *Movieguide* editor, exists because "religious people who are more conservative have less of a problem with using violence to defend themselves and/or to defend the lives of others." In addition, Baehr noted that religious conservatives "are also more likely to favor the death penalty than religious moderates."[26] Therefore, an appetite for movie violence only makes sense given other conservative/ evangelical values. In addition, evangelical films, like Mel Gibson's *The Passion of the Christ,* often revel in violence.

Evangelical Movies

The first evangelical films turned out to be low-budget indies financed by religious organizations and private donations. During the nineties Cloud Ten Pictures released some low-budget features based on the End of Days, including *Apocalypse, Tribulation,* and *Revelation.* These films feature amateurish performances and nonspectacular special effects. However, as evangelical numbers grew, Hollywood took notice, setting the stage for an evangelical invasion of mainstream Hollywood. The invasion, now in its early stages, promises to continue as long as audiences for conservative, religious-themed films remain robust.

The proliferation of evangelical films exposes mass audiences to the movement's underlying ideology and values. From modest beginnings, evangelical films now constitute a significant portion of Hollywood's output. Michael Tolkin's *The Rapture* (1991) marked the first appearance of evangelical content in mainstream Hollywood, although small, independently produced Christian films already screened at church events. Tolkin's subject, the "rapture" depicted in the Book of Revelation, presages Jesus's Second Coming and the End of Days in which the faithful are transported to heaven while the rest of the population perishes and, presumably, goes to hell. Mimi Rogers stars as Sharon, a beautiful young woman who converts to fundamentalist Christianity after a debauched existence as a barhopping swinger. Hearing of the coming Rapture, she takes Mary (Kimberly Cullen), her young daughter, to the desert to await the End of Days. There they encounter the Four Horsemen of the Apocalypse. The plot thickens after Sharon decides to kill Mary so she might ascend directly to heaven in death. After the Four Horsemen begin their grim reaping, the Apocalypse arrives in full force. At that time, mother and daughter are reunited in Limbo, where Sharon must choose whether or not to accept Jesus as her savoir. Unable to do so, she is left alone in a bleak, hellish landscape. Tolkin's film generated critical debate, amidst critical praise for Rogers's acting abilities, but did not inspire a sequel. Nearly a decade passed before evangelical films reappeared.

Andre Van Herden's *Revelation* (1999) envisions a post-Rapture world in which the Antichrist, Franco Malacousso (Nick Mancuso), fulfills biblical prophecy by persecuting Christians and demanding that every citizen on earth don virtual reality helmets on the "Day of Wonders," in which he will proclaim himself the true Messiah. Computer terrorism expert Thorold Stone (Jeff Fahey) fights against the virtual reality conspiracy with the assistance of a dedicated band of underground Christians.

Once again, the evil Antichrist mouths liberal maxims about protecting the weak and supporting everyone while engaged in a nefarious plot to take over the world and thwart prophecy. "You will renounce Jesus or you're going to die," he warns. In the Day of Wonders sequence Van Herden blocks out all scenery, leaving only the characters in a stark world of virtual reality. Stone, an atheist, struggles with his beliefs throughout most of the movie, but as prophecy unfolds he converts to Christianity, just in time to help save the world from evil forces.

The first evangelical film arrived in mall theaters during 2000, with Vic Sarin's *Left Behind* (2000), a low-budget film based on a novel by the Reverend Timothy LaHaye and Jerry B. Jenkins that, like *The Rapture,* chronicles the End of Days. Early in the film thousands of adults and children mysteriously disappear in an apocalyptic Rapture. Soon, the Antichrist, Nicolae Carpathia (Gordon Currie), appears and assumes control of the United Nations (UN). Next, he attempts to wrest control of the world's food supply to give Satan, his boss, the power of life and death over humans. *Left Behind* plays upon conservative distrust of the UN (a remnant of the McCarthy era), nuclear disarmament, and foreign nations' ganging up on the United States by unifying their currencies. Carpathia, the evil Russian Antichrist, seems a holdout from the cold war days. Sarin's film strongly condemns extramarital relationships. Airline pilot Rayford Steele (Brad Johnson) pays a heavy price for his flirtations with an attractive flight attendant. While his wife and daughter ascend to heaven in the Rapture, Steele must remain behind because of his indiscretions. The only kind of sexuality sanctioned in this film is that between married characters.

In 2001 Cloud Ten films released the next installment in the series, *Deceived: Left Behind—a World at War,* an unrated feature film starring Judd Nelson as Jack Jones. Directed by Andre Van Heerden and produced by Nicolas D. Tabarrok, the film explores evangelical themes by tying them into the search for extraterrestrial life. *Deceived* revolves around an observatory in California's Sierra Nevada mountains that apparently receives a powerful transmission from another world. However, the transmission turns listeners into psychotics who end up killing each other. The message comes not from another planet but directly from hell, designed to hasten the End of Days. Jack Jones and Kara Walsh, his former girlfriend, manage to prevent the evil transcription from leaving the observatory, thanks to God's answering their prayers. The film follows the standard evangelical format of emphasizing fidelity and male dominance while featuring modern interpretations of biblical prophecy.

The *Left Behind* series enjoyed modest box office returns, but it set the stage for more important films that followed, including Mel Gibson's *The Passion of the Christ* (2004), the first evangelical blockbuster despite Gibson's conservative Catholicism. Gibson's film depicting Christ's scourging and death premiered in conservative Catholic and evangelical churches across the country in 2003, where Gibson often appeared in person at advanced screenings. When *The Passion* officially opened on

Jesus (Jim Caviezel) undergoing scourging in Mel Gibson's *The Passion of the Christ* (2004), a favorite of the evangelical movement. (Copyright 2004 Newmarket Film Group)

Easter 2004, it instantly became a box office hit, earning more than $370 million in the United States and more than $670 million worldwide. More than any other film, *The Passion* signaled the arrival of conservative religious influence on Hollywood.[27] It appealed to conservative Christians of every denomination, while infuriating many Jews. While the film was still in production rabbis Marvin Hier and Abraham Foxman from the Simon Wiesenthal Center and the Anti-Defamation League (ADL) blasted Gibson's film as "new anti-Semitism." The ADL issued a news release in which it offered to "advise" the production company regarding the proper methods to depict Jews in the film. Upon the film's release, Foxman demanded that the Vatican condemn Gibson's film, and Hier of the Simon Wiesenthal Center unleashed an attack.[28] Gibson promptly denied charges of anti-Semitism, even though his father belonged to an anti-Semitic sect of Catholicism. The issue of anti-Semitism returned to the spotlight after Gibson's arrest in 2006 for DUI, in which the inebriated filmmaker reportedly berated one of the arresting officers with anti-Semitic epithets.

Faced with the overwhelming financial success that *The Passion* generated (it was one of the top-grossing films of 2004), and anxious to tap that new market, studios immediately gave green lights to additional religious-themed films, including an A-budget version of the *Left Behind* series, *The Exorcism of Emily Rose,* and *The Chronicles of Narnia: The Lion, the Witch, and the Wardrobe. Narnia,* made on a big budget despite its appeal to children, has been called a "$150 million tithe, Hollywood's biggest gift to Christians since Cecil B. DeMille's *The Ten Commandments.*" By the fall of 2006 *Narnia* had earned a hefty $744 million, making it one of the year's most profitable films.[29] The sequel, *The Chronicles of Narnia: Prince Caspian,* appeared in 2008, another example of the rising power of evangelicals in Hollywood.

Bill Corcoran's *Left Behind II: Tribulation Force* opened in 2005 in theaters throughout the country. Corcoran's film appears slicker and more professional than the earlier effort. It stars Kirk Cameron as Buck Williams, a popular television journalist. Williams teams up with a group of evangelical Christians who meets in an urban church. Airline Captain Rayford Steele (Brad Johnson) and his daughter Chloe (Janaya Stephens) also belong to the group, which forms after The Rapture instantaneously transports hundreds of millions of dedicated Christians, and every young child, into heaven. Thus the setting for the sequel immediately follows the focus of the action in the pilot film. Like the original, Corcoran's version features Antichrist Nicolae Carpathia (Gordon Currie), who, as a Russian, immediately evokes images of the USSR and the cold war. Carpathia's agenda as UN secretary-general begins with unifying the world's currencies, which, in the earth's chaotic state, does not present much of a problem to the charismatic Carpathia. Next, he establishes a world religion and crafts its mantra: "There is no heaven or hell, there is just us, here, now. Let us not look beyond ourselves, let us look to ourselves." The new "religion" hopes for world peace and a united, global

The White Witch (Tilda Swinton) and Peter Pevensie (William Moseley) in Andrew Adamson's *The Chronicles of Narnia: The Lion, the Witch, and the Wardrobe* (2005), a favorite with evangelicals. (Copyright 2005 Walt Disney Productions)

community. To religious conservatives, this amounts to the twin evils of liberalism and secular humanism.

Craig Baxley's *Left Behind III: The World at War* (2005) followed, becoming the first big-budget offering of the series. The Sony-produced version enjoyed robust box office sales, another sign of the growing popularity of evangelical films. Baxley's film portrays a clash between the Antichrist world leader Nicolae Carpathia (Gordon Currie) and U.S. president Gerald Fitzhugh (Louis Gossett, Jr.). After the United States descends into chaos, Fitzhugh converts to Christianity and fights Carpathia with the aid of the Militia, a small group of dedicated Christians. The film pits the Militia against the forces of the Antichrist, which resemble traditional liberals in their quest for peace through world unity. The Global Community (UN) demands gun control. Carpathia, the Antichrist, comes off in the film as a liberal. A follower explains, "He's always talking about the greater good and world peace." Furthermore, the Global Community, headed by Carpathia, oppresses Christians, suppresses the Bible as "hate literature," and confiscates private firearms. In this film privately owned firearms wielded by evangelicals ultimately save the world from Satan.

The *Left Behind* series evokes the earlier prefeminist world in which traditional marriages prevail and women play subordinate roles. The final denouement in the third installment occurs as a double wedding between protagonists Buck Williams (Kirk Cameron) and Chloe Steele (Janaya Stephens), while Captain Ray Steele marries Amanda White (Laura Catalano) after successfully rebuffing his ex-girlfriend Haddie Durham's (Chelsea Noble) sexual advances, thereby avoiding the mistake he made by dating Haddie during the first episode. Each character writes his/her wedding vows. Buck tells Chloe, "From the moment I met you I knew I had never known love before." Buck and Chloe's relationship epitomizes evangelical-style marriage by providing men with the leading roles ("I choose you to be my wife") and women with supportive roles ("To be yours and yours alone"). Characters in evangelical films find themselves punished for premarital and extramarital relationships, like Ray Steele's and Haddie Durham's. They discover happiness only by remaining chaste, like Buck and Chloe.

Catherine Hardwick's *The Nativity Story* (2006) continues in the religious tradition. Released just before Christmas 2006, the film follows the life of Mary and Joseph from the time that the angel appeared to Mary to the birth of Jesus in Bethlehem. The film depicts a variety of historical events sacred to Christians, including Mary's visit to Elizabeth, who, at an advanced age, is pregnant with John the Baptist; the journey of Mary and Joseph from Nazareth to Bethlehem; the journey of the Magi; the Star of Bethlehem; and the vengeful rage of King Herod. Screenwriter Mike Rich draws heavily from the Christian Gospels, and, to ensure acceptance among religious audiences, a number of Catholic, Protestant, and Jewish theologians were also consulted. The film depicts Jesus as a god who appears magically to serve as world redeemer.

Andrew Fleming's *Nancy Drew* (2007), a reprise of the classic girl detective novels of the past, received rave reviews from evangelical media and mixed or negative reviews from secular critics. Fleming's film stars Emma Roberts as Nancy Drew, girl detective. Drew achieves notoriety in her hometown of River Heights by thwarting a robbery of a church. Drew takes the thieves inside the church, which contains statues of Jesus and the saints, and the sacred setting helps her convince them to turn state's evidence. The film functions as a kind of Christian allegory, with Drew serving as a moral, virginal proponent of Christian morality. The blend of forties nostalgia and Drew's fresh-faced virginity, along with the Christian symbolism, guaranteed an enthusiastic reception among evangelicals. *Movieguide* awarded it four stars and commended it for its "very strong Christian worldview."[30]

Fleming's film is only one of many recent offerings designed to appeal to evangelicals, including *Bridge to Terabithia; Dreamer; The Chronicles of Narnia: The Lion, the Witch, and the Wardrobe;* and *Nancy Drew.* By 2009 *The Chronicles of Narnia: The Lion, the Witch, and the Wardrobe* and *The Chronicles of Narnia: Prince Caspian* had earned more than $1 billion in box office receipts.[31] This figure does not include the substantial earnings of evangelical-influenced films like *Bridge to Terabithia, Dreamer,* and the End of Days films. All of these films owe debts to Gibson's *The Passion of the Christ* for breaking the ice. The impressive financial success of evangelical films testifies to the growing influence of evangelicalism and its increasing impact on Hollywood films. Other recent evangelical films include *Beauty and the Beast: A Later-Day Tale* (2007), *The Pirates Who Don't Do Anything* (2008), *Resurrection* (2009), and a rumored Christian alternative to the Harry Potter series. The popular film series based on the novels of J. K. Rowling (2001–2009) inspired intense evangelical disapproval due to their themes of magic and sorcery, but until recently the movement has satisfied itself with attacking the Harry Potter films in reviews. Now it appears they will be answered in films.

Twentieth Century Fox paid a tribute to the evangelical movement in 2006 by creating a new division, Fox Faith, for Christian-oriented films. Fox began its outreach to evangelicals by selling low-budget Christian-based films on DVDs. These films feature no recognizable stars and include *Love Comes Softly, Woman Thou Art Loosed,* and *The Visitation.* These films sell at Christian retail outlets and in stores like Target and Wal-Mart. After the success of these ventures, Fox believes its new division will profit even more by producing bigger-budget Christian films. Fox, like Disney and others, continues to acknowledge the economic power of Christian audiences by producing more family-oriented films. A Fox executive explained that while the studio sought to avoid producing films with overt political overtones, like antiabortion features, it intends to focus the new division on "quality, story-driven entertainment that meshes with the values of our target audience."[32]

In 2006 *Jesus Camp,* a controversial documentary by Heidi Ewing and Rachel Grady about a Pentecostal children's summer camp located near Devils Lake, North Dakota, and run by the Reverend Becky Fischer, appeared. Three children who attended the camp in the summer of 2005—Levi, Rachael, and Tory (Victoria)—serve as the film's main characters, although it also features speakers from a prior conference held at Christ Triumphant Church in Lee's Summit, Missouri, most notably evangelist leader Ted Haggard. The subject of intense media interest, Ewing and Grady's film garnered an Academy Award nomination for Best Documentary, losing to Al Gore and Davis Guggenheim's *An Inconvenient Truth.* The controversy surrounds charges that the primary school–aged children were being indoctrinated with "far right" ideology, a charge vehemently disputed by the filmmakers and by evangelicals. Reverend Haggard, however, former head of the evangelical movement in the United States, charges that the film inadvertently demonizes evangelicals while inculcating a "sinister agenda." One scene features a cardboard likeness of President George W. Bush, which the children allegedly treat as a saint. The children learn that they hold the key to Jesus' return and as "Kids on Fire" must become an Army of God.[33] *New York Times* critic Steven Holden likened the idea of a children's army to the youthful Red Guards in Maoist China that wreaked havoc throughout that nation during the seventies. "It wasn't so long ago that another puritanical youth army, Mao Zedong's Red Guards, turned the world's most populous country inside out. Nowadays the possibility of a right-wing Christian American version of what happened in China no longer seems entirely far-fetched."[34]

Mainstream Influence

Religious conservatives increasingly influence Hollywood, even in apparently nonreligious films. Stephen Spielberg's *War of the Worlds* (2005), for example, echoes the millennial feel of evangelical End of Days films. Others, including the latest version of *The Exorcist,* also evoke biblical themes involving supernatural demons and spirits. In addition, studios now present Christian characters, even in minor roles, in more positive lights. Even television series now reflect religion's growing influence, including series like *Ghost Whisperer, Medium,* and *Three Wishes.* Each of these, like the above-mentioned films, evokes unseen worlds populated by spirits. Today's evangelical movement, like the New Age movement of the seventies and eighties, views events through a magical perspective.

Currently even A-budget films often bear the marks of behind-the-scenes religious pressure. Evangelical businessman Philip Anschutz produced Taylor Hackford's *Ray* (2004), an Academy Award–winning docudrama about singer Ray Charles. This film garnered an Academy Award for actor Jamie Foxx as well as one for Best Sound Mixing. Anschutz reportedly demanded that Hackford soften Charles's womanizing and drug addiction to render Charles more palatable to audiences, especially Christians. The 2005 DVD edition includes the major deleted scenes in an appendix. Some depict Charles smoking marijuana. Another shows Charles exploring his own sexuality for the first time, fondling and caressing a young woman's hand and forearm. Still another features Della, Charles's wife (Regina King), listening to a sermon in which a minister blasts Charles's music: "This is a colored man bringing the wrath of God down on other colored people. Stealing riches from the Lord and using them for the Devil's work." He concludes with "Ray Charles is gonna burn in hell!"

Today many films feature apocalyptic climaxes or End Times scenarios. A number of recent sci-fi films feature violent alien invasions, apocalyptic events by any reckoning. Films like *Independence Day* (1996), *Mars Attacks* (1996), *War of the Worlds* (2005), and *The Reaping* (2007) evoke Revelation-like images of impending doom. These are joined by films featuring apocalyptic avengers from the future (*The Terminator, Terminator 2: Judgment Day,* and *Terminator 3: Rise of the Machines*). These are joined by yet another group of apocalyptic films featuring terrorist-driven doomsday scenarios (*The Sum of All Fears, XXX, The Peacemaker*). Add this to films like

Armageddon (1998) and *The Day After Tomorrow* (2004), about the threat of annihilation by extreme global cooling resulting in a new Ice Age, and you have a pattern of paranoia about impending doom from factors outside of our control. But whether the threat comes from alien invasions, futuristic robots, international terrorists, asteroids from outer space, or global cooling, the effect on viewers is to cause anxiety and fear about an apocalyptical event beyond human control. It sounds very much like the End of Days.

Currently, conservative Christianity deeply permeates mainstream Hollywood films, and not only through end-of-days millennialism. Major studios now promote positive Christian characters. The sleazy Elmer Gantry–type charlatans of the past have transformed into friendly, clean Christian characters. Sylvester Stallone's *Rambo* (2008), for example, features a band of evangelical missionaries who are also doctors and other health care workers. Their mission is to minister to the Karen community in Burma (Myanmar). The church, which used to be markedly absent from movies, appears with increasing frequency, and filmmakers increasingly depict Christians and churches positively. For example, in the 2007 Disney film *Bridge to Terabithia*, directed by Gabor Usepo, the teenage stars, Jess Arrons (Josh Hutcherson) and Leslie Burke (Annasophia Robb), attend church services together. The seventh-grade couple enjoys a presexual relationship, which ends tragically with Leslie's drowning. The film leaves unexpressed the underlying sexual attraction between the two underage characters, focusing instead on their imaginary deep-woods kingdom, which comes into being through the creative power of their imaginations. This film, produced by Lauren Lavine and David Paterson, who also coproduced *The Chronicles of Narnia*, was widely shown on airplanes. Without the influence of evangelicalism and orthodox Catholicism on mainstream cinema, it is doubtful if a director would have included the church scene, since it serves no real narrative purpose. Usepo's film depicts positive images of the church, underlying its importance in the family and community.

Recent family films like *Dreamer, The Chronicles of Narnia*, and *Bridge to Terabithia*, and animated films like *Meet the Robinsons, Toy Story, A Bug's Life, Finding Nemo, Wall E*, and *Toy Story* are visible reminders of the power of conservative Christian audiences to persuade producers to offer G- and PG-rated films like these. In addition, a 2005 study revealed that R-rated movie production had declined by 12 percent over a ten-year period, and G-rated production rose 38 percent.[35] The success of these evangelical-friendly movies helped Hollywood's Christian-themed or Christian-friendly films to earn substantially more money than R-rated features, according to a recent study. Researchers compared the earnings of religious-themed films like *The Passion of the Christ, The Gospel of John*, and *The Chronicles of Narnia*, and Christian allegories like *Spiderman 3* and *Spiderman Returns*. The study also counted "morally uplifting" films like *Master and*

Commander, Piglet's Big Movie, Lilo and Stitch, The Rookie, Spy Kids 2, Cars, Charlotte's Web, The Queen, Invisible, Madagascar, Chicken Little, Pride and Prejudice, Because of Winn-Dixie, National Treasure, and *Collateral.* Researchers contrasted these earnings with the revenues of "non-Christian worldview" offerings, including *Fahrenheit 9/11, The DaVinci Code, Borat, Beerfest, Transamerica, Kill Bill 2, Latter Days, The Motorcycle Diaries, Harry Potter and the Goblet of Fire, The Ant Bully, The Black Dahlia, Jack-Ass, Number Two, Lady in the Water, Brokeback Mountain, V for Vendetta, Another Gay Movie, Saw II, Saved!, Bad Santa, Freddie vs. Jason,* and *Gigli.* The researchers found that those films expressing "very strong anti-Christian worldviews" earned, on average, around $18 million, while "very strong Christian worldview" films earned, on average, $65 million, or 3.5 times more.[36] In response to earnings like these, Hollywood is now more willing than ever before to fund Christian-oriented films.

Culture Wars

In 2006 a bitter dispute erupted over the game version of the popular *Left Behind* novels and films, depicting the End of Days, over the game's rules, in which players must either convert or kill non-Christians. Left Behind Games CEO Jeffrey Frichner argues that the game actually promotes pacifism because players lose "spirit points" each time they murder nonbelievers rather than convert them. Players gain "spirit points" each time they decide to make their character pray. To Frichner, a player of the Left Behind game becomes "a sort of a freedom fighter." Clark Stevens, codirector of the Campaign to Defend the Constitution, argues that the game promotes violence and intolerance, not pacifism. "Sure, there is no blood (the dead fade off the screen). But you are mowing down your enemy with a gun. It pushes a message of religious intolerance. You can either play for the 'good side' by trying to convert nonbelievers to your side or join the Antichrist." The Reverend Tim Simpson, president of the Christian Alliance for Progress, warned that "under the Christmas tree this year for little Johnny is this allegedly Christian video game teaching Johnny to hate and kill." The game's use of Muslim-sounding names for its villains also raises concerns about intolerance for mainstream Christians.[37] Violence and intolerance do not seem out of place among evangelicals, who focus much of their energy on targeting gays and abortion clinics.

Politics

The evangelical movement supports the neoconservative political movement of recent decades. Neoconservatives advocate a robust, aggressive U.S. foreign policy coupled with a strongly probusiness regulatory environment. Neocons distrust government at all levels and so happily advocate large federal budget deficits and massive tax cuts for the wealthier segments of the population. This movement, closely allied with conservative Christian and Jewish elements, finally gained political power and vastly increased influence with the election of George W. Bush. Bush's evangelicalism serves as an ideal accompaniment to his neoconservatism. Both elements contributed significantly to his elections in 2000 and 2004, as well as to the creation of Republican majorities in Congress in 1994 through 2006.

Evangelicals, as well as neoconservatives, blame Hollywood for many of the nation's ills. Ted Baehr explains that reform of Hollywood represents the road to political renewal. "The mass media creates [sic] the culture that elects the politicians and legislators who write your laws," he explains. "The politicians and legislators appoint the bureaucrats and judges who execute and interpret those laws. They also hire the government teachers and public school administrators who most likely educate your children." Therefore, argues Baehr, the key to political reform lies with cleaning up Hollywood. The mass media, according to Baehr, create "a culture that is so dumbed down and polluted with explicit sex, graphic violence, obscene language, and perversity that many Americans have lost all sense and sensibility."[38] Baehr's remarks echo many others in the evangelical and neoconservative movements, which greatly overlap each other.

MPAA Challenged

In a major triumph in its efforts to make Hollywood more pro-Christian the evangelical movement recently succeeded in reversing the long-standing MPAA rule mandating that any film containing a "theological element" receive at least a PG rating, not the more lucrative G rating. After the MPAA awarded *Facing the Giants* (2007) a PG for "evangelistic Christian elements" the ratings board received more than 15,000 e-mails from angry evangelicals protesting the rating.[39] Evangelicals viewed the MPAA policy as "anti-Christian bigotry." Christian groups, including a delegation from the Christian Film and Television Commission, lobbied Joan Graves, chair of the MPAA ratings board, about the issue. In response, Graves assured a group of evangelical leaders attending a meeting in Washington, D.C., that the MPAA would no longer automatically award PG ratings to films with religious content. Evangelical lobbyists then pressed Graves to appoint representatives from the evangelical community to the ratings board. Although she declined to make a commitment to add evangelicals to the ratings board, the issue will undoubtedly arise in the future as the movement's influence continues to expand.[40] With this decision, the MPAA acquiesced to Christian demands, bringing studios one step closer to embracing the evangelical code.

Gender Roles

Evangelicalism revived the flagging "good girl" archetypes of the Hays Code. Women in evangelical films either exhibit purity, or, if they do not, the filmmakers depict them as sinners. Female characters in evangelical films often begin as sinners and, after conversion to evangelicalism, end up adopting modest, conservative lifestyles. Evangelical women never stray from their husbands, nor do they engage in premarital sex. Chloe Steele of the *Left Behind* series remains chaste and, presumably, virginal throughout the films until her marriage to Buck Williams, unlike other female characters who succumb to premarital or extramarital sexual temptations. Evangelical women like Chloe serve in supportive roles, never in leadership positions. Their service can include scheduling appointments, preparing meals, or reading biblical verses to patients. Evangelical characters represent the cinematic equivalence of the "church woman."

Evangelical males dominate all relationships. They rarely cheat on their wives or girlfriends and always act as their protectors. If, like Captain Ray Steele in *Left Behind II*, they stray from the marriage bed they pay severely for their indiscretions. Similarly, Buck Williams, *Left Behind II*'s protagonist, remains chaste and pure, suppressing all desires, only favoring his platonic girlfriend Chloe with a discrete peck on the cheek as they bid farewell, perhaps for the last time. Like the heroes of the fifties classic Westerns, today's evangelical male characters represent the ultimate family values heroes: strong, silent, and commanding. Evangelical males model what many U.S. men fantasize about: complete domination over loyal, obedient wives. However, if today's demographic data are any indication, the evangelical code's role models are unrealistic and unavailable to most Americans.

Evangelical filmmakers are often challenged to create characters attractive enough and deviant enough to attract audiences. When evangelicals advocate celibacy for all except heterosexual married couples, one wonders how their filmmakers can create characters deviant enough to attract audiences. Oscar Wilde wrote that everyone must have a "redeeming social vice," so how is that possible with holier-than-thou evangelical characters? Can chastity attract audiences? At times, it has been difficult for evangelicals to create compelling characters simply because they must be held accountable to an unrealistic (as far as movies are concerned) code of conduct. In order to circumvent this problem some evangelical filmmakers provide their characters with interesting back stories of sexual transgression. *Left Behind*'s creators, for example, rely on this strategy for circumventing the evangelical prohibition against adultery and promiscuity.

Creating the Couple

For evangelicals, marriages are made in heaven, not on earth. They believe ardently in the deep, unspoken myth that God selects one ideal mate for everyone and makes their union possible if they truly believe in him. To evangelicals, relationships, like all other issues, constitute matters of faith. If people open their hearts to God and obey his commandments, they will be successful in finding mates. Once one's mate is found and wed, nothing can prevent complete happiness. Even after her Rapture, Captain Ray Steele remains faithful to his wife and longs for the time when they will reunite in heaven. Premarital and extramarital sex are left to the villains. Nicolae Carpathia, the evil Antichrist in the *Left Behind* series, enjoys the favors of many, including the beautiful but lustful Haddie. Unlike the villains, however, the protagonists remain chaste. Sex will be their ultimate reward, but only through the sanctity of marriage.

The evangelical movement continues to influence films, from Hollywood to the MPAA. The popularity of evangelical films like the *Left Behind* series; *The Passion of the Christ; The Chronicles of Narnia: The Lion, the Witch, and the Wardrobe;* and *The Nativity Story* illustrate the rising power of the movement. The recent popularity of evangelical-friendly films like *Dreamer* and *Bridge to Terabithia* will ensure even bigger budgets and more productions in the future. Today, Hollywood continues to target the vast evangelical audience with family-values films and films depicting the End of Days. The effect of evangelicals' efforts to change Hollywood has been little short of miraculous. According to an evangelical survey conducted in 2007 the percent of movies released with "positive moral content" increased from 26 percent in 1991 to 73 percent by 2006. Movies with Christian content increased 60 percent since 1999.[41]

Conservative religious-oriented audiences demand films that reflect positive views of religious themes. They seek films reflecting "family values," which often means films in which white males play leading roles, do not engage in fornication, and support nuclear families. Evangelicals support films with patriotic, pro-American themes and characters, as well as biblical themes. They prefer movies with clearly religious themes such as *Constantine, The Exorcism of Emily Rose, The Chronicles of Narnia: The Lion, the Witch, and the Wardrobe*, and *The Chronicles of Narnia: Prince Caspian* along with *The Passion of the Christ*.[42]

Evangelicals shun films that showcase secular, liberal, or progressive protagonists, like *Syriana, Good Night and Good Luck, Brokeback Mountain, Breakfast on Pluto, Transamerica, Casanova, The Constant Gardener, Match Point, State of the Union, Mr. and Mrs. Smith, North Country, The Family Stone, Dear Wendy, Rent,* and *The New World,* among many others. These films contain socialist, communist, or anti-American propaganda, according to the article.[43] They obviously present themes and issues repugnant to evangelicals. Today, powerful evangelicals like Ted Baehr lobby Hollywood to "clean up" their offerings by making them more palatable to evangelicals. Baehr's editorials appear regularly in the *New York Times* and the *Wall Street Journal.* His growing stature in the industry exemplifies the potency of the evangelical movement in Hollywood.

Evangelicals hold Darwin's Theory of Evolution as little more than subtle Satanism. Nathan Frankowski's *Exposed: No Intelligence Allowed* (2008) documents the fierce discrimination allegedly employed against adherents of the Theory of Intelligent Design. Frankowski's documentary, narrated by Ben Stein, who cowrote the script, depicts a patently evil cabal arrayed unfairly and unprofessionally against innocent adherents to Intelligent Design. These scientists are fired, denied tenure, and otherwise harassed by bureaucrats who are depicted as mindless idiots and Nazis. Despite the film's heavy hand, it may illuminate turf-guarding by highly placed members of academe. The movie's marketing plan, masterminded by Premise Media, involves free tickets for evangelicals. The same company handled marketing for *The Passion of the Christ* and *The Chronicles of Narnia.* In each of these cases, the company premarketed the movie to evangelicals and other conservative Christian and Jewish congregations.

The Valenti Code allows greater permissiveness and increased realism in films. Nudity, banned by the Hays Office, has steadily increased to reflect contemporary mores. As early as 1997 critic Molly Haskell observed that "time was when you could pretty much get through an entertainment season without having to confront the human body in its unadorned state. Now you'd need Bible-belt blinders to escape the omnipresent spectacle of flesh."[44] Sexual subject matter and graphic language have now become the norm in Hollywood. A 2004 study undertaken by the Harvard School of Public Health from 1992 and 2003 found evidence for "ratings creep" and concluded that "the MPAA appears to tolerate increasingly more extreme content in any given age-based rating categories over time." Kimberly Thompson concluded that "when you look at the average, today's PG-13 movies are approaching what the R movies looked like in 1992." Furthermore, noted Thompson, "Today's PG is approaching what PG-13 looked like a decade ago."[45] Changing public attitudes toward the permissible limits of sexual behavior on and off screen have resulted in "ratings creep." *In the Cut, The Cooler,* and *South Park* make the necessary compromises in order to earn R ratings, whereas, twenty or thirty years ago, they would certainly have received the dreaded X designation.

Evidence recently emerged that the number of R-rated movies in the top twenty-five, consisting of the highest box-office grosses, declined significantly between 1996 and 2005, owing partly to evangelical pressure. In 1996, according to Ted Baehr and

Tom Snyder, nearly half, or twelve, included "explicit sex and/or sexual nudity." In 2005 only three sexually explicit films made it into the top twenty-five. Perhaps more telling is the fact that by 2005 nearly 96 percent of the top twenty-five movies contained "morally uplifting or Christian content, up from only 62 percent in 1999."[46] Clearly, these data reveal a sea change in movies during the past decade, brought about in large measure by the evangelical movement.

Naturally, the emerging evangelical code contains strong elements of puritanism and political conservatism, along with remnants of McCarthyism. The movement includes powerful pressure groups intent on imposing their values on Hollywood. The studios, for their part, pay heed to this vocal movement. As a result, audiences increasingly find films sanitized and rendered Christian-friendly without the necessity of any outside assistance from the official censors. Mainstream movies routinely incorporate positive Christian characters and showcase evangelical themes. Evangelical films condemn sexual promiscuity and endorse chastity, orthodoxy, and sobriety. With large studios like Twentieth Century Fox and Disney providing big budgets for evangelically oriented films, the movement's power and influence promise to increase in the future.

The growing power of evangelical audiences signals the probability of even greater evangelical influence on Hollywood in coming seasons. Family values movies like *Madagascar, Charlie and the Chocolate Factory, The Incredibles, Finding Nemo, The Chronicles of Narnia,* and *Dreamer* found success at the box office, inspiring other producers to create family-oriented films. Hot new production companies like Mandalay-Prelude Faith-Based Films also help feed Hollywood's growing appetite for family-oriented, faith-based feature films. The growing success of Disney/Pixar and other animation producers also feeds demand for more family-based films. The financial success of all family-oriented films, especially the religious-themed offerings, guarantees even greater audience exposure. Currently, top evangelical spokespersons like Ted Baehr command Hollywood's attention. As long as they continue to have access to studios through individual/organizational clout and through Christian focus groups and evangelical filmmakers, the movement will continue to shape film history.

At the moment conservative Christians pose a threat to movie realism, sensuality, and sexuality. Evangelicals have already altered the motion picture landscape considerably, and their influence promises to increase. Eventually, however, the movement's influence must surely wane. Eventually the public may tire of religious-oriented films, just as they have with other genres and movements. The pendulum swings in many directions. Evangelicalism, like McCarthyism, may eventually pale. Sales at the box office and sales and rentals of DVDs will ultimately determine the fate of the evangelical code. Only when revenues fall for faith-based films will producers focus on other genres.

Hollywood takes seriously the threat of a new religious boycott, which could well mean the difference between financial health and illness. Eventually, despite censors, filmmakers produce the kinds of films desired by audiences by giving them what they want. However, the movement's power and influence may have already crested and begun to run out of energy. During the fall of 2006 leaders of the evangelical movement held emergency meetings across the country in an attempt to reverse what they viewed as an alarming trend among teenagers to leave the movement. They also met for soul-searching after dramatic Democratic gains in 2008. Recent studies indicate that if current trends continue, only a tiny percent of today's teenage population will be evangelicals when they reach adulthood. As conservative Christians continue to flex their strength, their struggles with religious moderates are rending many Protestant churches into conservative and moderate wings. However, the current dearth of youthful converts and other signs of internal dissatisfaction signal a waning of power and influence. Even if that happens, a new coalition of conservatives will eventually rise to take their place as the pendulum swings once again. Evangelicals now face an ideational turnaround that finds some of the movement's stalwarts out of work and out of touch while newer leaders emerge. As founders Jerry Falwell and James Dobson pass from the scene, a younger generation of popular ministers and theologians like Rick Warren and Bill Hybells advocate widening the agenda to include combating climate change, addressing global poverty, and combating racism. The 2008 presidential elections exposed deep divisions among evangelicals, with many abandoning the Republican Party for the first time. These and other signs inspired the phrase "End Times for evangelicals."[47] The evangelical movement appears at a crossroads, with some wedded to the old issues of antihomosexuality and antiabortion, while others long for an expanded social agenda that would move the movement toward the social and political center. Which way will the movement turn? Whichever the direction, the fact remains that movies will certainly be affected.

CHAPTER SEVEN

Code Reform

Virtually everyone perceives the powerful changes taking place in movies. Most realize the increasing levels of violence and sex in films. Realistic depictions of contemporary sexual mores are becoming scarce while bleak, dystopian narratives of contemporary life proliferate. Today's postmodern thrillers express angst, pessimism, anger, violence, and chaos. Movie censorship, currently rendered through the MPAA, shoulders much of the blame for increasing movie violence. Today's dystopian features include *The Road to Perdition, Rambo,* the *Saw* series, *Independence Day, Hostel, Hannibal, Gladiator,* and *The 300,* many of which are fine films, yet each reflects deep social conflict centered around the current Production Code.

Beneath the surface of the censorship wars lurk powerful pressure groups possessing both overt and covert agendas. Some, including evangelicals, advocate strict limitations on filmic depictions of sexuality, humanism, and feminism, while liberals and progressives advocate restrictions on movie violence. Statistically, evangelical audiences prefer feature films rated "R" for violence more than mainstream audiences do. However, liberals and progressives often denounce violent features. In the current censorship battles religious groups like the Christian Coalition, Focus on the Family, and the World Council of Evangelicals compete with the American Civil Liberties Union (ACLU), the National Association for the Advancement of Colored People (NAACP), and the National Organization for Women (NOW) for influence over the form and content of Hollywood films. Ideological conflicts between these groups translate into controversies over movie ratings. The controversies raised often result in censorship through banning or financial penalties (having to reshoot and reedit scenes) for filmmakers and distributors.

Censorship, varying from strict to lax, appears and reappears throughout film history, although the faces of the censors and the names of the agencies change from era to era. When viewed from a historical perspective, strategies to evade or thwart pressure groups appear remarkably similar over time, while would-be censors of every era resort to similar tactics to control movies. Therefore, one may draw interesting conclusions by viewing censorship wars up close. The result is a fascinating glimpse into the hidden world of movie censorship. Censorship wars provide unique opportunities to witness the deep ideological gulfs over society's most sensitive issues, ranging from social issues like abortion and promiscuity to political issues involving socialism and communism.

Sex

Pioneer filmmakers immediately learned the power of sex to attract audiences, and just as quickly ignited conservative ire and disapproval. Movie sex created censorship, and sexuality continues to play a central role in movie ratings conflicts. Early movies from the turn of the twentieth century like *Fatima, Dolorita, The Kiss,* and *The Gay Shoe Clerk* depict sex at a deep level, unleashing unexpected approbation. These movies outraged adherents of Victorian morality who deemed sexuality "improper" for middle-class people. Concerned citizen groups attempted at first to regulate movies through blue laws and fire regulations regarding theater operation, but after 1907, when Chicago established a board using police powers to enforce Victorianism in movies, cities and states began censoring movies for sexual depictions. During the Hays Code era, official America appeared squeaky clean, and movies reflected that atmosphere. Politicians might get away with an occasional "damn" or "hell," like "give 'em hell Harry" (Truman), but filmmakers never could. Instead, they learned to conceal sexual themes through coded behavior and speech, and in so doing they crafted many movie classics.

Early battles over sexuality reveal deep cultural schisms over gender roles, courtship rules, and behavioral boundaries. Clashes quickly developed between advocates of a realistic view of sexuality and those demanding limiting or denying sexuality. Marty Kline labels the latter "erotophobes," those who fear and despise sexuality. Kline labels those who revere and respect human sexuality "erotophiles." Kline sees these two forces locked in an epic struggle, with both sides convinced of the correctness of their positions and the weakness and folly of their opponents' positions.[1] The history of cinema often reflects power struggles between puritanical elements and permissive forces. In fact, struggles over sexuality erupt throughout film, usually surfacing as film ratings controversies. A close examination of these controversies reveals two opposing perspectives locked in perpetual battle.

Kline's analysis divides individuals into prosex erotophiles and antisex erotophobes. Kline probes their attitudes toward such issues as feminism, liberalism, and multiculturalism. To erotophobes, women should remain in the home, or at least be identified in some way with the "traditional" nuclear family, particularly as it appeared in the fifties. For social and religious conservatives, sex stems from naughty yet pleasurable impulses that humans must learn to control. The sex act is reserved for procreation only, and social conservatives, including evangelicals and orthodox

Catholics, characterize adultery and infidelity as sins representing unnatural human behavior. Officially, they perceive homosexuality as sinful, not biological. Above all, they demand family values films rated no higher than PG-13 in which Christian values and lifestyles prevail. Unofficially, evangelicals prefer violent R-rated features. This contradiction exemplifies a deep division among evangelicals. On the one hand, they abhor violent R-rated movies, yet on the other they consume them more often than nonevangelicals.

Early film history exemplifies Kline's observations regarding sex wars. Erotophiles like Edison and Porter supported freer depictions of sexuality, while erotophobes, including members of the clergy and some of the mayors and police commissioners of several large cities, advocated strict limits on film content, advertising, and audience age. In fact, a strongly erotophobic reaction to early films arose as soon as observers noticed the almost hypnotic attraction of moving images as entertainment. The spectacle of movies catering to working-class immigrants also proved alarming to many middle-class and elite observers. Pioneering filmmakers and distributors responded with legal tactics that were doomed initially to failure. The situation remains essentially the same today. The two factions, erotophiles and erotophobes, continue to clash over movies, but today their interactions are often institutionalized and mediated through committees and self-regulatory organizations.

Erotophobes learned to apply various forms of pressure to the movie industry to ban sexual depictions, nontraditional relationships, any hint at impiety, and a variety of other sensitive issues. As a result of pressure from powerful groups and individuals, many early films depicting sexuality suffered censorship in the form of excised images and scenes or being banned completely. In a later period McCarthyists also forced changes in films and banning, although the chief concerns were more political than social. However, McCarthyists succeeded in suppressing a number of film noir seductresses and inspired a series of cynical "bad cop" noir.[2] Although early industry critics were most upset by film sexuality, they also banned films glorifying stories about outlaws and crimes, like Jesse James and the sensational Stanford White murder trial. Religious films also drew intense scrutiny and criticisms. McCarthyists, in their turn, opposed the freer sexuality of liberal "social problem" films as well as the increasingly probing film noir genre. To McCarthyists, communism and socialism equaled unbridled sexuality, and female communists in anticommunist movies depicted their deepest fears about female sexuality. Ironically, the anticommunist genre produced some of the most blatantly erotic female characters since pre-code days (*Red Menace*).

Censored in their ability to depict sex realistically, filmmakers long ago invented a code of symbols, double entendre, and innuendo to convey sexuality. Instead of directly depicting sexual actions or dialogue, filmmakers learned to simply show characters headed toward a bedroom or walking offscreen with each other. Audiences learned to decode these and other actions connoting but never denoting sexuality. Filmmakers created symbolism and innuendo, and audiences filled in the rest. Filmmakers grew adept at substituting symbols like luxuriant drags on cigarettes, lingering glances, and playful toying with trinkets as substitutes for sex. Symbols and double entendre dialogue created a subtext of sexuality without necessarily offending censors.

Throughout movie history filmmakers have strategized about the sex in their movies, parsing out portions of nudity, racy dialogue, and compromising scenes designed to attract audiences that eventually become negotiated and mediated between censors and producers. Long ago they developed alternative endings, official disclaimers, and other tactics designed to foil censors. From the beginning filmmakers used the legal system to combat censorship. Although their early efforts proved fruitless, by 1965 they had achieved a significant victory over censors when the Supreme Court outlawed prior censorship. However, by many accounts that ruling never went into effect as censors learned to adapt to court rulings and disguise their censorship under legally acceptable rubrics.

The consequences of movie censorship include a reduction in realism and explicit dialogue in exchange for decent ratings. The process involves editing, reediting, and now often reinserting disputed scenes in DVD versions available for rent or purchase. In addition, over the years filmmakers created ploys, strategies, and procedures designed to minimize the censors' bite. They created entire genres like screwball comedy and film noir in order to thwart censors, and in so doing brought some of Hollywood's greatest movies to the screen. The relationship between censor and censored remains tight, since censors owe their very existence to filmmakers, who long ago learned how to handle their harshest critics.

Violence

Pioneering filmmakers soon learned to embellish their films with violence as well as sex. Although sex attracted large audiences to penny arcades and nickelodeons, violence also served as an equally effective audience lure. Thus, from the earliest days of cinema, violence emerged as a powerful audience draw, proving almost as effective as sex in attracting audiences. And these films were rarely banned or censored, unlike the early ones employing sex as an audience lure. As subsequent Production Codes suppressed sex, filmmakers turned increasingly toward violence as a safer lure than sex.

Like earlier codes, the Valenti Code suppresses sexuality and related issues much more than violence. Although the code warns that films should affirm "the basic dignity of human life," it fails to prohibit brutality or graphic violence. Why did Valenti avoid the issue of violence? Perhaps the reason is that violence is not taboo, whereas many forms of sexuality are. Some argue that film violence stems from the general

Naomi Malone (Elizabeth Berkley) does a pole dance in Paul Verhoeven's controversial *Showgirls* (1995), a film categorized by many as "soft porn." (Copyright 1995 United Artists)

violence of society. Since we live in a violent culture, with high crime rates and frequent military adventures, it should come as no surprise that movies contain high levels of violence. Terrorism and counterterrorism also contribute to the overall level of violence. Screen violence therefore reflects wider societal violence, which in turn mirrors film violence.

The Valenti Code not only tolerates violence; from its inception it unleashed it upon the public with a vengeance. After the current MPAA rating system went into effect in the late sixties films like Arthur Penn's *Bonnie and Clyde* (1968), George Roy Hill's *Butch Cassidy and the Sundance Kid* (1969), and Fred Zinnemann's *The Wild Bunch* (1969) marked a watershed with regard to depictions of violence. They included graphic scenes, often filmed in slow motion, for the first time. Penn, Hill, and Zinnemann realized that the new Production Code allowed graphic violence, whereas it placed steep obstacles in the path of depictions of sexuality. Although the trend toward violent films actually began during the film noir and classic Western periods of the forties and fifties, the Valenti Code greatly accelerated that trend. Hollywood studios have relied increasingly on graphic violence to enhance realism and attract audiences. In fact, Hollywood's proviolence reputation stems from its efforts to avoid the more controversial sexual allures while relying on the safer (from the MPAA's perspective) allure of violence. Cinematic violence, though commonplace, is rarely boring, and it is not prohibited by the Valenti Code, whereas most serious sex is. In that sense, the current code's effects on film violence echo the Hays Code's tolerance of violence. As long as Production Code enforcers have to choose between permitting film violence or film sex, they will select violence.

Gangster films, long suppressed by the Hays Code, exploded during the Valenti era, which proved friendlier to the genre, especially with regard to violence. Francis Ford Coppola's *The Godfather* (1972), now considered the best gangster film ever made, initiated a cycle of movies featuring crime bosses, including *The Godfather II* and *III, Mean Streets* (1973), *Once Upon a Time in America* (1984), *The Untouchables* (1987), *Miller's Crossing* (1990), *Goodfellas* (1990), *Reservoir Dogs* (1992), *Carlito's Way* (1993), *Casino* (1995), *Donnie Brasco* (1997), *Road to Perdition* (2002), *The Departed* (2006), and *American Gangster* (2007). Gangster films of the Valenti era flourish, thanks to the Valenti Code's relaxing of older prohibitions against glamorizing gangster heroes. With its relative tolerance for violence and its refusal to censor subject matter directly, the Valenti Code created the best atmosphere for the gangster genre since the pre-code era.

The recent rise of violent films spawned new archetypes, particularly "bad boy" criminals, starting with Freddy and all the other slasher villains, along with violent characters from more recent movies like *Fight Club, Training Day, Cold Mountain,* and *Saw IV,* among many others. *The Silence of the Lambs's* Hannibal Lecter (Anthony Hopkins) and all the other mass murderers descended from Ed Gein, the Wisconsin farmer–turned–mass murderer who made garments from the skin of his victims and reputedly engaged in cannibalism. Hollywood filmmakers who have cribbed details from Gein's life owe him a huge creative debt. In addition to serial killers like Gein and Lecter (and *Dirty Harry's* zodiac killer) are hundreds of copies, including the psychopathic terrorists of the action/adventure genre (*True Lies, Terminator, Air Force One, XXX, End of Days*). Many of these villains are violent, Nazi-like terrorists who will stop at nothing to get their way. They are perhaps manifestations of some of society's most disturbing tendencies. The current rating system promotes these violent characters. In the long run, horrific levels of cinematic violence can be laid directly at the MPAA's door.

Mark Harris charges the MPAA with a gross violation of its duty to protect children from violent images. First, he cites the usual litany of criticism of the Production Code: "Indies have it harder than studio films, naked men are naughtier than naked women, and almost any sex is worse than almost all violence." However, to Harris, the problem runs deeper. "The MPAA has never decided whether its job is guidance or rule making. As a result, four ratings—G, PG, PG-13, and R—are merely advisory." It leads to leniency with regard to violence. "The raters tell parents what's in a movie and let them decide whether to take their kids," explains Harris. "But the fifth rating—NC-17—carries the force of law: It's the only stage at which raters decide their judgment should overrule yours."[3]

One might expect violence to permeate R-rated thrillers, or at least PG-13 features, but currently even G-rated films also reveal similar violent trends. One study found a high correlation between violent depictions and films made for children. Disturbingly, the researchers found that animated movies aimed at children contain significantly more violence than nonanimated features. Animated films rated G by the MPAA received a significantly higher content-based score for violence on average than nonanimated films rated G. Firearms also appeared in a large number of G films. The authors found significantly higher gross revenues for PG-13 and R-rated films that received MPAA warnings for violence compared with those films that did not.[4] Clearly, movie violence attracts larger audiences than nonviolent films.

Since sex becomes more subject to censorship, filmmakers turned to violence to sell movies to mass audiences, including children. A 2004 study revealed that nearly all of the PG-13 movies marketed to children contain significant levels of violence, posing an emotional health risk for adolescents.[5] It turns out that nearly all PG-13 films, which are supposed to be marketed to families and younger children, contain significant amounts of violence. Incredibly, Hollywood deliberately targets teenagers with violence-laden films. To what extent can youth violence be blamed on Hollywood models? That question might make for a lively debate someday.

Can movie violence provide unanticipated social benefits? In 2008 researchers at the University of California announced the results of an extensive study into the effects of violent movies on violent crime from 1995 to 2004. Professor Gordon Dahl and Professor Stefano DellaVigna discovered that showing violent films cut violent assaults in the United States by, on average, about 52,000 a year over the decade. Comparing national crime reports, cinema ratings, and movie audience data, they discovered that violent crime decreased significantly on days with larger theater audiences for violent films. Violent crime rates on those days decreased even more precipitously after midnight, leading to the conclusion that significant numbers of potentially violent criminals opt to view violent films instead of perpetrate violent deeds. For them, going to violent movies substitutes for other activities like drinking, taking drugs, and engaging in violent behavior. After midnight, violent crime rates drop even further on violent-movie nights, probably because a significant portion of the audience watched movies instead of consuming alcohol and drugs, which are often associated with violent behavior.[6] This study reveals a potentially therapeutic aspect of cinematic violence. Watching violent movies may stimulate a handful of copycat criminals into committing violent crimes, but it appears to have the opposite effect on criminals in general. The idea that movies might provide sublimation of certain violent impulses among some of the audience argues against suddenly banning film violence, especially because that might inadvertently stimulate violent crimes. Therefore, some violent movies might just turn out to contribute to law, order, and social stability. If advocates of the suppression of violent movies knew of this unanticipated benefit they might have to reexamine their positions.

Gender Roles

Gender roles reflect some of society's most deep-seated attitudes, beliefs, and prejudices. The development of cinematic gender roles reveals a fascinating history of social and sexual taboos. From the beginning, producers employed sexy female characters to lure male viewers through erotic dancing, flirtatious behavior, and lack of clothing. During the pre-code period flapper/vamp characters like Jean Harlow's Lil, Marlene Dietrich's Blonde Venus, and Mae West's Lady Lou proved irresistible to audiences. The twenties ushered in gold-digging, sexy, slinky vamps wearing revealing clothes, smoking cigarettes, and drinking bootleg liquor. These characters owe a huge debt to the early nickelodeon females like Fatima, Dolorita, and many others. In fact, the femmes noir of the forties and fifties also owe a debt to the early nickelodeon vamps.

By the late twenties and early thirties, female characters routinely slept their way up the corporate ladder and seduced men into satisfying their whims and desires. Many, like *Blonde Venus, Gold Diggers of 1933,* and *She Done Him Wrong,* feature sexy costuming and ornate dance numbers. Their popularity testifies to the allure of social-climbing, sexy women on the silver screen. These early stars like Clara Bow, Jean Harlow, Marlene Dietrich, and Mae West embodied the "new woman" emboldened by woman's suffrage, an increase in manufacturing and office work for women, and changes in the family. They may have been forced into prostitution for their family's survival, or motivated by financial and social gains, but these females definitely threatened the older, Victorian ideal of conventional, conservative wives and mothers.

Pre-code male protagonists often fall into the category of action-adventurer "swashbuckler" heroes portrayed by Douglas Fairbanks Sr., Rudolph Valentino, and Ramon Navarro, or the "bad boy" gangsters defined by James Cagney and Paul Muni. Critics dubbed them "male vamps," likening them to the femmes fatales of Hollywood. These liberated males embody masculine fantasies about seducing and dominating women. Interestingly, the male characters that played opposite the sexy female vamps were often depicted as clueless victims unaware of social reality, like Jean Harlow's first husband, played by Chester Morris, in *Red-Headed Woman* and Mae West's many consorts in *She Done Him Wrong.*

Hays censors banned bold, openly sexual female characters and replaced them with saucy-tongued screwballs competing with and for men. The women of screwball comedy represent officially sanitized versions of the pre-code vamps. No longer dropping sexy one-liners or acting like gold diggers, stars like Claudette Colbert, Katharine Hepburn, and Rosalind Russell popularized the new career woman of the thirties. These characters, although not as freewheeling and liberated as their pre-code counterparts, skated on the edge of the permissible, hiking up their skirts to lure motorists into picking them up, raising pet leopards, or taking a man's job of reporting for a big-city newspaper. Early Hays Code females challenged the definition of acceptable female behavior without technically violating the rules, but the resulting screwball characters, although vastly entertaining, seem a far cry from real Depression-era women of any social class. In retrospect, interactions between odd-ball characters from the upper classes appear irrelevant amidst unemployment, idle farmworkers, and bread lines. Those settings would not appear in mainstream movies until John Ford's *The Grapes of Wrath* (1940) and *Tobacco Road* (1941).

The Hays Code encouraged bumbling, bemused screwball heroes and sanitized "G-men" crusaders instead of pre-code swashbuckling, bad boy heroes. Musical comedies showcased the talents of Fred Astaire and Dick Powell, who sang and danced their way to stardom. Powell starred in Busby Berkeley's racy *Gold Diggers of 1933* as well as its Hays Code successor *Dames* (1934). Hays Code musicals appeared tame compared to sexy pre-code extravaganzas.

During the first half of the twentieth century male characters evolved from swash-buckling adventurers and colorful bootleggers to the lost souls of thirties' comedies and their cousins in melodramas like *Gone With the Wind* and *The Thin Man* series. The Hays Code, by inspiring new genres and transforming older ones, for a time tamped down outward disobedience and demanded conformity. However, as public attitudes gradually relaxed with rising prosperity filmmakers created new strategies of adherence to the letter but not the spirit of code censorship. As the thirties drew to a close darker heroes emerged. Victor Fleming's *Gone With the Wind* (1939) features Rhett Butler (Clark Gable) and Scarlett O'Hara (Vivien Leigh), two rebellious mis-fits. John Ford's *The Grapes of Wrath* (1940) features Tom Joad (Henry Fonda), just released from prison after serving a sentence for manslaughter, who then sets out at the end to organize farmworkers in California. If Joad, Butler, and O'Hara weren't outlaws enough, within a few short years film noir characters that functioned at the edges of society and often barely skirted the edge of the law emerged.

Wars profoundly affect censorship as censors turn their attention to depictions of the conflict. World War II served as a powerful distraction for Joseph Breen's Production Code Administration, which focused more on promoting patriotism than policing movies. Returning veterans felt little empathy with Victorian morality, forcing the Production Code to relax, allowing female seductresses for the first time since the pre-code era. These characters dominated thrillers for three decades, seducing men while luring them into lives of crime. They embody male fears of female ascendancy during the wartime defense buildup, which witnessed 10 million women joining the formerly all-male workforce in defense industries. These new characters, showing socially deviant gender roles for nearly independent women, were played by Barbara Stanwyck, Lana Turner, Rita Hayworth, Veronica Lake, Lauren Bacall, and Ingrid Bergman, among many others. They competed successfully with men in the workplace as well as the bedroom. They have been described as "bitches, harpies, and shrews." In fact, these potent femme noir characters not only made fools of men but usually seduced them into committing various felonies, including murder. As dangerous, deadly seductresses, femmes noir embodied male fears of growing female assertiveness, epitomized by the Rosy the Riveter campaign organized by the War Department. Harking back to pre-code vamps, femmes noir behaved wickedly and audaciously, often appearing deceptive, ruthless, and deadly. These characters went far beyond the harmless though enticing man-chasing vamps of the twenties and thirties. These dangerous, duplicitous characters reflect male insecurity over the nascent feminist movement during the war that turned gender roles upside down. Rosie the Riveter and the millions of her hardworking women comrades embodied the rise of a powerful social force that would become scarce during the postwar period, driven off the screen by McCarthyism.

McCarthy-era films stereotyped communists, particularly females, as loose, atheistic, and unscrupulous, while depicting anticommunists as upstanding, family-oriented patriots. During the polarized McCarthy era female communists in film prey upon hapless males and, lacking the restraints of Christianity or conservatism, indulge in lustful orgies with their victims. Ironically, the communist characters in these films often appear more interesting than the anticommunists. Anticommunist females embody Victorian-era family values.

McCarthyism fostered embittered male protagonists that, like *High Noon*'s Marshal Kane, rely ultimately on only themselves against ruthless gang members and aliens. No doubt, McCarthyism influenced Fred Zinnemann's depiction of the Frank Miller gang as a pack of ruthless thugs who wish to tear down social stability and structure. Will Kane becomes something of a lost soul and reluctant warrior, a common McCarthy-era motif for male characters who had lost much of their former potency. The era's anticommunist films have long since been forgotten, except for thinly veiled sci-fi thrillers like *Invasion of the Body Snatchers*. In these films and many others McCarthyism stimulated a new kind of hero: loner, isolated, opposed by forces of authority. The movement also stimulated a new kind of villain: arbitrary, cruel, and arrogant. The McCarthy era inspired a series of "bad cop noirs" featuring corrupt law enforcement officers, perhaps reflecting public distrust of authorities. The underlying message of McCarthy-era movies became don't trust those in authority.

Like anticommunist films, evangelical films also often feature female seductresses, but instead of communists they have now become secular hedonists. *Left Behind* set the tone by depicting venal, corrupt seductresses as foils for the nurturing, family-values females that play supportive roles to male leads. Whatever their earlier transgressions, evangelical females renounce sexual freedom or forgo any possibility of achieving heaven. Unfaithful males receive the same fate, but they may redeem themselves by adopting a cleansing of their ways. Other evangelical male characters symbolize God or Jesus, like the lion in *The Chronicles of Narnia* and Jesus in *The Passion of the Christ*.

Powerful signs of evangelicalism pervade many contemporary movies. Even animated films increasingly bear the subtle stamp of evangelicalism. *Jonah: A Veggie Tale* (2002) features healthy vegetable characters that are also religious. The protagonist is an asparagus spear named Jonah, a Hebrew prophet (voice of Phil Vischer) who praises God from the back of a giant caterpillar. When God commands Jonah to go to Nineveh, a wicked Babylonian city, Jonah refuses, then learns some bitter lessons about disobeying God's commands.

For contemporary movie buffs, Hollywood's "good girls" represent a minority compared with its "bad girls." Good girl characters like Heidi, Mary Bailey, and Pollyanna often appear infantilized if not actual children. Contemporary good girl characters also include children, as in *Dreamer, The Chronicles of Narnia,* and *Bridge to Terabithia.* Adult good girls also feature in evangelical films, including the *Left Behind* series, but they often possess sexy back stories prior to their conversion to evangelicalism. Conservative movements like McCarthyism and evangelicalism prefer good girls in their female roles and violent action/adventure heroes like Rambo in their male roles.

Villains of evangelical films range from unctuous liberals to versions of the Antichrist. Whatever their names may be, though, beneath the surface they are all liberals, humanists, and secularists, the movement's chosen antagonists. Like McCarthyism, evangelicalism focuses on liberalism and attacks it at every opportunity. Villains like *Left Behind*'s UN secretary-general Nicolae Carpathea represent Clinton-era liberals. Even *The Passion of the Christ*'s High Priest Calaphas, a Jew, not only evokes anti-Semitism but is also a veiled attack on liberalism, or at least an evangelical conception of egotistical, legalistic liberals.

Creating the Couple

The history of movie coupling provides fascinating insights into this vital activity. Most movies depict some form of romantic relationship, and the socially acceptable boundaries for those relationships vary dramatically over time. Pre-code films celebrated the union of seductresses played by Jean Harlow, Marlene Dietrich, Barbara Stanwyck, and Mae West with bad boy protagonists played by James Cagney, Paul Muni, Douglas Fairbanks Sr., and Rudolph Valentino. These filmic relationships often proved transitory. Characters in pre-code movies tend to undergo a sexual awakening in which their attitudes toward sex became more cynical and realistic. No doubt, these movie themes reflected profound social changes happening during the Jazz Age and the Great Depression.

During the Hays Code relationships went underground and under the covers—
they became subliminal, nuanced, and less realistic than during the pre-code era. At
first, the Hays Code banned seductresses as "gold diggers," but soon witty, seductive
screwball heroines, followed by film noir femmes fatales, appeared. The Hays period
witnessed a weakening of male roles, from swashbuckler action heroes or bad boy
charmers of the pre-code period to lost-soul screwball heroes or effete singers and
dancers in musicals. With the advent of film noir, screen males grew even weaker,
behaving like lost-soul archetypes: patsies, dupes, and victims. Relationships proved
toxic and continued their downward track for decades.

Film noir males often underestimate the beautiful femmes fatales they encounter
in many films, from the forties until today. Although the females often prove duplicitous, males also appear bemused or duplicitous themselves. A number of film noirs
feature males acting as double agents for the government and for organized crime or
Nazi Germany (*The Dark Corner, The House on 92nd Street*). Private detectives also
play duplicitous, shady roles in noir thrillers like *Double Indemnity, Sunset Boulevard,
The Lady from Shanghai, The Postman Always Rings Twice,* and many more. Noir
males often lose in competition with aggressive, smart femmes fatales. They, themselves, seldom appear honest or forthright. Starting in the late forties, with the rise of
McCarthyism, male and female characters retreated even deeper into symbolism,
innuendo, and double entendre.

World War II combat films ushered in a new era where females focused on supporting their husbands and raising families, as in *Thirty Seconds over Tokyo.* Combat
films also featured a new kind of hero: a tough, brave team player, not a loner. Team-
oriented heroes predominate in combat films like *Dive Bomber, Air Force, Guadalcanal Diary, Flying Leathernecks, They Died with Their Boots On, Thirty Seconds over
Tokyo, Twelve O'clock High, Sahara, D-Day,* and *The Sixth of June,* to name a few.
Wartime demanded courage and obedience to the chain of command, and spouses
functioned more as assistants than as opponents. The need for wartime discipline
inspired many combat films. Combat heroes played by John Wayne, Dana Andrews,
Humphrey Bogart, Montgomery Clift, Robert Mitchum, and Robert Montgomery
proved popular as long as the war lasted. *Thirty Seconds over Tokyo*'s couples embody
supportive, not combative, relationships. Lieutenant Jed Lawson's (Van Johnson)
wife, Ellen (Phyllis Thaxter), upon learning that her husband is shipping out,
promises, "Oh, Ted, I'm going to write you a letter every day you're gone. I know
they won't deliver them. I won't even mail them, but I'm going to write them anyway. That way we'll kind of be in touch. That way we'll feel close."

After the war social problems that had been swept under the rug during the
war reemerged with a vengeance. Films like *The Best Years of Our Lives, Till the
End of Time,* and *From Here to Eternity* depicted dysfunctional relationships,
reflecting the war's more negative aspects. *The Best Years of Our Lives*' Fred Derry

(Dana Andrews) becomes estranged from his wife, Marie (Virginia Mayo), and falls in love with young Peggy Stephenson (Theresa Wright) instead. *From Here to Eternity*'s First Sergeant Milton Warden (Burt Lancaster) falls for Karen Holmes (Deborah Kerr), an officer's wife. These relationships appear dysfunctional, yet they were tolerated by the later Hays Code under Joseph Breen and Geoff Shurlock. The reason is that loveless marriages were suddenly fair game for filmmakers intent on exposing social problems. As Ashton D. Trice and Samuel A. Holland observe, postwar filmmakers, suddenly free of the military-dominated Production Code, focused on homegrown problems and thorny issues.[7] The heroes of these films, played by Dana Andrews, Robert Mitchum, Montgomery Clift, Frank Sinatra, and Burt Lancaster, appear lustful, sensitive, and reflective, not bold, courageous, and good team players, as the earlier combat heroes usually were. Their spouses, too, have changed, and not for the better. Often victims of what the military currently refers to as posttraumatic stress disorder, protagonists in these films are part of the walking wounded. They often spar verbally with their mates and usually end up leaving them.

The postwar period inaugurated a long period of problematic relationships in real life, depicted poignantly in film noirs, social problem films, and family melodramas. Alfred Kinsey documented the hidden side of relationships for the first time. One study reveals that at least one-fourth of marriages will end in divorce. In addition, a large number of married people suffer from addictions and psychosomatic disorders.[8] If Hollywood mirrors problems besetting society, then romantic relationships must be very fragile indeed.

The Valenti Code, like the earlier Hays Code, inspired new genres and character types. Memorable female characters include the seductresses that serve as heroines/villains of neo-noir, including *Body Heat*'s Matty Walker, *Basic Instinct*'s Catherine Trammel, and *The Last Seduction*'s Wendy Kroy. These duplicitous, powerful, and ultimately dangerous women replaced the sexy flappers and vamps of the pre-code period, as well as the saucy heroines of screwball comedy played by Claudette Colbert and Katharine Hepburn. Today, Uma Thurman as The Bride in *Kill Bill* has replaced Katharine Hepburn as Hildie in *His Girl Friday* as the quintessential gutsy female ready to take on men on her own turf. Today's action heroines like The Bride serve as an update to the sultry seductresses of the film noir and neo-noir movements.

The Valenti Code affords some freedom in depicting relationships, more than under previous codes, but with Valenti a new breed of femme fatale heroine, the neo–femme noir, arose. These new characters inherited much from the classic femme noir fatale, but embellished the role with even more violence and duplicity. Heroines of neo-noir flaunt their sexuality as never before, seducing often pathetically weak males and then ensnaring them in deadly schemes. Today's seductresses pose life-threatening challenges to men as never before. No longer content merely to ensnare weak males in plots to murder their husbands, the new femmes fatales may recruit their male counterpart into a "murder for hire" business (*The Last Seduction*), loot their fortunes and have them committed to a mental institution (*Dream Lover*), or avenge their brutal treatment against both men and women (*Kill Bill*). These characters correspond to the third-wave feminism of recent decades that endorses females ready, willing, and eager to satisfy their sexual appetites. These characters ooze sexuality and respond to it as natural and normal.[9]

The Valenti Code, with its notorious tolerance for violence, continues to subtly encourage dangerous, even psychotic characters, both male and female. However, for every murderous femme fatale many ultraviolent male action heroes stand willing and able to kill both males and females. The most recent *Rambo* (2008) protagonist (Sylvester Stallone) butchers scores of bad guys in the latest edition of the sequence, and the Terminator wields violence and death as effortlessly as classic gangster heroes dealt fatal blows to their gangland rivals. Today's characters, both males and females, indulge in over-the-top amounts of violence. The result is to cast male and female relationships as dangerous, duplicitous, and deadly.

Under the evangelical code homosexuality remains one of the most sensitive issues in film. Under past codes, the issue remained in the closet, occasionally suggested but never consummated until recently. During the pre-code era gay characters appeared in early biblical romances like Cecil B. DeMille's *The Ten Commandments* (1923). Overtly gay characters did not appear in films until the sixties and seventies with films like *Midnight Cowboy* (1968), *The Boys in the Band* (1970), and *Sunday, Bloody Sunday* (1971). Currently, gay characters may serve as stars, as in *Brokeback Mountain* (2005). Homosexuality, like adultery and premarital sex, has gradually become more respectable in films, but the result has also been more criticism leveled at Hollywood by social conservatives.

MPAA Image

In another sign of the tarnished MPAA image, the online *Urban Dictionary* defines it ironically as "a great moral teacher, proving to everyone that nudity and sexuality are more harmful to young people than depictions of graphic violence. A beating, beheading, disembowelment, immolation, crucifixion, dismemberment? No problem! But catch a brief glimpse of a breast or a patch of pubic hair? Pornography!"[10] The first direct attack on the MPAA in a motion picture occurred in 1999 in Trey Parker's *South Park: Bigger, Longer, and Uncut* (1999). Parker, still bitter about the NC-17 rating awarded his 1997 animated feature *Orgazmo,* inserted an animated character's comments regarding the organization: "Remember what the MPAA says; Horrific, deplorable violence is okay, as long as people don't say any naughty words!"

Kirby Dick's *This Film Is Not Yet Rated* inaugurated a minor culture war over the issue of censorship. Some critics seized the opportunity occasioned by Dick's film to bash the MPAA, while others defended the current ratings system. The fact that Dick's film sparked a backlash of criticism suggests that he succeeded in his original intention of exposing inconsistencies in the MPAA.

Although the major studios avoid realistic depictions of sexual relationships due to the structural imbalances exposed by *This Film Is Not Yet Rated*, a small number of independent filmmakers elect to depict adult sexuality precisely because Hollywood refuses to touch it. Major studios prefer films depicting violence, but that leaves sex to the indies. Indie filmmakers like John Waters, Trey Parker, and Kevin Smith assiduously explore issues of adult sexuality, constantly risking NC-17 ratings. However, mainstream filmmakers like Stephen Spielberg, James Cameron, and Michael Bay, who command A budgets, gravitate toward violence-filled films, thereby avoiding NC-17 ratings. They would rather stick with a tried-and-true box office lure than risk depicting adult relationships in order to avoid ratings problems.

Rarely have films from the majors received NC-17 ratings, yet controversial indie films, including *Orgazmo, Boys Don't Cry, Clerks II, South Park, A Dirty Shame*, and *Lust, Caution*, routinely receive these ratings. If major studios submitted these films, they would immediately negotiate for and receive R ratings. The major studios have the resources to reedit scenes, protest decisions, and effect compromises. So, in that respect, the current code reinforces the advantages big studios possess over indies. In that sense, the code reinforces Hollywood's status quo. The NC-17 rating, therefore, becomes an immensely powerful tool to marginalize indie filmmakers, thereby helping to ensure the major studios' industry domination.

Code Reform

Finally, bowing to pressure from outraged critics and filmmakers, the MPAA recently made weak attempts to correct the major abuses of the system and thereby to resurrect some semblance of respect for NC-17 films, but this cause appears hopeless. Currently, the NC-17 equates with X, which spells sex and potential trouble. When major studios produce relationship-oriented films, such as Bernardo Bertolucci's *In the Cut*, Wayne Kramer's *The Cooler*, and Woody Allen's *Match Point*, the MPAA threatens NC-17 ratings to force reediting. *In the Cut* currently exists in two versions, NC-17 and R, both of which appear in the DVD version. This process of "negotiation" with the MPAA necessarily softens and blunts films' edges, often rendering them less than realistic, and certainly less so than the producers originally intended.

Increased pressure by independent filmmakers and film critics already achieved changes, as the MPAA now contemplates retiring or revising the NC-17 rating. Rumors surfaced in 2007 about new rules in the offing for film ratings. However, as with all former codes, reform proceeds at a glacial pace. One proposal calls for a new NC-21 rating, replacing NC-17 and to be reserved for only the most pornographic films. Those deemed nonpornographic would receive R ratings. This proposal would allow excellent yet racy films that previously garnered NC-17 ratings to be viewed by younger audiences. Only blatant pornography and ultraviolent films would be banned from teenage audiences. With pornography restricted to legal adults, older teenagers might watch serious nonpornographic films depicting adult relationships.

The NC-21 rating raises the issue of what defines "pornography." No clear definition of pornography exists, partly because what may appear pornographic to some might strike others as artistic, satirical, or otherwise enjoyable and redeemable. Many films once labeled pornographic find themselves on the classics shelf today, including pre-code films, screwball comedies, film noirs, and even older sex films like *Behind the Green Door* and *Deep Throat*. Roger Ebert advocates a different approach through a new "A" rating that would appear between today's R and NC-17 ratings. "A" stands for "artistic," so racy films deemed worthwhile could be viewed by older teenagers and shown in mall theaters. This rating might encourage serious depictions of adult relationships, if the ratings board deemed the film to be of sufficient social and artistic worth.[11]

Hollywood's fascination with violent R, PG-13, and recently even G features results in increasing public disapproval of movies. Audrey Totter, one of the original femmes fatales of film noir, charges that addiction to violence saps Hollywood creativity and robs movies of power. She believes that "Hollywood should police itself" but fears there's "too much money to be made." Audience demand for violence drives producers to turn out more violent movies. "As long as people go to see the violent movies . . . Hollywood will keep churning them out." The problem is that "there is always a new youth market that hasn't been initiated yet to the violence."[12] As long as box office success remains dependent on violence to attract audiences, producers will find little incentive to produce nonviolent films.

As Totter and many others note, today's movies, with a few exceptions, fail to depict romantic relationships realistically or compellingly. Critic A. O. Scott contrasts contemporary filmic relationships with those of the Hays Code period. Scott charges that the standard PG-13 romantic tearjerker "nowadays treads so delicately in fear of giving offense to someone somewhere that it wanders into blandness and boredom." The situation has become so dire that Scott concludes that "the movies made under the Production Code are far more sophisticated, and far less timid, than what we see today." The main reason for today's blandness and timidity is the Valenti Code's failure to protect filmmakers from social and religious pressure groups. Increasingly, the Valenti Code itself bears the main responsibility for the skewed, dismal state of romantic movies today.[13]

Today, in order to depict sex realistically, filmmakers must accept NC-17 ratings, despite financial hardships. Directors like Bernardo Bertolucci, John Waters, and Ang Lee recently defied CARA and decided to release their films unrated rather than accept NC-17 ratings. Bertolucci was overruled by his studio and Waters also compromised in the end, but Lee, in defense of his *Lust, Caution* (2007), refused to cut sex scenes to suit censors and received a punitive NC-17 rating. Was the sacrifice worth it? Financially, no, but artistically, probably. After congratulating Lee for his courageous decision to ignore the censors and follow his artistic instincts, Roger Ebert observed that Lee's "moments of full frontal nudity avoid the awkwardness of most movie sex scenes in which the lovers, although alone, carefully mask their naughty bits. The scenes are not edited for erotic effect, it must be observed, but are treated in terms of their psychological meaning."[14] Lee's film went on to win Best Picture at the Venice International Film Festival and many nominations for Best Foreign Language Film from Golden Globe and other organizations. Would it have received these honors if it was cut for an R rating?

Today's censorship wars may well be rendered obsolete by technology as filmmakers discover that they can merely restore censored footage in DVDs, feeding a growing aftermarket of sales and rentals. Increasingly, DVDs contain not only the theatrical version but also their original uncut versions, often featured as "deleted scenes." Studios market these restored versions as "unrated," "uncensored," or "European." Computer-downloaded versions also evade the code by reinserting offending scenes and deletions, even capitalizing on the appeal of "banned" or "censored" material. Currently, many films bypass theatrical release entirely, opting for the more lucrative aftermarket. Given these strategies, one must question whether movie censorship can survive this technological revolution.

Can Hollywood actually function smoothly without regulation? Will social conservatives tolerate creative filmmaking? In fact, Hollywood must possess a Production Code in order to withstand pressure from antagonistic organizations and social and political movements. Without a Production Code, filmmakers risk strict governmental censorship. Although the Supreme Court outlawed prior censorship, other forms of censorship prove equally potent. But whatever the eventual censorship system of the future, one thing is certain: it will possess flaws and inequalities and will always produce unanticipated consequences. At the same time, it will undoubtedly wield a profound influence on Hollywood movies for years to come.

Selected Filmography

Pre-Code

Thomas Edison's *Fatima: Coochie Coochie Dancer* (1896) features the Middle Eastern gyrations of Fatima, a popular dancer at the 1893 Chicago World's Fair. Length: one minute. In 1907 Chicago's censorship board affixed a large stain covering Fatima's body on the print showing in Chicago.

Thomas Edison's *Fatima: Muscle Dancer* (1896) is another version of Fatima gyrating seductively in a revealing costume.

William Heise's (producer Thomas Edison) *The Kiss* (1896) features May Irwin and John Rice, two actors in John McNalley's Broadway play, engaging in a one-minute kiss that scandalized social conservatives.

The Edison Film Company's *The Dolorita Passion Dance* (1897) features a young woman dancing the "Danse-du-Ventre, the famous Oriental muscle dance" in front of some seated musicians.

Edwin S. Porter's *The Gay Shoe Clerk* (1903) depicts a young shoe clerk (Edward Boulden) fitting a young woman with a shoe while she suggestively raises her long skirt hem above her ankle. Soon he steals a kiss, infuriating the girl's mother, who rushes her out of the store.

Edwin S. Porter's *The Great Train Robbery* (1903) depicts a train robbery crosscut with shots of a pursuing posse. Porter adapted parallel editing to make this the first coherent narrative movie.

Cecil B. DeMille's *The Cheat* (1915) depicts a wayward wife (Fannie Ward) who flirts with a Burmese businessman (Sessue Hayakawa) and eventually kills him in self-defense. Her husband (Jack Dean) takes the blame for the crime.

D. W. Griffith's *The Birth of a Nation* (1915) was one of the first feature-length movies with thousands of extras depicting battles in the Civil War. The film glorifies the Ku Klux Klan as the saviors of the South and stimulated intense controversy.

Maurice Tournier's *A Girl's Folly* (1917) depicts a young girl (Doris Kenyon) who falls in love with a popular movie actor (Robert Warwick) and decides to move in with him, shocking lingering Victorian sensibilities.

In Cecil B. DeMille's *The Ten Commandments* (1923), part one depicts Moses leading the Israelites out of Israel. Part two depicts the commandments in action in contemporary San Francisco.

King Vidor's *The Big Parade* (1925) depicts a young man (John Gilbert) impulsively joining the army during World War I and losing a leg in combat. The film's antiwar theme and depictions of casual wartime sexuality generated controversy.

Cecil B. DeMille's *Madame Satan* (1930) features a deceived wife played by Kay Johnson who struggles to unleash her repressed sexuality so that she can win her husband's (Reginald Denny) affections.

Mervyn LeRoy's *I Am a Fugitive from a Chain Gang* (1931) stars Paul Muni as Robert Burns, a real-life example of miscarriage of justice who wrongly imprisons an innocent bystander for armed robbery. Censors fretted over LeRoy's depiction of Georgia chain gangs, but the producer ignored their protestations.

William Wellman's *Public Enemy* (1931) stars James Cagney as Tom Powers, an Al Capone–like Chicago gangster. Many objected to Wellman's glorification of a crime boss, as he was depicted as an attractive social rebel.

Joseph Von Sternberg's *Blonde Venus* (1932) stars Marlene Dietrich as multitalented Helen, billed as "Blonde Venus" in the role of nightclub singer. Dietrich delivers a memorable rendition of "Hot Voodoo" dressed scantily as a primitive African.

Jack Conway's *Red-Headed Woman* (1932) features a sizzling Jean Harlow as Lil, a sexual adventuress willing and able to trade physical intimacy for financial gain. She cuckolds her husband (Chester Morris), then attaches herself to an older, wealthier businessman. In the end she acquires a wealthy Frenchman and retains her lover (Charles Boyer) as chauffeur. The film's blatant and unrepentant sexuality infuriated many at the time.

Cecil B. DeMille's *The Sign of the Cross* (1932) forms the last of DeMille's pre-code biblical narratives, and depicts the emperor Nero (Charles Laughton) burning Rome and making Christians into scapegoats. The Empress Poppaea (Claudette Colbert) falls for Marcus Superbus (Fredric March), who in turn loves another. The plot was ripe for sexual innuendos, much to the censors' displeasure.

Lowell Sherman's *She Done Him Wrong* (1934) stars Mae West as Diamond Lou, a reprisal of her successful Broadway role in *Diamond Lil.* Lou seduces every male in sight while delivering sexy one-liners. West helped outwit censors, and much of the original script remains intact.

Hays Code

Frank Capra's *It Happened One Night* (1934) stars Claudette Colbert and Clark Gable as star-crossed lovers suddenly thrown together on the road. Although the two originate from different social classes (she's upper; he's middle) they eventually become attracted to each other and fall in love. Mixing of social classes was also slightly taboo at that time but not as taboo as the pre-code gold digger movies, which were banned. Capra's film became a pattern followed by others in the "screwball" comedy genre.

William Keighley's *G-Men* (1935) stars James Cagney as an FBI agent with a criminal background. Cagney's Brick Davis embodies the pre-code gangster hero now on the side of law enforcement. Keighley got away with glorifying a macho urban fighter by having him switch sides and fight for law and order.

Howard Hawks's *Bringing Up Baby* (1938) pits a wealthy zany played by Katharine Hepburn against a bumbling college professor played by Cary Grant. Their social class differences spiced up their romance but avoided overt censorship.

Raoul Walsh's *High Sierra* (1941) features an unglamorous small-time gangster, Mad Dog Earl (Humphrey Bogart), who breaks out of jail and hides in the Sierra Nevada Mountains in California. Walsh succeeded in deglamorizing Earl, and the movie received a seal from the Production Code Administration.

John Huston's *The Maltese Falcon* (1941) features Humphrey Bogart as private detective Sam Spade, who encounters a dangerous murderer named Brigid O'Shaughnessy (Mary Astor), who hires him on a pretense. Spade struggles against a vicious gang of criminals headed by Casper Guttman (Sydney Greenstreet). Spade turns over Brigid to the police even though the two are intimates, one of the few times in the film noir genre in which the male protagonist lives to defeat his female antagonist.

Howard Hughes's *The Outlaw* (1941) features Jane Russell in revealing blouses as the girlfriend of Billy the Kid and Doc Holliday. Hughes struggled against Breen's reluctance to approve this film, which finally occurred. Now, it is recognized as a minor classic and an interesting example of Hays Code censorship.

Sam Wood's *King's Row* (1942) stars Robert Cummings and Ronald Reagan as boyhood friends growing up in a small town who encounter incest, sadism, and nymphomania. The Breen Office battled fiercely over this film, and Wood ended up accommodating some of Breen's objections while choosing to ignore others. This is truly a "censorship classic."

Billy Wilder's *The Lost Weekend* (1945) features Ray Milland as Don Birnham, an alcoholic who attempts suicide after a weeklong binge. This film faced censorship attempts by powerful lobbyists from the alcohol industry.

Tay Garnett's *The Postman Always Rings Twice* (1946) features sultry Lana Turner as a faithless wife who dallies with a drifter played by John Garfield. The two plot to murder the cuckolded husband but come to a bad end. This film embodies film noir sexuality, with Garfield easily succumbing to Turner's seduction.

Fred Zinnemann's *High Noon* (1952) features Gary Cooper as Marshal Will Kane, a just, fair law enforcement officer who experiences danger as a result of the government's releasing from prison a former prisoner who had vowed revenge on Kane. The marshal seeks assistance from his fellow townspeople, including his deputy, but no one stands up for him against the fierce Frank Miller gang except his Quaker bride, played by Grace Kelly. The PCA struggled in vain against the sex and violence in this film.

Otto Preminger's *The Moon Is Blue* (1953) could not be permitted by the Hays Code. Preminger's film depicts two middle-aged male bachelors, played by William Holden and David Niven, who vie for the affections of a young actress played by Maggie McNamara. Preminger's film depicts changing romantic relationships and features saucy dialogue salted with previously banned words. As a result, Preminger decided to release the film without a seal of approval from the censors.

Lazlo Benedek's *The Wild One* (1954) stars Marlon Brando as Johnny, the leader of a motorcycle gang. The gang takes over a small town in California, where the members are magnets for the local girls. Censors forced Benedek to insert a disclaimer scene at the end in which a police officer lectures about youth crime.

Joseph L. Mankiewicz's *Guys and Dolls* (1955) is a musical comedy based on Damion Runyon's popular stage play about a gambler (Marlon Brando) who seduces a Salvation Army officer (Jean Simmons) to win a bet. Censors attempted to suppress much of the gambling as well as the obviously sexual relationships in the film, but Mankiewicz managed to retain much of the original Broadway bawdy qualities.

Otto Preminger's *The Man with the Golden Arm* (1955) chronicles the struggle of a heroin addict named Frankie Machine (Frank Sinatra) to free himself of his addiction. The Hays Code forbade films about drug addiction, so Preminger released the film unrated, just as he had *The Moon Is Blue* two years earlier. These actions helped undermine the legitimacy of the Hays Code.

Elia Kazan's *Baby Doll* (1956) features a seemingly underage girl, Baby Doll (Caroll Baker), who is legally married although not yet consummated to Archie Lee (Karl Malden). Baby Doll, although supposedly nineteen years old, looks and acts much younger, sleeping in a crib and dressing as a child throughout the film. This movie stimulated a sharp attack by the Catholic Legion of Decency, and the producer ultimately pulled it from distribution.

Stanley Kubrick's *Spartacus* (1960) challenged the censors by including a bisexual character, Crassius (Laurence Olivier), and barely disguised Roman orgies. Kubrick was able to avoid total censorship by setting his movie in the classical past.

McCarthy Code

William Wyler's *The Best Years of Our Lives* (1946) showcases problems afflicting returning military personnel after World War II. The returning veterans, played by Fredric March, Dana Andrews, and Harold Russell, experience marriages gone sour, job discrimination, and adjusting to society after becoming handicapped. These issues vexed Americans and disturbed the era's political conservatives, who forced films that highlighted social problems out of theaters.

Abraham Polonsky's *Force of Evil* (1948) stars John Garfield as Joe Mores, slick gangster lawyer to the local crime boss Ben Tucker (Roy Roberts). Polonsky's film depicts social institutions, including the police, as totally corrupt and controlled by mob bosses. Denied a seal of approval, Polonsky released it independently. He was blacklisted throughout the McCarthy period.

Howard Hawks's *Red River* (1948) features authoritarian rancher Tom Dunson (John Wayne), who ultimately comes to terms after a violent struggle with his adopted son, played by Montgomery Clift, who represents a post-McCarthy world.

R. G. Springsteen's *The Red Menace* (1949) stars Robert Rockwell as Bill Jones, a distinguished war veteran who becomes ensnared by the local communist cell after being seduced by one of its members (played by Barbara Fuller). Hanne Axman plays Nina Petrova, the only decent female around, who falls in love with Jones. The two ultimately become betrothed.

Robert Stevenson's *I Married a Communist* (1950) stars Robert Ryan as a business executive with a hidden, radical past that makes him easy prey for the local communist cell. Thomas Gomez plays the head communist, and the entire film projects a "better dead than red" message.

Otto Preminger's *Where the Sidewalk Ends* (1950) is a "bad cop" noir featuring a flawed detective (Dana Andrews) who loses his temper and kills suspects in a prefiguring of the "Dirty Harry" protagonists decades later. These flawed leaders reflect McCarthy-era pessimism about government and law enforcement due to McCarthyism's excesses.

Robert Wise's *The Day the Earth Stood Still* (1951) features Michael Rennie as Klaatu, a being from an advanced civilization who journeys to earth to save humanity from a devastating nuclear war. Wise's film served as an indirect indictment of contemporary cold war politics and McCarthyism.

Leo McCrary's *My Son John* (1952) stars Dean Jagger and Helen Hays as a couple who discover that their son, played by Robert Walker, is a secret communist agent. This film, and many others, preyed on anticommunist hysteria fostered by the McCarthy movement.

Herbert Biberman's *Salt of the Earth* (1954) documents a New Mexico zinc miners' strike involving Hispanic miners. The film reveals mistreatment by the mine operators of their Hispanic workers while they shower their white workers with better wages and working conditions. This film would not have been awarded a PCA seal of approval, and it was released independently to be screened in union halls and other small venues.

Gordon Douglas's *Them* (1954) depicts an invasion of gigantic ants that mutated due to radiation from the bombing of Hiroshima. Like many classic sci-fi movies this one exudes paranoia about invasions of deadly beings, which were often communists in disguise.

Don Siegel's *Invasion of the Body Snatchers* (1956) depicts aliens formed from giant vegetable pods that appear identical to real humans and that murder their human twins in a bid to take over the world. Siegel's film serves as the quintessential McCarthy-era paranoid sci-fi thriller.

Orson Welles's *Touch of Evil* (1957) was the last of the classic A-budget film noirs, and it is the most memorable of the "bad cop noirs" featuring flawed law enforcement officers. Officer Hank Quinlan (Welles) plants evidence on suspects and exhibits anti-Mexican racism.

Stanley Kubrick's *Spartacus* (1960) presents the struggle between McCarthyites and everyone else as analogous to the massive slave rebellion during the height of the Roman Empire. Kubrick stars Kirk Douglas as Spartacus, who ignites a rebellion of slaves that threatens to topple the Roman Empire.

George Clooney's *Good Night and Good Luck* (2005) documents the historic clash between journalist Edward R. Murrow and Senator Joseph McCarthy that helped speed McCarthy's eventual political fall. Clooney's film was attacked by contemporary supporters of McCarthy, who are often labeled "neo-McCarthyists."

Valenti Code

Mike Nichols's *Who's Afraid of Virginia Woolf* (1966) touched off a storm of criticism due to strong, sexually suggestive language and its plot involving George (Richard Burton), a college professor, and his wife, Martha (Elizabeth Taylor). The two spouses misbehave after a young couple comes to their house for dinner. Phrases like "angel tits" and "hump the hostess" infuriated critics and censors, and eventually the MPAA awarded a seal provided the producers include proper disclaimers and prohibit underage minors from attending.

Arthur Penn's *Bonnie and Clyde* (1968) depicts a romanticized version of the exploits of Bonnie Parker (Faye Dunaway) and Clyde Barrows (Warren Beatty), the Depression-era bank robbers. Penn's film brought to the screen new levels of graphic violence, especially in the final scene in which the pair is blown to bits by hundreds of machine gun bullets spraying from the guns of concealed law enforcement officers. This scene marked a turning point as other filmmakers followed Penn's example and saturated their R-rated movies with graphic violence.

George Roy Hill's *Butch Cassidy and the Sundance Kid* (1969) tells the romanticized story of Western outlaws Butch Cassidy (Paul Newman) and the Sundance Kid (Robert Redford). As in *Bonnie and Clyde*, these outlaws are cut to pieces by the Bolivian military in a graphic scene.

Sam Peckinpah's *The Wild Bunch* (1969) achieved notoriety for its graphic violence, especially in an opening bank robbery scene and in the finale, in which the outlaw gang, led by Pike Bishop (William Holden), is cut to pieces by elements of the Mexican army.

Mike Nichols's *Carnal Knowledge* (1971) follows the sexual history of two college roommates, Jonathan (Jack Nicholson) and Sandy (Art Garfunkel), and their sexual experiences with various women over a period of decades. Because it was deemed "artistic" Nichols's film received an R rating from CARA, not an X.

Bernardo Bertolucci's *Last Tango in Paris* (1972) stars Marlon Brando as an aging expatriate in mourning after his wife's recent suicide. While shopping for an apartment in Paris he encounters a young, beautiful bride-to-be named Jeanne (Maria Schneider). The two begin an impassioned sexual relationship in which they promise not to reveal personal information about themselves because Jeanne will soon marry her fiancé. Due to its frankly sexual nature, especially in its positive treatment of premarital sexuality, the MPAA awarded it an X rating.

Philip Kaufman's *Henry and June* (1990) received the first NC-17 rating for depicting the ménage à trois between author Henry Miller (Fred Ward); his wife, June (Marina de Maderos); and fellow writer Anais Nin (Uma Thurman). This film raised much controversy even though it received a restrictive rating.

Pedro Almodovar's *Tie Me Up, Tie Me Down* (1990) depicts a mental patient, played by Antonio Banderas, who kidnaps and binds a dope-addicted former porn star, played by Victoria Abril. It turns out that he was only interested in settling down with her, not in terrorizing or killing her. Despite this gesture toward the MPAA, though, Almodovar's film failed to receive an R rating due to one explosive sex scene, clinching an NC-17 rating.

Paul Verhoeven's *Basic Instinct* (1992) focuses on a police search for an ice-pick murderer in San Francisco. Michael Douglas plays Nick, a police detective who finds himself strongly attracted to the chief suspect in the case, a crime novelist named Catherine Trammel (Sharon Stone). Scriptwriter Joe Eszterhas embellished the film with sexy copulation/bondage scenes, explicit dialogue, and lesbian lovemaking. It serves as a fine example of neo-noir filmmaking.

Barry Levinson's *Disclosure* (1994) continues the neo-noir theme of a femme fatale (Demi Moore) sexually harassing her underling, played by Michael Douglas. This role reversal illustrates well the dangerous femmes noir of the nineties and two thousands.

Nicholas Kazan's *Dream Lover* (1994) follows the neo-noir formula, with Madchen Amick in the role of the femme fatale wife who has her wealthy husband, played by James Spader, committed for insanity so she can loot his assets and flee the country.

John Dahl's *The Last Seduction* (1994) features Wendy Kroy (Linda Fiorentino) as a faithless wife who cajoles her husband into stealing and selling prescription medicine, then steals the money and sets herself up in another town as a telemarketing manager. She seduces Mike (Peter Berg) into murdering her husband and serving as a chief assassin in her murder-for-hire ring.

Oliver Stone's *Natural Born Killers* (1994) introduced Mickey (Woody Harrelson) and Mallory (Juliette Lewis) Knox, a husband and wife couple from hell. The couple begins by killing Mallory's father Ed (Rodney Dangerfield), who openly molests his daughter and threatens to rape her. After dispatching both of Mallory's parents the couple goes on a killing spree, outing any who become seduced by Mallory's beauty and seeming openness to sex. Mallory functions as a femme fatale in the same mold as other neo-noir seductresses.

Stanley Kubrick's *Eyes Wide Shut* (1999) depicts a happily married physician played by Tom Cruise who explores a steamy, surreal sexual underworld after learning from his wife, played by Nicole Kidman, that she has been having powerful fantasies about sex with a stranger. Kubrick's film pushed censorship limits regarding sexuality.

Wayne Kramer's *The Cooler* (2003) exemplifies the current policy of negotiating ratings. Kramer's erotic thriller, featuring William H. Macy and Maria Bello, received an NC-17 rating initially, but the producers ultimately negotiated an R rating after appealing to the MPAA. The Valenti Office especially disliked a scene featuring Macy performing cunnilingus on Bello but eventually allowed it.

Bernardo Bertolucci's *The Dreamers* (2003) depicts a ménage à trois between Matthew (Michael Pitt), a U.S. exchange student living in Paris, and a French brother and sister named Theo (Louis Garrel) and Isabelle (Eva Green). The MPAA threatened an NC-17 rating over three minutes of sex shots, but Bertolucci at first refused to make any cuts. However, the studio evoked its contract calling for delivery of an R-rated feature, and Bertolucci was forced to make the cuts in the U.S. version. The "European version," available on DVD, retains the censored shots.

Kirby Dick's *This Film Is Not Yet Rated* (2006) documents how the CARA ratings board actually operates and interviews filmmakers and critics disgruntled with the current system. Dick's documentary exposed the MPAA ratings system to public scrutiny for the first time and resulted in some minor reforms by CARA.

Evangelical Code

A. M. Kennelly's *Power of the Cross* (1916) became the first motion picture officially condemned by the Catholic Church, which also excommunicated its director.

Cecil B. DeMille's *Sign of the Cross* (1932) outraged Catholics for its attack on religious bigotry, thought by many to be a veiled attack on the Catholic Church. Officially, however, religious opposition focused on Claudette Colbert's (Poppaea) nudity as she bathes in a supposed bath of ass's milk.

Richard Brooks's *Elmer Gantry* (1960) stars Burt Lancaster as Gantry, a fast-talking, hard-drinking salesman who falls in love with a female evangelist going by the name of Sister Sharon Falconer (Jean Simmons). Gantry's philandering ways and Falconer's charlatan demeanor generated intense criticisms of this film by religious conservatives.

John Huston's *The Night of the Iguana* (1964) stars Richard Burton as defrocked Episcopal priest the Reverend T. Lawrence Shannon who is guiding a busload of middle-aged Baptist women in Mexico. When an underage passenger played by Sue Lyon forms an attraction to Shannon the official chaperone vows revenge on the minister. This film scandalized religious conservatives, who began advocating stricter censorship.

Michael Tolkin's *The Rapture* (1991) marked the first appearance in mainstream Hollywood of the End of Days, in which the faithful are transported to heaven while the rest of the population perishes. Mimi Rogers stars as Sharon, a beautiful young woman who converts to fundamentalist Christianity after a debauched existence as a barhopping swinger. She takes Mary (Kimberly Cullen), her young daughter, to the desert to await the End of Days and there Sharon decides to kill Mary so that her innocent daughter might participate in the Rapture.

Andre Van Herden's *Revelation* (1999) envisions a post-Rapture world in which the Antichrist, Franco Malacousso (Nick Mancuso), fulfills biblical prophecy by persecuting Christians and demanding that every citizen on earth don virtual reality helmets on the "Day of Wonders," on which he will proclaim himself the true Messiah. Computer terrorism expert Thorold Stone (Jeff Fahey) fights against the virtual reality conspiracy with the assistance of a dedicated band of underground Christians.

Vic Sarin's *Left Behind* (2000) is a low-budget film based on a novel by the Reverend Timothy LaHaye and Jerry B. Jenkins that, like *The Rapture*, chronicles the End of Days. Early in the film thousands of adults and children mysteriously disappear in an apocalyptic Rapture. Soon the Antichrist, Nicolae Carpathia (Gordon Currie), appears and assumes control of the United Nations.

Andre Van Heerden's *Deceived: Left Behind, a World at War* (2001) stars Judd Nelson as Jack Jones, who goes to an observatory in California's Sierra Nevada Mountains that apparently received a powerful transmission from another world. However, the transmission turns listeners into psychotics who end up killing each other. The message comes not from another planet but directly from hell, designed to hasten the End of Days.

Mel Gibson's *The Passion of the Christ* (2004) became the first evangelical blockbuster. Gibson's film depicts Christ's scourging and death. The film premiered in conservative Catholic and evangelical churches across the country in 2003, where Gibson often appeared in person for advanced screenings. The success of this film led to an evangelical movie explosion.

Andrew Adamson's *The Chronicles of Narnia: The Lion, the Witch, and the Wardrobe* (2005) depicts a magical world discovered by some children in which champions of good and evil battle each other for supremacy. The story derives from a C. S. Lewis novel and contains a thinly disguised Christian theme complete with a lion king (symbolizing God) who tips the battle in favor of the side of good.

Bill Corcoran's *Left Behind II: Tribulation Force* (2005) stars Kirk Cameron as Buck Williams, a popular television journalist. Williams teams up with a group of evangelistic Christians that meets in an urban church. Airline captain Rayford Steele (Brad Johnson) and his daughter Chloe (Janaya Stephens) also belong to the group, which forms after the Rapture instantaneously transports hundreds of millions of dedicated Christians, and every young child, into heaven. Cameron and Steele, with assistance from other group members, defeat the Antichrist's plot to take over the world.

George Miller's *Happy Feet* (2006) is an animated feature about Mumble, a young emperor penguin who is born unable to sing. Instead, Mumble displays a natural talent for dance, unheard of among emperor penguins. Mumble experiences difficulty relating to the other penguins, a situation that prompted some evangelical critics to label him a thinly disguised gay penguin. A conflict erupted over the widespread opposition to this children's film on the part of conservative Christians.

Katherine Peterson's *Bridge to Terabithia* (2007) features a teenage boy named Jess Aarons (Josh Hutcherson) who befriends a new girl in his school, played by Anna-Sophia Robb. She helps him discover a magical world called Terabithia in which the forces of good and evil clash violently. Peterson's film bears a strong resemblance to *The Chronicles of Narnia* and is, in fact, part of a series of religious-themed movies that includes *Narnia*.

Notes

Chapter One

1. Michael Medved website, www.michaelmedved.townhall.com. See also Michael Medved, *Hollywood versus America* (New York: Harper Collins, 1992).

2. Roger Ebert website, www.rogerebert.com.

3. Gerald Gardner, *The Censorship Papers: Movie Censorship Letters from the Hays Office, 1934 to 1968* (New York: Dodd, Mead, 1987), 179.

4. Tami D. Cowden, Caro LaFever, and Sue Viders, *The Complete Writer's Guide to Heroes and Heroines* (Hollywood, CA: Lone Eagle, 2000).

5. Virginia Wright Wexman, *Creating the Couple: Love, Marriage, and Hollywood Performance* (Princeton, NJ: Princeton University Press, 1993), ix.

Chapter Two

1. Frank Miller, *Censored Hollywood: Sex, Sin, and Violence on Screen* (Atlanta: Turner, 1994), 24.

2. IMDB website, http://www.imdb.com/title/tt0285087.

3. Miller, *Censored Hollywood*, 24.

4. www.youtube.com/watch?v=O6IqCaAYfXQ.

5. www.youtube.com/watch?v=Q2X_BZpnWFc.

6. "The Nickelodeon," in Gerald Mast, ed., *The Movies in Our Midst: Documents in the Cultural History of Film in America* (Chicago: University of Chicago Press, 1982), 43.

7. Ibid., 51–56.

8. Edward Wagenknecht, "Came the Dawn," in Wagenknecht, *The Movies in the Age of Innocence* (Norman: University of Oklahoma Press, 1962), 78–79.

9. Eileen Bowser, *The Transformation of Cinema, 1907–1915* (Berkeley: University of California Press, 1990), 49.

10. Miller, *Censored Hollywood,* 24.

11. Ibid., 25.

12. Ibid.

13. IMDB website, www.imdb.com/title/tt0313010.

14. Miller, *Censored Hollywood,* 25.

15. Gregory D. Black, *Hollywood Censored: Morality Codes, Catholics, and the Movies* (Cambridge, UK: Cambridge University Press, 1994), 10.

16. Charles V. Tevis, "Censoring the Five-Cent Drama," in Mast, *The Movies in Our Midst,* 69.

17. Ibid., 69–70.

18. Walter Prichard Eaton, "A New Epoch in the Movies," in Mast, *The Movies in Our Midst,* 106.

19. Annette Kuhn, *Cinema, Censorship, and Sexuality: 1909–1925* (London: Routledge, 1988), 18.

20. Richard Wormser, "D. W. Griffith's *The Birth of a Nation,*" PBS website, www.pbs.org/wnet/jimcrow/stories_events_birth.html.

21. Mast, *The Movies in Our Midst,* 139.

22. Robert Sklar, *Movie-Made America: A Cultural History of American Movies* (New York: Vintage, 1994), 127.

23. Dawn B. Sova, *Forbidden Films: Censorship Histories of 125 Motion Pictures* (New York: Checkmark Books, 2001), xi.

24. George R. Gordon, *Erotic Communication: Studies in Sex, Sin, and Censorship* (New York: Hastings House, 1980), 110.

25. Sova, *Forbidden Films,* xi.

26. Ibid., 49.

27. Mark A. Vieira, *Sin in Soft Focus: Pre-Code Hollywood* (New York: Harry N. Abrams, 1999), 8.

28. Sklar, *Movie-Made America,* 60–61.

29. Sova, *Forbidden Films,* 11.

30. Ashton D. Trice and Samuel A. Holland, *Heroes, Antiheroes, and Dolts: Portrayals of Masculinity in American Popular Films, 1921–1999* (Jefferson, NC: McFarland, 2001), 17.

31. Sova, *Forbidden Films,* 13.

32. Ibid., 270–271.

33. Jack C. Ellis and Virginia Wright Wexman, *A History of Film,* 5th ed. (Boston: Allyn and Bacon, 2002), 131.

34. Black, *Hollywood Censored,* 57–59.

35. Lea Jacobs, *The Wages of Sin: Censorship and the Fallen Woman Films— 1928–1942* (Berkeley: University of California Press, 1995), 32–34.

36. Black, *Hollywood Censored,* 65–70.

37. Thomas Doherty, *Pre-Code Hollywood: Sex, Immorality, and Insurrection in American Cinema, 1930–1934* (New York: Columbia University Press, 1999), 2.

38. See Vieira, *Sin in Soft Focus;* Sklar, *Movie-Made America.*

39. Sova, *Forbidden Films,* 247.

40. Thomas Schatz, *Hollywood Genres: Formula, Filmmaking, and the Studio System* (New York: McGraw Hill, 1981), 82.

41. Sova, *Forbidden Films,* 55.

42. Thomas Doherty, *Pre-Code Hollywood: Sex, Immorality, and Insurrection in American Cinema, 1930–1934* (New York: Columbia University Press, 1999), 2–3.

43. Schatz, *Hollywood Genres,* 81.

44. Miller, *Censored Hollywood,* 54–55.

45. Black, *Hollywood Censored,* 116–121.

46. Jacobs, *The Wages of Sin,* 31–33.

47. Julie Burchill, *Girls on Film* (London: Virgin Books, 1986), 13.

48. Jacobs, *The Wages of Sin,* 5–12.

49. Trice and Holland, *Heroes, Antiheroes, and Dolts,* 9.

50. Elizabeth Hamilton, *When I'm Bad I'm Better: Mae West, Sex, and American Entertainment* (Berkeley: University of California Press, 1997), 173–187. See also Doherty, *Pre-Code Hollywood,* 183–186; Vieira, *Sin in Soft Focus,* 112–116.

51. Gilbert Seldes, "The Movies in Peril," in Mast, *The Movies in Our Midst,* 429.

Chapter Three

1. Frank Miller, *Censored Hollywood: Sex, Sin, and Violence on Screen* (Atlanta: Turner Publishing, 1994), 39–40.

2. Raymond Moley, "The Birth of the Production Code," in Gerald Mast, ed., *The Movies in Our Midst: Documents in the Cultural History of Film in America* (Chicago: University of Chicago Press, 1982), 317.

3. Quoted in Andrew J. Rausch, *Turning Points in Hollywood History* (New York: Kensington, 2004), 62.

4. Olga J. Martin, "The Legion of Decency Campaign," in Mast, ed., *The Movies in Our Midst,* 333–339.

5. *Chicago Daily Tribune,* June 5, 1934, quoted in Martin, "The Legion of Decency Campaign," 334.

6. Ibid., 335.

7. *Variety,* June 15, 1934, quoted in Martin, "The Legion of Decency Campaign," 336.

8. Martin Quigley, "Decency in Motion Pictures (1937)," in Gerald Mast, ed. *The Movies in Our Midst,* 340.

9. http://www.selfstyledsiren.blogspot.com/2008/05/hollywoods=censor=joseph=i
=breen=and.html.

10. Christopher Beach, *Class, Language, and American Film Comedy* (Cambridge, UK: Cambridge University Press, 2002), 18.

11. Maria DiBattista, *Fast-Talking Dames* (New Haven, CT: Yale University Press, 2001).

12. Katherina Glitire, "The Same, but Different: The Awful Truth about Marriage, Remarriage, and Screwball Comedy," *Cineaction* 54: 3–5.

13. Miller, *Censored Hollywood*, 93.

14. Ibid., 88–89.

15. Gerald Gardner, *The Censorship Papers: Movie Censorship Letters from the Hays Office, 1934–1968* (New York: Dodd, Mead, 1987), 184.

16. Chandler cited in Andrew J. Rausch, *Turning Points in Film History* (New York: Kensington, 2004), 116.

17. Gardner, *The Censorship Papers,* 40–44.

18. William Marling, *The American Roman Noir: Hammett, Cain, and Chandler* (Athens: University of Georgia Press, 1995), 254–255.

19. Eddie Muller, *Dark City Dames: The Wicked Women of Film Noir* (New York; HarperCollins, 2001), 1.

20. Gardner, *The Censorship Papers,* 179–181.

21. Ibid., 27.

22. Ibid.

23. Ibid.

24. Ibid., 184.

25. Miller, *Censored Hollywood*, 147–148.

26. Ibid., 148–149.

27. Leonard J. Leff and Jerold L. Simmons, *Dame in the Kimono: Hollywood Censorship and the Production Code* (Lexington: University Press of Kentucky, 2001), 204–206.

28. Miller, *Censored Hollywood*, 148–149.

29. Arthur Schlesinger, "When the Movies Really Counted," in Mast, ed., *The Movies in Our Midst,* 420.

30. Jack Vizzard, *See No Evil* (New York: Simon and Schuster, 1970), quoted in Mast, ed., *The Movies in Our Midst,* 695.

31. Gardner, *The Censorship Papers,* 35–37.

32. Miller, *Censored Hollywood*, 160–163.

33. Ibid.

34. Gardner, *The Censorship Papers,* 169–172.

35. Ibid., 201–203.

36. Dawn B. Sova, *Forbidden Films: Censorship Histories of 125 Motion Pictures* (New York: Checkmark Books, 2001), 28.

37. Ibid., 29

38. Steven Rebello, *Alfred Hitchcock and the Making of Psycho* (New York: Dembner Books, 1990). See also Janet Leigh, *Psycho: Behind the Scenes of the Classic Thriller* (New York: Harmony, 1995).40. Gardner, *The Censorship Papers*, 92–94.

39. Vito Russo, *The Celluloid Closet: Homosexuality in the Movies* (New York: Harper and Row, 1987), 63.

40. Miller, *Censored Hollywood*, 186.

41. Gardner, *The Censorship Papers*, 92–94.

42. Gregory D. Black, *Hollywood Censored: Morality Codes, Catholics, and the Movies* (Cambridge, UK: Cambridge University Press, 1994), 183–184.

43. Robert Lang, *Masculine Interests: Homoerotics in Hollywood Film* (New York: Columbia University Press, 2002), 7–8; Paul Buhle and David Wagner, *Radical Hollywood: The Untold Story Behind America's Favorite Movies* (New York: New Press, 2002); and Thomas Schatz, *Boom and Bust: American Cinema in the Forties* (Berkeley: University of California Press, 1997), 265.

Chapter Four

1. John P. Diggins, *The American Left in the Twentieth Century* (New York: Harcourt, Brace, Jovanovich, 1973), 129.

2. Digital History website, www.digitalhistory.uh.edu.

3. Gerald Gardner, *The Censorship Papers: Movie Censorship Letters from the Hays Office, 1934–1968* (New York: Dodd, Mead, 1987), 164–165.

4. Paul Buhle and Dave Wagner, *Radical Hollywood: The Untold Story behind Hollywood's Favorite Movies* (New York: New Press, 2002), 325.

5. Wise Bread website, www.wisebread.com/fbi-considered-its-a-wonderful-life-communist-propaganda.

6. Gardner, *The Censorship Papers,* 39.

7. Richard W. Hanes, *The Moviegoing Experience: 1968–2000* (Jefferson, NC: McFarland, 2003), 21.

8. Andrew J. Rausch, *Turning Points in Film History* (New York: Citadel, 2004), 137–138.

9. Andrew Saris, ed., *The Film Director's Encyclopedia* (Detroit: Visible Ink, 1998), 393.

10. Buhle and Wagner, *Radical Hollywood,* 324.

11. Paul Buhle and Dave Wagner, *Blacklisted: The Film Lover's Guide to the Hollywood Blacklist* (New York: Palgrave Macmillan, 2003), 76.

12. Buhle and Wagner, *Radical Hollywood,* 379–380.

13. www.moderntimes.com/blacklist.

14. Eleanor Roosevelt, "My Day," October 29, 1947 (syndicated column).

15. See James L. Lorence, *The Suppression of the Salt of the Earth* (Albuquerque: University of New Mexico Press, 1999).

16. Buhle and Wagner, *Radical Hollywood,* 421.

17. Ibid., 418–421.

18. www.noIndoctrination.org.

19. Ann Coulter, "I Dare Call It Treason," June 25, 2003 (syndicated column).

20. Joan Kennedy Taylor, "Separating State and Culture," *Association of Libertarian Feminists* 77 (Winter 2001), 21, quoted on Brainwashing 101 website, www.brain-terminal.com/video/brainwashing-101.html.

21. www.matthewturner.co.uk/Blog/2006/10/urgent-spam-from-david-horowitz .html.

22. Brainwashing 101 website, www.brain-terminal.com/video/brainwashing-101.html.

23. Ted Baehr, ed., *Movieguide: A Family Guide to Movies and Entertainment* 21, no. 5 (March 4, 2006): 38.

24. Ibid.

Chapter Five

1. Samuel Goldwyn, "Hollywood in the Television Age," in Gerald Mast, ed., *The Movies in Our Midst: Documents in the Cultural History of Film in America* (Chicago: University of Chicago Press, 1982), 639.

2. Chester Morrison, "3-D: High, Wide, and Handsome," in Mast, *The Movies in Our Midst,* 647.

3. Encyclopedia.com, www.encyclopedia.com/doc/1G2-3434500950.html.

4. Tim Dirks, "Film History of the 1960s," AMC Film website, www.hollywood center.com/timeline.html.

5. Frank Miller, *Hollywood Censored: Sex, Sin, and Violence on Screen* (Atlanta, GA: Turner, 1994), 203–205.

6. Ibid., 201–205.

7. Jon Lewis, *Hollywood Versus Hard Core: How the Struggle over Censorship Saved the Modern Film Industry* (New York: New York University Press, 2002), 307.

8. www.wikipedia.org/wiki/This_Film_Is_Not_Yet_Rated.

9. Pauline Kael, "On the Future of Movies," in Mast, *The Movies in Our Midst,* 734–736.

10. Jim Windolf, "Stephen Spielberg," *Vanity Fair* (January 2, 2008).

11. Peter Biskind, *Easy Riders, Raging Bulls: How the Sex-Drugs-and-Rock N Roll Generation Saved Hollywood* (New York: Simon and Schuster, 1998), 307.

12. Jack Valenti, "How It All Began," www.mpaa.org/Ratings_HowItAll Began.asp.

13. Janet Maslin, "Film Views: Is NC-17 an X in a Clean Raincoat?" *New York Times*, February 23, 2009.

14. Ibid.

15. Dawn B. Sova, *Forbidden Films: Censorship Histories of 125 Motion Pictures* (New York: Checkmark, 2001), 171.

16. Ibid., 34–36.

17. Mark Harris, "NC-17: Fatally Flawed," *Entertainment Weekly* 940 (June 22, 2007).

18. Kimberly M. Thompson and Fumie Yokota, "Violence, Sex, and Profanity in Films: Correlation of Movie Ratings with Content," *Medscape Today* (July 12, 2004).

19. Fumie Yokota and Kimberly M. Thompson, "Violence in G-Rated Animated Films," *Journal of the American Medical Association* 283, no. 20 (May 24, 2000): 31.

20. Theresa Webb, Lucille Jenkins, Nickolas Browne, Abdellmonen A. Afifi, and Jess Cross, "Violent Entertainment Pitched to Adolescents: An Analysis of PG-13 Films." *Pediatrics* 119, no. 6 (June 2007): 1219.

21. Quoted in David Edlestein, "Blame Blockbuster, Not the MPAA," *Slate* (July 22, 1999), www.slate.com/id/1270.

22. www.urbandictionary.com/define.php?term=MPAA.

23. www.wikipedia.org/wiki/This_Film_Is_Not_Yet_Rated. See also Gregory D. Black, *Hollywood Censored: Morality Codes, Catholics, and the Movies.*

24. Quoted in Eddie Muller, *Dark City Dames: The Wicked Women of Film Noir* (New York: Regan, 2001), 196.

25. Ibid., 229.

26. Jonathan M. Freedman, *Media Violence and Its Effect on Agression: Assessing the Scientific Evidence* (Toronto: University of Toronto Press, 2002), preface.

27. Albert Bandura, "The Power of Social Modeling: The Effects of Television Violence," www.stanford.edu/dept/bingschool/rsrchart/bandura.

28. MPAA website, www.mpaa.org.

29. Pamela McClintock, "MPAA, NATO Reform Ratings System," *Vfilm* (January 16, 2007).

30. Quoted in "MPAA Tries to Remove NC-17 Stigma," www.variety.com/article/VR1117960864.html.

31. Valenti, "How It All Began."

32. "Movie Answer Man," November 16, 2003, www.rogerebert.com.

33. Mary Ann Johanson, "Anti-MPAA: Female Sex and Male Violence—The Divide in Movie Ratings," *Online Film Critics Society* (November 1999).

34. Roger Ebert, "The Dreamers," *Chicago Sun-Times,* February 13, 2004.

35. "Study Finds 'Ratings Creep': Movie Ratings Categories Contain More Violence, Sex, Profanity Than Decade Ago," Harvard School of Public Health press release, July 13, 2004,www.hsph.harvard.edu/presss/releases/press07132004.html.

36. Christine Rosen, "Female *Fight Club:* 'Pummel-Me Feminism,'" *Wall Street Journal,* April 25, 2005.

37. Sova, *Forbidden Films*, 123.

38. Sharon Waxman, "The Mystery of the Missing Moviemakers," *New York Times,* February 4, 2007, 11.

39. "MPAA Embraces NC-17," *Entertainment Online*, January 23, 2007, www.variety.com/article/VR1117960864.html.

40. Kim Masters, "Harvard Tells Hollywood to Ban Cigarettes from Kids' Movies," *Slate*, April 16, 2007.

41. Scott Bowles, "Cloudy Picture for MPAA Smoking Scrutiny," *USA Today*, May 10, 2007.

42. Jon Lewis, *Hollywood Versus Hard Core*, 7.

43. Jack Valenti, "How It All Began."

Chapter 6

1. Dawn B. Sova, *Forbidden Films: Censorship Histories of 125 Motion Pictures* (New York: Checkmark, 2001), xi.

2. Ibid., 276.

3. Dan Gilbert, "Religion in American Film" www.barnard.columbia.edu/religion/pages/right.html.

4. George F. Will, "What Goeth Before the Fall," *Washington Post*, October 5, 2006.

5. Boyd Farrow, "Hollywood Missionaries," *New Statesman*, November 21, 2005.

6. Quoted in *Baptist Press*, October 11, 2007.

7. Nathan Gonzales, "Beware: Evangelical Polling Ahead," *Rothenberg Political Report*, August 23, 2008.

8. "Religion and the Presidential Vote," Pew Research Center for the People and the Press, December 6, 2004.

9. Chris Hedges, "Radical Christian Right Preaches Liberal Evil," *Alter Net*, April 10, 2007.

10. "American Priests Consecrated in Dispute," *Chicago Tribune*, August 31, 2007, 18.

11. Mark Gauvreau, "Joe McCarthy's Jesuit," *American Spectator*, July 21, 2005, www.spectator.org/archives/2005/07/21/joe-mccarthys-jesuit.

12. Focus on the Family, www.focusonthefamily.com.

13. Leslie E. Smith, "Living in the World, but Not *of* the World: Understanding Evangelical Support for *The Passion of the Christ*," in Michael Beherenbaum and J. Shawn Landres, eds., *After the Passion Is Gone: American Religious Consequences* (Walnut Creek, CA: Altamira, 2004), 49.

14. Anonymous, "Cheated by the Affirming Church," *Christianity Today*, December 1, 2004.

15. Becky Ellis, "Won't Get Schooled Again," *Briarpatch* (March–April 2008).

16. Ted Baehr and Tom Snyder, "It's the Media, America!" *Movieguide* 22, nos. 1–2 (December–January 2007), 60–61.

17. Bruce Fieler, "Teach, Don't Preach the Bible," *New York Times*, December 21, 2005, A35.

18. Sova, *Forbidden Films*, 176–177.

19. Pew Forum on Religion and Public Life, February 26, 2009, pewforum.org.

20. John Leland, "*Brokeback:* Conservative Christians Try Reviews, Not Protests, for Controversial Movies," *New York Times,* December 26, 2005.

21. Ibid.

22. U.S. Conference of Catholic Bishops Movie Reviews, www.usccb.org/movies/archivedmoviereviews.

23. Sherry McMurray, "Happy Feet," Christian Spotlight on Entertainment, www.christ.ananswers.net/spotlight/movies/2006.html.

24. www.movieguide/org.

25. Gabriel Snyder, "At B.O., Pious Show No Bias," *Variety* (June 29, 2005).

26. Ibid.

27. www.boxofficemojo.com/movies/?ID=passionofthechrist.htm.

28. J. Shawn Landres and Michael Berenbaum, eds. *After the Passion Is Gone: American Religious Consequences* (Walnut Creek, CA: Altamira, 2004), 2-3.

29. www.the-numbers/com/movies/series/ChrroniclesofNarnia.php.

30. *Movieguide* 22, no. 8 (April 4, 2007): 42.

31. www.the-numbers.com/movies/series/ChroniclesofNarnia.php.

32. Sharon Waxman, "Fox Unfeils a Division for Religion-Oriented Films," *New York Times*, December 17, 2006, B8.

33. *Jesus Camp* website, www.jesuscampthemovie.com

34. Steven Holden, "Children's Boot Camp for the Culture Wars," *New York Times*, September 22, 2006.

35. Profitability Study of MPAA-Rated Movies, Commissioned by the Dove Foundation, Grand Rapids, Michigan, May 2005, www.dove.org/research/DoveFoundation.

36. *Movieguide* 21, nos. 22–23 (November–December 2006): 13.

37. Ilene Lelchuk, "'Convert or Die' Game Divides Christians," *San Francisco Chronicle*, December 12, 2006, 1.

38. Ted Baehr, "How to Redeem Our Dumbed-Down Culture," *Movieguide* 21, nos. 18–19 (September 2006): 34.

39. John Jalsevac, "Facing the Giants Rated PG for 'Mature Themes', Not Christianity," LifeSiteNews.com, June 20, 2006, www.lifesitenews.com/Idn/2006/jun/06062001.html.

40. "Hollywood Agrees Not to Engage in Anti-Christian Bigotry," *Movieguide* 21, nos. 16–17 (August 2006): 27.

41. "Movieguide's Impact on Current Trends in the Movie Industry," *Movieguide* 22, nos. 19–20 (September 2007): 31.

42. Sam Ward, "Hollywood," *USA Today*, February 12, 2006.

43. Ted Baehr and Tom Snyder, "Winds of Positive Moral Change Are Blowing in Hollywood," *Movieguide* 21, nos. 16–17 (August 2006): 28–29.

44. Molly Haskell, *Holding My Own in No-Man's Land: Women and Men and Films and Feminists* (New York: Oxford University Press, 1997), 189.

45. "Study Finds 'Ratings Creep': Movie Ratings Categories Contain More Violence, Sex, Profanity Than Decade Ago," *Harvard School of Public Health* press release, July 13, 2004, www.hsph.harvard.edu/press/releases/press07132004.html.

46. "Movieguide's Impact on Current Trends in the Movie Industry," *Movieguide* 22, nos. 19–20 (September 2007): 31.

47. David D. Kirkpatrick, "End Times for Evangelicals?" *New York Times Magazine* (October 28, 2000).

Chapter 7

1. Marty Kline, *America's War on Sex: The Attack on Law, Lust, and Liberty* (Westport, CT: Praeger, 2006), 1.

2. Martin Rubin, *Thrillers* (Cambridge, UK: Cambridge University Press, 1999), 102–103.

3. Mark Harris, *Entertainment Weekly* (June 15, 2007), www.ew.com/ew/article/0,,20042869,00.html.

4. Kimberly M. Thompson and Fumie Yokota, "Violence, Sex, and Profanity in Films," *Medscape Today* (July 12, 2004), www.medscape.com/viewarticle/480900.

5. Theresa Webb, Lucille Jenkins, Nickolas Browne, Abdellmonen A. Afifi, and Jess Cross, "Violent Entertainment Pitched to Adolescents: An Analysis of PG-13 Films," *Pediatrics* 119, no. 6 (June 2007): 1219.

6. Gordon Dahl and Stefano Delle Vigna, "Does Movie Violence Increase Violent Crime?" *Social Science Research Network* (January 2008), www.papers.ssrn.com/so13/papers.cfm?abstract_id=1082697.

7. Ashton D. Trice and Samuel A. Holland, *Heroes, Antiheroes and Dolts: Portrayals of Masculinity in American Popular Films, 1921–1999* (Jefferson, NC: McFarland, 2001), 77.

8. Frank Miller, *Censored Hollywood: Sex, Sin, and Violence on Screen* (Atlanta: Turner, 1994), 51.

9. Kirby Dick, "Bad Ratings," *Los Angeles Times*, January 24, 2007, A25.

10. *Urban Dictionary*, www.urbandictionary.com.

11. www.rogerebert.com.

12. Eddie Muller, *Dark City Dames: The Wicked Women of Film Noir* (New York: HarperCollins, 2001), 196.

13. "Lust, Caution," October 5, 2007, www.rogerebert.com.

14. Ibid.

Index

About the Author

Tom Pollard is professor of social sciences at National University in San Jose, California. He taught in higher education for thirty years after receiving his Ph.D. in American studies at the University of Kansas. He has had a lifelong interest in movies and film. His most recent books (both coauthored with Carl Boggs) are *The Hollywood War Machine: U.S. Militarism and Popular Culture* (Paradigm 2007) and *A World in Chaos: Social Crisis and the Rise of Postmodern Cinema* (2003). He has published more than twenty articles, essays, and reviews in several academic journals, most of them in the area of film and popular culture. He has been involved for more than ten years in the making of documentary films, the most recent being a work that chronicles the sixtieth anniversary of World War II in the Battle of Peleliu, titled *Once We Were Enemies*. His most recent documentary is *Crystal Feat/Crystal Clear*, a collaborative work involving Canadian filmmakers. His documentaries have appeared on BBC, Discovery Channel, the Life Network, the Canadian Broadcasting System, and various PBS channels. His other documentaries include *Paradise Bent: Boys Will Be Girls in Samoa*, *The Maya Pompeii*, and *Weird Homes of North America*, all shown at major film festivals worldwide.

MEDIA AND POWER
David L. Paletz, Series Editor
Duke University

PUBLISHED IN THE SERIES

Spinner in Chief: How Presidents Sell Their Policies and Themselves
Stephen J. Farnsworth

Netroots: Online Progressives and the Transformation of American Politics
Matthew R. Kerbel

The Age of Oprah: Cultural Icon for the Neoliberal Era
Janice Peck

Sex and Violence: The Hollywood Censorship Wars
Tom Pollard

Art/Museums: International Relations Where We Least Expect It
Christine Sylvester

*Mousepads, Shoeleather, and Hope: Lessons from the Howard Dean
Campaign for the Future of Internet Politics*
Zephyr Teachout and Thomas Streeter et al.

FORTHCOMING IN THE SERIES

From Cronkite to Colbert: The Evolution of Broadcast News
Geoffrey Baym

Creative Destruction: Modern Media and the End of the Citizen
Andrew Calabrese

Evil and Silence
Richard Fleming

Media and Conflict: Escalating Evil
Cees J. Hamelink

Social-Issue Documentaries: Strategies for Political Impact
David Whiteman